SPIRAL GUIDES

Travel with Someone You Trust®

NEW ZEALAND

Contents

the magazine 5

- ✦ Shaky Isles
- ✦ People with *Mana*
- ✦ No More Meat and Three Veg
- ✦ Weird and Wonderful Wildlife
- ✦ The New Zealand Experiment
- ✦ From Mansfield to Middle Earth
- ✦ Sweaty Jerseys and the Auld Mug
- ✦ Best Of... ✦ TranzAlpine Train Adventure

Finding Your Feet 33

- ✦ First Two Hours
- ✦ Getting Around
- ✦ Accommodation
- ✦ Food and Drink
- ✦ Shopping
- ✦ Entertainment

Around Auckland 47

Getting Your Bearings ✦ In a Day
Don't Miss ✦ Downtown Auckland ✦ Auckland Harbour
✦ Auckland War Memorial Museum ✦ Hauraki Gulf
✦ Bay of Islands ✦ Coromandel
At Your Leisure ✦ 10 more places to explore
Where to... ✦ Stay ✦ Eat and Drink ✦ Shop
✦ Be Entertained

Central Plateau 77

Getting Your Bearings ✦ In a Day
Don't Miss ✦ Mount Tarawera and Buried Village
✦ Thermal areas ✦ *Hangi* and cultural performance
✦ Tongariro National Park
At Your Leisure ✦ 8 more places to explore
Where to... ✦ Stay ✦ Eat and Drink ✦ Shop
✦ Be Entertained

Written by Veronika Meduna
Where to... sections by Mavis Airey

Copy edited by Nia Williams
Page layout by Nautilus Design (UK) Limited
Verified by Michael Mellor
Indexed by Marie Lorimer
Original photo shoot by Andy Belcher

Edited, designed and produced by AA Publishing
© Automobile Association Developments Limited 2002
Maps © Automobile Association Developments Limited 2002
Reprinted November 2002
Reprinted November 2003

Published in the United States by AAA Publishing,
1000 AAA Drive, Heathrow, Florida 32746.
Published in the United Kingdom by AA Publishing.

ISBN 1-56251-759-7

Cover design and binding style by permission of AA Publishing

Color separation by Leo Reprographics
Printed and bound in China by Leo Paper Products

109876543

A01994

the magazine

Earth forces break through the surface at Wai-o-tapu

Previous page: The Maori challenge is the traditional reception for visiting strangers

Geologically speaking, New Zealand is a teenager. Massive earth forces ripped the landmass from its parent continent only 90 million years ago and the young country's final character is still in the making. In places, the islands' mountainous spine continues to grow and, occasionally, the landscape gives in to volatile mood swings and explodes.

New Zealand is perched on the collision zone between two gigantic chunks of the Earth's crust. The Pacific and Indian-Australian tectonic plates grind against each other, sometimes causing disaster but also creating some unique landscapes, and making New Zealand one of the world's most dynamic places to live. In their lifetime, New Zealanders are likely to experience several earthquakes and volcanic eruptions, landslides, floods, droughts and the occasional cyclone – not to mention seasonal extremes in weather conditions. It's all just part of the New Zealand experience.

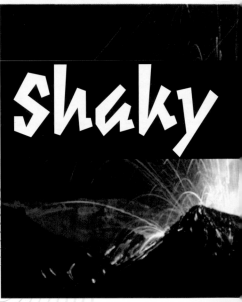

Shaky

A Dynamic Land

The boundary between the tectonic plates runs right through the country – from the Bay of Plenty through Wellington and along the entire length of the South Island. The plates move at about the same rate as fingernails and hair grow: about 25mm per year.

In the North Island this friction has caused volcanic eruptions and earthquakes,

Mount Ruapehu is the most active of three volcanoes in Tongariro National Park

but it also created the extraordinary thermal areas of the Central Plateau (▶ 85–88) and the spectacular peaks of Tongariro National Park (▶ 90–92). The mountains along the line from White Island (▶ 95) – a smouldering volcano off the Bay of Plenty – to Tongariro are the southern furnaces of the Pacific Ring of Fire, a chain of volcanoes stretching from Alaska through the Philippines, Indonesia and Japan to New Zealand.

The South Island experiences regular tremors and landslides; but without the Alpine Fault (which runs along the length of the Southern Alps and continues to push up the mountains), the island's craggy spine would not be such a magnificent wonderland of snow-topped peaks, glaciers, lakes and fjords.

The 1886 eruption of Mount Tarawera left a gaping wound in the Earth

The Human Cost

The nation's archives are stacked with photographs of natural disasters. Memories of the devastation and human losses caused by the 1931 Napier earthquake (▶ 97) still linger, and scars in the landscape are testimony to a powerful 1987 tremor at Edgecumbe, in the Bay of Plenty. Longer ago, the Mount Tarawera explosion

The Legend of the Ring of Fire

Maori mythology offers a beautiful explanation for the Ring of Fire: Nga-toro-i-rangi, an ancient priest and explorer, travelled to Aotearoa and decided to climb up Mount Tongariro to claim all the land he could see from the summit. But there was another traveller on his way to do the same thing, so the sage called up a storm to discourage his competitor. However, he was caught in the chilling gale himself and had to call on his sisters, in the distant homeland of Hawaiki, to send him fire to keep him warm. Elders came with flax bags of glowing embers, but in their haste several embers burnt through the bags, falling where today's volcanoes still feel their fire.

Grumbling
Mount Ruapehu
regularly
disrupts life
around its base

(➤ 82–84), buried several villages and destroyed spectacular sinter (rock deposit) terraces, a major tourist attraction at the time.

However, more recent eruptions, such as Mount Ruapehu's in 1995, have caused minimal damage because modern technology allows geologists to monitor the mood of each active volcano. Even the sleeping volcanoes dotting Auckland's cityscape (➤ 53) are under constant scrutiny. The current cones are considered extinct, but the volcanic field below them is only dormant and could well open up new vents. Nevertheless, Aucklanders sleep easily – they know they'll get about three weeks' warning, courtesy of increasingly sensitive monitoring techniques.

New Zealand's capital, Wellington, is bracing itself for a spectacle of another kind. The city straddles a fault line that last caused a major earthquake in 1855. The

New Zealand experiences 10,000 to 15,000 earthquakes each year, but most are too weak to be noticed. However, a few are greater than magnitude 6 on the Richter Scale – big enough to cause major destruction if they strike a town. This risk has prompted city planners to protect public buildings. The Parliament complex (► 108–110) and Te Papa (► 111–112) in Wellington now sit on earthquake-proof foundations.

quake, which registered 8.2 on the Richter Scale, was felt from Auckland to Dunedin, and Wellington – still only a small town at the time – watched buildings tumble and a new landscape grow as the tremor raised the coast by up to a staggering 6m. The quake added a strip of new land to the entire southern coastline, uplifting some 5,000sq km of land. The capital is now having to face the growing likelihood of another "Big One" sometime soon.

Four Seasons in One Day

Apart from the forces within, New Zealand is exposed to extreme weather changes. The long and narrow islands can sometimes experience freezing hailstorms on one coast and desiccating sunshine on the other. As if earthquakes and volcanoes weren't enough, New Zealand also experiences extremes in weather. From the subtropical climate of the far north to the temperate southern regions, the difference in temperature can be several degrees. The islands' maritime climate means that the weather changes with amazing rapidity, and you should come prepared for four seasons in one day.

White Island is an inhospitable moonscape of hissing craters

PEOPLE WITH
MANA

"Haere mai, haere mai" are some of the first words you're likely to see on arriving in New Zealand, welcoming you to Aotearoa, the Land of the Long White Cloud. Maori language and culture are experiencing a renaissance, expressed in a proud celebration of Maori leaders, rebels and visionaries.

No official event is complete without a Maori ceremony. Te Reo Maori, the Maori language, is taught in mainstream schools and used in parliamentary debates, and many of its words have entered New Zealand English. This renewed interest comes after generations of Maori traditions being discouraged in an ill-conceived belief that Maori

The Treaty of Waitangi was written in both English and Maori

The Treaty of Waitangi

The Treaty of Waitangi was drawn up in 1840 and eventually signed by more than 500 tribal chiefs. Under its terms, chiefs ceded their sovereignty to the British Queen in exchange for protection and the same rights as British citizens. However, the meaning of "sovereignty" was muddled in translation and the document remains controversial. The treaty guaranteed Maori the possession of their land and resources, but land was in fact confiscated and relations between the chiefs and the Crown quickly deteriorated.

Background: A full facial tattoo, or *moko*, is a sign of a chief's high ranking

would want to assimilate with the European settlers' way of life, and could do so more easily if they forgot their own culture. Today, however, the goal is to embrace cultural diversity and to find a way for Maori and *Pakeha* – and the many other ethnic groups of New Zealand – to live together in a fairer society. The process is not without tensions: Maori are still disadvantaged in many ways. But they are proud to celebrate the achievements of their cultural heroes – people with *mana* (spiritual authority).

✂ **Hone Heke Pokai** (*c*1810–50), a Maori leader in the far north, became the first tribal chief to add his name to the Treaty of Waitangi in 1840 (➤ 63–64). Before long, though, Maori began to fear that the Europeans would observe the treaty's principles of partnership only until they were in a position to seize the land. Hone Heke regretted his role and expressed his growing resentment of British sovereignty by cutting down one of its symbols, a shipping-signal flagstaff on Maiki, overlooking Russell, not once but four times.

✂ In September 1887, **Horonuku Te Heu Heu Tukino** (1821–88) gave away one of his tribe's most precious possessions – the three sacred peaks that today form Tongariro National Park (➤ 90–92). The far-sighted paramount chief of the Ngati Tuwharetoa people realised that giving the land to the government would prevent its being sold off in small slices. The area became New Zealand's first – and the world's fourth – national park, preserving the mountains' spiritual significance for those who still live in their shadow.

✂ In 1893, **Sir Apirana Ngata** (1874–1950) became the first Maori to graduate from a New Zealand university. He had grown up in the Ngati Porou communities of the East Coast (➤ 182–185) and saw it as his

High-ranking women wore *moko* only on the chin and lips

Moko were carved into the skin with bone chisels and blue pigment

mission to save his people from social disintegration and eventual extinction. He helped them to develop and farm their land, while also encouraging them to preserve their culture and maintain their own identity.

Dame Whina Cooper (1895–1994) was an active campaigner for many years, founding the Maori Women's Welfare League. She became a national representative of peaceful protest in her 80s, when she led thousands of Maori on a rally. For two months in 1975 she headed the Maori land march from Northland to Parliament in Wellington (➤ 108–110), to dramatise the Maori's determination to retain their land and culture. Her actions and views were a driving force behind the cultural renaissance that gathered momentum in subsequent years.

In the Name of Progress?

Following Abel Tasman's and Captain James Cook's 17th and 18th century explorations, European sealers and whalers began to arrive in about 1790. While they plundered the coasts, timber traders felled the massive kauri trees in Northland (➤ 70), bringing firearms, and contagious diseases to which Maori had no resistance. Influenza alone wiped out thousands, and muskets sparked intertribal warfare. New Zealand was annexed by Britain in 1838, became a self-governing British colony in 1856 and a dominion in 1907.

Te Arikinui Dame Te Atairangikaahu (born 1931) is a monarch without a state but she is influential in Maori affairs. The arrival of Europeans prompted leaders of the largest tribes to form a confederation for a stronger voice and Te Arikinui is the group's sixth – and first female – paramount chief. One of her greatest moments came in 1995 at a ceremony to celebrate the first settlement of Maori claims under the Treaty of Waitangi. Her tribe, the Tainui, who live along the mighty Waikato River, were given land and money to compensate for losses in the first century of colonisation.

A Maori Glossary

Aotearoa New Zealand
Aroha love
Awa river
Haere mai welcome
Haka dance
Hangi earth oven
Hongi pressing noses in greeting
Iwi people, tribe
Kai food, eat
Karakia prayer
Kia ora a common greeting
Koha gift
Kaumatua male elder
Kuia female elder
Mana spiritual power, authority
Maunga mountain
Moana lake, sea
Pa fortified village
Pakeha person of European descent
Tapu forbidden, sacred
Waka canoe

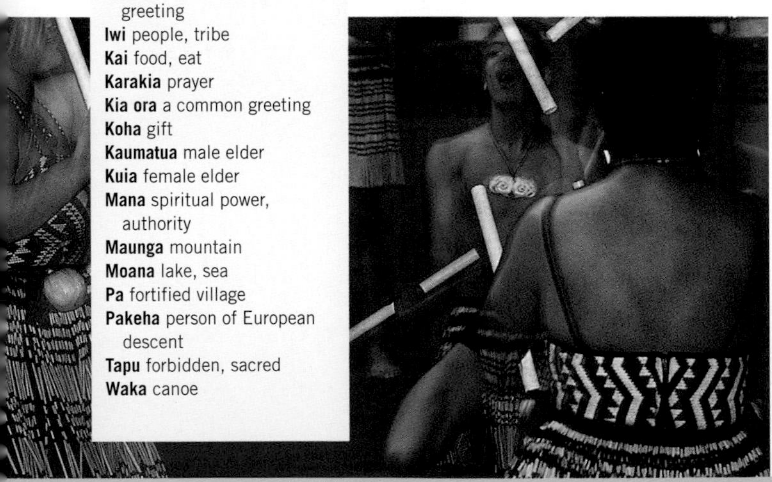

Stick dances once prepared young warriors for battle

No more meat and three veg

Juicy and sweet delights combine in a tropical fruit pavlova

New Zealand is known as an adventure destination, but the possibilities go beyond the purely physical. Your taste buds will also get some exercise, a treat or a challenge.

The annual Wildfoods Festival in Hokitika on the West Coast is not for the timid palate. It's the culinary equivalent of a bungy jump. You have to let go of the idea that food is meant to look pleasant. Roasted grubs, sea slugs, worm fritters and all sorts of other "bush tucker" are served up during a weekend around March each year to a crowd of wildfood aficionados. If you have the courage to swallow one of these unconventional delicacies, you'll at least be rewarded with a strong sense of achievement.

> **"The culinary equivalent of a bungy jump"**

Not for the Fainthearted

The Hokitika gathering is one of the gastronomic highlights of the West Coast (▶ 141–142) social calendar. It's grown from small beginnings in 1990, with fewer than 30 stalls and just under 2,000 visitors, to a wild gourmet extravaganza where almost 20,000 people are catered for by 100 food stalls. Old favourites are huhu grubs, possum nuggets, and fat larvae 5cm long and tasting of peanut butter, but each year new specialities appear on the menu. Start with stinging

- Nowhere in New Zealand is far from the ocean. The seafood industry is a fast-growing export earner, and, at NZ$1.43 billion, trails only the traditional dairy, meat and forestry industries.
- A highly prized asset of the country is the Greenshell mussel, a delicious and tender native of New Zealand's shores, which is farmed by aquaculture in the Marlborough Sounds (▶ 113–116), the Coromandel (▶ 65–66) and Stewart Island.
- Despite today's wider choices, fish and chips remain a favourite take-away food. New Zealanders spend more than NZ$75 million on "greasies" every year.

nettle soup or weed salad, and then choose between water buffalo fillets, barbecued wallaby, fried locusts, braised steer, mussel kebab and wild boar. Then try chocolate truffles laced with juicy earthworms for dessert and wash it all down with locally made gorse or manuka wine. And to help the digestion, how about a worm slammer – earthworms pickled in vodka?

Cosmopolian Dining

The number of New Zealand's fully licensed restaurants has more than tripled to over 1,500 since the early 1990s, supplemented by hundreds of smaller eateries, fast-food outlets and more than 2,000 fish and chip shops. It may not sound a lot, but just walk down Auckland's Ponsonby Road, Christchurch's Oxford Terrace or Wellington's Courtenay Place, and you'll find cafés and restaurants jostling for space and customers.

From fine-dining establishments to the hole-in-the-wall sandwich bar, there are plenty of culinary temptations in the

Left: Hot boulders are used to steam food in its own juices
Second left: Peter Thornley is one of New Zealand's best known chefs

A Quick Guide to the Best New Zealand Wines

WHITE

Sauvignon Blanc: New Zealand's most famous wine, especially when it's from Marlborough. Typically, it has a gooseberry and grassy character with a dry style that's refreshing as an aperitif or with seafood. *Cloudy Bay Sauvignon Blanc* is an elegant, fragrant example from a top maker (around $25). If you don't like gooseberries in your wine, try *Villa Maria Reserve Clifford Bay Sauvignon Blanc*, a more restrained style from a different part of Marlborough (around $25).

Chardonnay: These range from big, buttery and full of oak to lighter styles designed to go with food. *Neudorf Moutere Chardonnay* (around $40), from Nelson, has won international acclaim as one of New Zealand's best.
Bucking the Kiwi trend, Auckland winemaker Michael Brajkovich has achieved cult status with his Burgundian-style *Kumeu River Kumeu Chardonnay* (around $35).

Riesling: A brilliant food wine, excellent value, and best made in the South Island. Canterbury is a leader in the variety, and the Giesen family, originally from Germany, has a special flair

cities and a wealth of gastro-nomic experiences in rural areas. Cooking styles represent the United Nations, slightly skewed towards the Pacific Rim, with indigenous influences. Ingredients are a mix of home-grown and exotic, but are always fresh.

Kiwi Fusion

New Zealand has always produced superb ingredients – meat, poultry, vegetables, seafood and fruit – but New Zealanders have not always been as open to new culinary ideas as they are today. There was a time when roast lamb, accompanied by bland vegetables, was the most exciting meal. Meat and three veg is still a classic, but as a nation of immigrants, New Zealanders couldn't help but be exposed to outside influences. After simmering in conservative juices, Kiwis have whipped up a fusion of tastes and now have the best of many worlds, with the strongest influences from Asia, the Pacific Islands and the Mediterranean. (➤ 41–42 for more on the country's best food and restaurants.)

(➤ 41–42 for more on the country's best food and restaurants.)

Second right: Sun-drenched Waiheke Island produces fine wines. Right: A barbecue with seafood and meat is a Kiwi tradition

for it. Try the *Giesen Canterbury Reserve Riesling* (around $20). *Framingham* is a Riesling specialist in Marlborough, making dry, classic off-dry and sweet, late-harvest styles (around $20).

Sparkling: New Zealand sparkling wines range from cheap sweet fizz to traditionally made, bottle-fermented brut in the Champagne style. *Cellier Le Brun* showed Marlborough how to do it, and still makes one of the best: *Le Brun Family Estate Daniel No 1* (around $30).

RED

Pinot Noir: New Zealand is one of the few countries capable of producing world-class Pinot Noir. The best comes from Martinborough and the South Island. It's hard to make, quantities are small, and it's expensive. Two of the finest from different regions are *Ata Rangi Pinot Noir* from Martinborough (around $50) and *Felton Road Pinot Noir* from Central Otago (around $40).

Cabernet Sauvignon/Merlot: Hawkes Bay is one of the few regions in New Zealand able to ripen Cabernet Sauvignon consistently. Merlot is often blended in to soften its tannins. Te Mata's *Coleraine* (around $50) and *Awatea* (around $35) are fine variations on the theme.

New Zealand is a favourite among wildlife tourists, who arrive armed with binoculars, underwater goggles, cameras and high hopes of catching a glimpse of some extraordinary creature. Few realise that their first wildlife encounter is likely to be with a possum stretched out flat on the road.

New Zealand is home to some of the world's rarest and strangest animals: plump, sweet-smelling parrots that have forgotten how to fly, ancient, wrinkly reptiles that once shared the planet with dinosaurs, heavily armoured insects the size of mice, and the fluffy, flightless kiwi, the national symbol. The country is like a Noah's Ark, floating in the southern Pacific carrying a precious cargo of unique creatures.

At Kaikoura, sperm whales dive to about 1,000m but they are capable of reaching 3,000m

Weird & Wonderful

When New Zealand broke off from the super-continent Gondwana millions of years ago, its only animals were birds, reptiles and insects. The only land mammals were bats. Without the threat of predators or competition from opponents, birds didn't need to fly and insects could grow to palm size. But there are now a number of stowaways and to ensure the survival of legitimate passengers, many New Zealanders regard it as their civic duty to stand on the accelerator if they see one of these squatters on the side of the road.

The Possum Problem

Possums are the worst. The standard joke about New Zealand is that the country has more sheep than people – but possums outnumber the two added together. More than 60 million emerge

Giant sperm whales regularly visit the coast off Kaikoura

An Experiment Gone Wrong

Possums were introduced from Australia in 1848 to launch a fur trade. They are now found in more than 90 per cent of the country.

from their sleeping holes each night to crunch on 20,000 tonnes of vegetation, mostly the shoots of indigenous trees. Australia's eucalyptus trees contain natural toxins but New Zealand's trees

Wildlife

have no defence mechanisms. Apart from stripping native forests, possums rob birds of their food supplies. Similarly, stoats and ferrets, which feast on the eggs and chicks of native birds, make any attempt at breeding a difficult undertaking.

While the public roadkill effort may initially come as an unpleasant surprise to visitors, it is but a small part of a huge effort to keep such undesirables in check. At a cost of more than NZ$100 million per year, a variety of methods, including poisoning and trapping, is used to keep pests at bay and to help visitors take home memories of truly wild encounters.

Feathered Favourites

One of the most memorable wildlife experiences is watching penguins come ashore after their day's fishing. If you are in the right place at the right time, you'll see some of these "tuxedo-wearers" waddle ashore or perform an elaborate welcome ritual with their mate. The Otago Peninsula (► 166–167) is a good place to see yellow-eyed penguins and at Milford Sound (► 158– 160) you

There are only 2,500 to 3,000 breeding pairs of Fiordland crested penguins in New Zealand

Kakapo treasure: only about 60 parrots survive on offshore islands

might encounter Fiordland crested penguins.

There are several other peculiar birds. The cheekiest is the kea (alpine parrot), which you're likely to encounter around Arthur's Pass (➤ 139– 140) where it breeds in rocky crevices. The flightless and night-active kiwi is almost impossible to see in the wild, unless you venture as far south as Stewart Island; because they nest on the ground, their eggs and chicks are sitting targets for introduced predators such as stoats and ferrets, and the birds have almost disappeared from the mainland. But there are several kiwi houses in the country – for example at the Whakarewarewa thermal reserve (➤ 85–88) – and they've been reintroduced to the Karori Wildlife Sanctuary in Wellington (➤ 118), where you can hear them, and maybe even spot them, during an evening walk.

New Zealand is surrounded by hundreds of offshore islands. Like lifeboats around a vessel with a valuable load, these islands provide safe havens for endangered species. Kapiti (➤ 120) is one of the most accessible islands, where you can see plump wood pigeons and the vivacious kaka (forest parrot) swoop through native trees.

Marine Mammals
Whales, dolphins and seals live around New Zealand's 13,000km of coast-line. The

best place to see all three is Kaikoura (➤ 146) on the east coast of the South Island. Sperm whales are abundant all year, chasing giant squid in the deep underwater canyons off the coast. Dolphins cruise the bays around Kaikoura in large pods, and they are also reliably found in the Bay of Islands (➤ 62–64). Hector's dolphins, the smallest species, are unique to New Zealand and regularly visit Akaroa Harbour (➤ 134) in summer to have their young. If you're looking for seals, follow your nose. The blubber-wrapped torpedoes are so well camouflaged on the rocky coastline they are hard to spot, but their fishy smell gives them away.

Kea have a soft spot for rubber and every year insurance companies deal with claims for damage to windscreen wipers, sealings on doors and windows, and for shredded bicycle seats.

Nothing is safe from the curious kea

Every year, as many 1,000 fur seals are entangled and drowned in the nets of fishing trawlers

New Zealand fur seals were almost wiped out by hunters but are now on the increase

The New Zealand experiment

As a small nation of resourceful people far away from everybody else, New Zealand can afford to swim against the stream and try things others might not dare to consider.

Leading the flock

1893: NZ is the first country to give women the vote.
1948: Major protests against the exclusion of Maori players from a rugby tour of South Africa.
1981: Protests against a visit by the South African Springbok rugby team divide the country.
1985: NZ's anti-nuclear policy leads to the refusal of a visit by the USS *Buchanan* warship.
1994: NZ ratifies the Protocol on Environmental Protection to the Antarctic Treaty, banning mining for at least 50 years.

One of the country's most controversial political decisions – to declare itself a nuclear-free nation in the mid-1980s and to spearhead protests against nuclear testing in the Pacific – caused major strife at the time but is now viewed with envy by many countries.

During the same period, the government launched some radical economic reforms that transformed the country from a welfare state with an income based on subsidised agriculture to one of the world's most liberal free-market economies. Farmers' subsidies disappeared, import tariffs were dropped, government departments were privatised, state assets were snapped up by overseas interests and a

Top: In 1995, the Greenpeace ship *Rainbow Warrior* was bombed in Auckland Harbour before it could join a protest against French nuclear testing Centre: Auckland Harbour skyline

controversial Goods and Services Tax (GST) was added to almost everything. New Zealand was one of the first countries to give up trade barriers in an effort to make the country more interesting to overseas investors.

But the bubble burst with the worldwide stock market crash in 1987. Despite an economy in the doldrums, successive governments continued the push for privatisation and, eventually, the economy started to recover during the mid-1990s. But by that time New Zealand also had an unprecedented 10 per cent unemployment rate and an ever-widening gap between rich and poor.

Internet cafés help bring the world to New Zealand

New Zealanders are some of the most wired people in the world. About 47 per cent of them have a computer at home and 25 per cent have an internet connection. In fact, New Zealand ranks seventh in the world in the number of internet connections. Most schools have their own websites and use computers in teaching, and 85 per cent of websites in New Zealand are those of businesses.

Vital statistics

• Agriculture is New Zealand's economic backbone: almost 70,000 farms cover more than 16 million ha grazed by 50 million sheep, 10 million cows and half a million pigs.
• About four-fifths of New Zealanders are of European origin, from Britain, the Netherlands, former Yugoslavia and Germany. Maori make up about 14 per cent of the population; the next largest ethnic group (5.6 per cent) is Pacific Islanders.
• Nearly 30 per cent of land is set aside as national parks and other protected areas. There are 14 national parks, 20 forest parks, about 3,500 reserves and some 61,000ha of protected private land.

Today, most New Zealanders enjoy a living standard equivalent to that of other developed countries, and many businesses have grown into international companies. But some people are looking back with tinges of regret as they watch the once sacrosanct ideals of equality, state welfare and unionism apparently taking a back seat behind more corporate philosophies.

Nevertheless, New Zealanders remain open to new challenges and have held on to their adventurous and non-conformist spirit. They have taken to the internet like ducks to water (see panel), but have no qualms about speaking out about their unease regarding high-tech developments in biotechnology, for example.

Not so long ago, New Zealand writers and painters were convinced that the only way to find fame and fortune was by leaving their island home behind. But things have changed since writer Katherine Mansfield embarked on her voyage to London. Now film stars flock to New Zealand to slip on a hobbit costume and roam the depths of Middle Earth.

From Mansfield

Star-spotting became a favourite pastime in Wellington during the 18 months it took to shoot the epic three-film adaptation of JRR Tolkien's trilogy *The Lord of the Rings*. Strict secrecy surrounded every scene and filming location, but intrepid fans spied out locations, climbed trees for a better glimpse of Cate Blanchett or Liv Tyler, and prowled Wellington's pubs, clubs and bars in the hope of spotting a hobbit or an elf.

Film Friendly

While the filming of the trilogy in 1999 and 2000 put New Zealand firmly on Hollywood's map, it is only one of a dozen productions choosing to shoot Down Under. High on the side of an snowy peak in the Southern Alps, Hollywood star Chris O'Donnell hung on to the edge of an ice shelf in the

dizzying high-altitude thriller *Vertical Limit* (2000). At about the same time, dinosaurs walked the earth in Canterbury, courtesy of a BBC television crew using New Zealand's primeval landscapes to represent the wilderness in *The Lost World*. And during the 1990s, the dense, subtropical bush of Northland provided the stage for Warrior Princess Xena's small-screen somersaults and punches.

Although she never returned to her native country, many of Katherine Mansfield's stories are set in New Zealand

Colin McCahon is one of New Zealand's leading contemporary painters. His landscape paintings began attracting international attention during the 1970s and the value of his works has topped a million dollars. One of his most famous paintings, the Urewera mural, made headlines when Maori activists stole it from the Department of Conservation centre in Te Urewera National Park. The theft – and later return – was part of a symbolic action to highlight ongoing grievances.

to Middle Earth

The magnet for much of the cinematographic interest in New Zealand is Peter Jackson, the cheerful force behind *The Lord of the Rings*, who previously shot the 1996 comic chiller *The Frighteners* in and around Wellington and Lyttelton (▶ 144–145).

The appeal of New Zealand to the world's moviemakers is not new. As early as 1912, pioneer French film maker Gaston Melies found new landscapes for his dramatic short films, and in the 1920s a Hollywood studio shot *Venus of the South Seas* in Nelson.

Several Hollywood productions – including *Midnight Run*, starring Robert de Niro – set up shoots in New Zealand during the 1980s. Soon, the country became a popular location, not only because of the choice of scenic backdrops, but because employing film and television crews in New Zealand is relatively inexpensive. Wellington, where Peter Jackson worked on his first amateur flicks, now has an office whose sole function it is to make the capital a film-friendly city and to cut through the red tape for movie directors.

New Zealand's diverse and unspoilt landscapes were the perfect backdrop for *The Lord of the Rings*

Ring Things

• *The Lord of the Rings* employed more than 3,000 people, mostly New Zealanders.
• Carpenters, weavers, painters, sculptors, glass blowers and armourers all had to sign confidentiality agreements in their contracts.
• Several shops and cafés decided to rename themselves as something borrowed from Tolkien's imagination.
• Income in bars, a petrol station and shops near the Wellington studios multiplied. Real-estate prices soared.
• Peter Jackson was given permission to film in Tongariro National Park (▶ 90–92), but was not allowed to use horses or helicopters.

American actor Michael J Fox starred in *The Frighteners*, which featured special effects created by a New Zealand company

The Lord of the Rings trilogy is the second most expensive movie production worldwide and the largest overseas production to come to New Zealand. In comparison, the budgets of New Zealand films fade into insignificance.

International productions
Titanic NZ$470 million
The Lord of the Rings NZ$360m
Waterworld NZ$283m
Godzilla NZ$226m
Star Wars – The Phantom Menace NZ$217m

New Zealand productions
The Frighteners NZ$28m
The Piano NZ$10m
What Becomes of the Broken Hearted NZ$5m
Heavenly Creatures NZ$3.7m
Once Were Warriors NZ$2m

Artistic Merit

The country's literary scene has also come of age, with New Zealand writers winning international and domestic fiction awards. Katherine Mansfield is regarded as one of New Zealand's finest literary exports and the achievements of her short life continue to be celebrated at her birthplace in Wellington (► 117). Keri Hulme is best known as the author of the Booker Prize-winning novel *The Bone People*, but she has also produced many short stories and volumes of poetry. Another Maori writer who is creating waves internationally is Witi Ihimaera. The former diplomat and New Zealand consul to the United States became the country's first Maori writer to publish a novel in English. Since *Tangi* in 1973, he has become a prolific chronicler of crucial social issues affecting Maori people.

In visual arts, the country's most internationally famous artist is Dunedin-born Frances Hodgkins (1869–1947), whose watercolours and oil paintings are part of the permanent exhibitions at galleries in Wellington and Dunedin.

Xena actress Lucy Lawless is a New Zealander

SWEATY JERSEYS AND THE AULD MUG

Sport is an essential part of everyday life in New Zealand and a major source of national pride. Winning athletes are treated to a hero's welcome when they return; failure to win a coveted trophy sends the nation into collective mourning.

New Zealanders are passionate about sports – whether it's on the field or in front of the TV. More than 90 per cent of young people are actively involved in at least one sport, either through school or clubs, and more than half are involved at a competitive level. Over 80 per cent of women and 60 per cent of men participate in one or more sports or leisure activity.

Rugby

Rugby union is the main national sport – some would say obsession – with 140,000 Kiwis playing club rugby. The national players, the All

Top and above: Fervent fans and Maori rituals contribute to the All Blacks' success

The man on New Zealand's $5 banknote is one of the country's enduring heroes – Sir Edmund Hillary. Respected for his modesty and down-to-earth nature, "Sir Ed" used the fame that followed his and sherpa Tenzing Norgay's ascent of Mount Everest in 1953 to raise funds to build hospitals and schools in Nepal.

Sir Edmund Hillary epitomises the spirit of adventure and determination to which many New Zealanders aspire

Blacks, are among the most successful teams in the world. Their season starts in February with the Super 12 competition and ends with the National Provincial Championships in late October. Their every move is recorded in the nation's memory, and many New Zealanders can recite names of players going back decades. Like film stars elsewhere, rugby players fill the tabloid pages, especially since rugby

Yachting

New Zealand's biggest sports coup happened in 1995, not on the rugby field but on the ocean, and not even in New Zealand but off the southern Californian coast, when a group of yachties took home the world's oldest sporting trophy. In 144 years, the America's Cup had left its case in the USA only once, to spend a season with the Australian team in 1983. New Zealand's first real challenge

Many New Zealanders love messing around in a yacht or motorboat

became a professional sport in 1995. The team is famous for performing the Te Rauparaha Haka, a Maori war chant, before each match, a tradition dating from the 19th century.

was mounted in 1988 in San Diego. Amid legal wrangles and accusations, the defenders' *Stars and Stripes* beat New Zealand challenger *KZ1*. Three further unsuccessful challenges followed, but in 1995, New Zealand's *Black Magic* finally broke the spell. The Kiwi syndicate's leader, Peter Blake (who was later awarded a knighthood for his yachting achievements), made a casual remark on TV about wearing red socks as a lucky charm, and within a few days there were no red socks left in the shops. Such was the cup fever that churches rescheduled services for Sunday afternoons because the races happened in the mornings, and some businesses didn't

bother to open until after each race. Huge crowds came to welcome the sailors and the "Auld Mug" as they arrived at Auckland, and the team spent several days being showered with confetti as they travelled the regions from victory parade to victory parade.

Five years later, at the dawn of the new millennium, the spectacle was repeated in the Hauraki Gulf (► 60–61) and Auckland's Viaduct Basin (► 54) was the place to be for every self-respecting Kiwi. The Italian Prada team sailed

Below: The Pipeline Bridge bungy jump near Queenstown is 102m of pure adrenaline

Bottom left: At 23, Stephen Fleming became the youngest ever captain of New Zealand's cricket team

Can You Hackett?

Bungy jumping veteran A J Hackett is one of the driving forces behind New Zealand's reputation as an adventure sports destination. He has developed four jump sites in the Queenstown area (► 168–169) and is touring the world in search of more. However, bungy jumping is no New Zealand invention. On Pentecost, one of the islands in Vanuatu, men have been jumping off high wooden towers for centuries – with their feet attached to elastic vines. In the 1970s, this ancient ritual inspired the Oxford University Dangerous Sports Club to try it for themselves.
A J Hackett saw a video and was hooked. He spent some time testing latex rubber cords before making a series of jumps, first from a ski-field gondola 91m above the snow, and then, in June 1987, from the Eiffel Tower, launching an entire industry.

Move While You Can

Christchurch-based extreme multisport champion Steve Gurney holds the record for the annual Coast-to-Coast race. Athletes meet at a beach on the West Coast and then run, cycle and kayak across the Southern Alps to a beach in Christchurch on the east coast. Gurney can do it in 10 hours and 47 minutes, about twice as long as the TranzAlpine needs to cross the island (► 30–32), and he's won seven times. New Zealanders also invented the Southern Traverse, where competitors cover about 450km in five or six days, following the race motto "sleep if you dare, move while you can".

through the challenger races to face the defending New Zealand team in what became the first finals in the cup's history without an American team. *Black Magic* won easily and Auckland began gearing up to host the next defence, at the beginning of 2003.

Outdoor Life

Easy access to wilderness areas and the ocean is one of the reasons for most Kiwis' sporting passion. It would be difficult to grow up in New Zealand without spending significant amounts of time hiking in the mountains, fishing the rivers or riding the surf. Another reason is that Kiwis are natural competitors: once they get involved, they want to be the best. It's perhaps not surprising that some of the craziest and most challenging outdoor endurance competitions and adventure sports began in New Zealand. Whether it's bungy jumping, sailing or extreme endurance races, chances are that a Kiwi holds the record.

Yachts set sail in Auckland's harbour during trials for the America's Cup

New Zealand's sporting heroes

- **Jean Batten** smashes Amy Johnson's solo flight time between England and Australia by six days in 1934. In 1935, the "Garbo of the Skies" becomes the first woman to make the return flight. In 1936 she makes the first direct flight between England and New Zealand and then the fastest trans-Tasman flight.
- **Jack Lovelock** wins Olympic gold in the 1,500m in 1936.
- **Murray Halberg** wins Olympic gold in the 5,000m in 1960 and holds five national titles for 1 mile and 3 miles.
- **Peter Snell** is a triple gold medallist in middle-distance running and becomes the fastest man to run the mile in 1962.
- **Mark Todd** wins Olympic gold in three-day eventing, riding Charisma, in 1984 and 1988.
- **Barbara Kendall** wins Olympic gold for boardsailing in 1992.
- **Danyon Loader** wins Olympic gold in swimming, 200m and 400m freestyle in 1996.
- **Rob Waddell** wins Olympic gold in singles rowing in 2000.
- **The Black Ferns**, the New Zealand women's rugby team, win the World Championships in 2000.

BEST OF ...

Ninety Mile Beach actually stretches, unbroken, for 56 miles

Take a dolphin-watching tour

Auckland is New Zealand's largest city

Best Beaches

New Zealand is like one big beach. With 13,000km of coastline, you're never far from the ocean and you could easily design an itinerary that includes a daily walk on the beach. At **Tunnel Beach**, southwest of Dunedin, you'll find giant sandstone bluffs and a hand-hewn tunnel built by one of the city's early settlers just to give his family access to a beautiful little cove (the 1.5km walk to the beach is closed during the lambing season in August and September). **Ninety Mile Beach** in Northland (➤ 69) is a great sunset location, and for a wild surf try **Piha Beach**, west of Auckland (➤ 68) or **Gillespies Beach** (➤ 181), on the West Coast.

Best Wildlife Views

Swimming with **dolphins** at Kaikoura (➤ 146) or in the Bay of Islands (➤ 62–64) could move you to tears of joy. It's one of the most emotional wildlife experiences to be in the water with hundreds of the graceful creatures. Watching dolphins ride the bow wave of a boat in Milford Sound (➤ 158–60) comes close, and seeing a **sperm whale** relaxing on the water off Kaikoura is awe-inspiring. Hearing the high-pitched call of a **kiwi** tingles the spine, but seeing one in the wild on Stewart Island is unforgettable.

Best Exercise

• Hire some **inline skates** to dart along Wellington's waterfront or squeeze into a kayak for a paddle on the harbour.
• In Auckland, you can be the **skipper of a super-yacht** for a few hours (➤ 54), and see how exhausting it can be.
• In flat Christchurch, the best way to do your sightseeing is **on foot or a bike**.

Best City Views

• Mount Victoria and the cable car terminal in **Wellington's** Botanic Garden (➤ 178) give stunning views over the capital.
• In **Auckland**, zoom up the Sky Tower (➤ 52–53) or drive up to One Tree Hill (➤ 67).
• In **Queenstown**, the top station of the gondola is a good place to be in the evening (➤ 156).
• **Christchurch** (➤ 132–133) looks great from a hot-air balloon.

Best Parks

• **Hagley Park** in Christchurch (➤ 133)
• **Botanic Garden** in Wellington (➤ 178)
• **Eden Garden** in Auckland (➤ 68)
• **Auckland Domain** (➤ 59)
• **Queenstown rose gardens** (➤ 157)

Best Public Facility

The grass-roofed public toilets in the small town of **Kawakawa**, south of the Bay of Islands (➤ 62–64) are the last piece of artful architecture by Friedensreich Hundertwasser. The celebrated eccentric Austrian architect and painter chose the sleepy town as his retirement home and also transformed some of the shop fronts on the main street in his trademark colourful style.

Best Adrenaline Rushes

• Bungy jumping at night (➤ 168–169)
• Zorbing in water (➤ 101)

Best Boat Trip

A cruise of **Milford Sound** (➤ 158–160) is hard to beat as far as the drama of the dripping landscape is concerned, but **Doubtful Sound** offers a more remote kind of wilderness experience (➤ 160).

Unbeatable views from the Sky Tower

Christchurch: city of gardens

Cruising Milford Sound

Tranquil Doubtful Sound

The coast-to-coast traverse of the Southern Alps is one of the great rail journeys of the world. From the Pacific to the Tasman Sea, the TranzAlpine chugs through 231km of the South Island's ruggedly beautiful scenery, keeping a leisurely pace as it negotiates long-legged viaducts and narrow tunnels.

Christchurch's railway station is a glass-fronted modern structure in the middle of an industrial wasteland. It's an incongruous start to a scenic rail journey, but the sense of anticipation among the small crowd gathered at the and Greymouth (➤ 141), providing the only means of transport for people who needed to cross the Main Divide in bad weather. Rain, wind and snow frequently shut down the western leg of State Highway 73, which cuts

TranzAlpine Tr

TranzAlpine platform is palpable. Surprisingly, many of the people waiting to board the train are seasoned travellers who've already seen much of the world's most breathtaking scenery, but are still open to be inspired by stunning landscapes. Others look forward to one of the highlights of their holiday. And then there are the veteran trainspotters, eager to inspect the locomotive and to compare "specs".

A diesel engine pulls a long line of pale blue carriages up to the platform. Not so long ago only ramshackle railcars travelled along the narrow-gauge track between Christchurch (➤ 132–133)

an almost parallel route through the mountainous immensity of the South Island's alpine spine.

Today the TranzAlpine is still popular with regular travellers between the lush and wild West Coast (➤ 141–143) and the orderly Canterbury Plains, but the comfort level of the modern carriages reflects the growing number of travellers and rail buffs on the train. About 200,000 people have travelled on the TranzAlpine every year since it was launched as a tourist attraction in 1987.

For the first 20 minutes of the half-day journey to Greymouth, the train speeds – relatively speaking – through

Above: Photo opportunities abound on this stunning trip

suburbia and the city's rural outskirts to Rolleston, where it leaves the main south line to veer west towards the mountains. As the TranzAlpine rumbles through the flat alluvial Canterbury Plains, passing rolling pastures, deer and ostrich farms and small rural townships, there's plenty of time to socialise with your neighbours. The seating arrangement encourages this, with a line of tables each

ain Adventure

surrounded by four upholstered chairs, with just enough space to spread out a newspaper or eat your lunch.

Springfield, a former railway service centre about an hour from Christchurch, marks the start of the long alpine haul to Arthur's Pass (➤ 139–140). Here, the bush-clad foothills start stretching beyond the tree line, exposing the first raw rock faces and bare summits.

As the TranzAlpine enters a labyrinth of gorges and hills, it crosses the first viaduct, which spans more than 200m across the dry shingle bed of the Kowhai River.

For the next hour, the journey becomes a scenic and

spectacular slide show. No fewer than 16 short tunnels act as the light switch between stupendous vistas of magnificent deep-cut river canyons and soaring mountains. About 85km from Christchurch, the rust-coloured "T" of the Staircase Viaduct connects two tunnels and, at 73m (3m higher than Christchurch Cathedral), marks the highest of a sequence of tall steel bridges the TranzAlpine has to cross on its way through the mountains, until it emerges into the broad valleys of the Waimakariri and Bealy rivers. In summer, the braided Waimakariri (Maori for "cold water") runs through its wide

Above: The alpine landscapes of Canterbury

gravel bed in trickles and streams, but after a storm it swells to a thunderous river that carves the landscape.

The alpine sheep stations in this area are some of the largest in the country and a tribute to the determination of farmers who still graze their flocks in the steep hills surrounding the fertile river flats. While most of the high-country homesteads reflect the wealth of Canterbury's oldest farming families, the railway stations along the way are often no bigger than a spacious goat shed, albeit in the most scenic of settings.

alpine township to explore some of the nearby walks. As the train starts its steep down-hill ride to the West Coast, it disappears into the 8.5km Otira Tunnel for more than ten minutes. At the time of the Otira Tunnel's construc-tion in 1923 it became famous as the longest tunnel in the British Empire. It was the final link between the east and west coast.

At the other end the land-scape is dramatically different. Dense and luscious rainforest hangs in fronds over the track and huge flax bushes push against the embankment.

Left: Make sure you get a window seat
Right: Nature and people coexist in the wilderness

Arthur's Pass, 737m above sea level, is the end point of the climb. The TranzAlpine stops for a short break, but several passengers usually decide to stay at the tiny

Gems on the western leg include the Otira Hotel, Tara-makau River, rich in fish and greenstone, vast patches of sweating rainforest and the trout-filled Lake Brunner.

Planning Your Journey

• The TranzAlpine makes the return trip every day. It leaves Christchurch at 9 am and arrives in Greymouth at 1:25 pm, then leaves Greymouth at 2:25 pm for the return journey, arriving back in Christchurch at 6:35 pm.

• Most visitors travel one way and explore the West Coast for a day or two before returning on the train or by car or bus. Make your bookings as early as possible, particularly if you're planning to travel during the summer holiday period in December and January, by calling 0800 802 802 (toll-free) or 00 64 4 498 3303 from overseas. You can also write to Tranz Scenic, Tranz Rail Ltd, Private Bag, Wellington, New Zealand, or fax 00 64 4 498 3090 (www.tranzrailtravel.co.nz/ tranzScenic/theTranzAlpine/overview.asp). Tranz Rail's reservations centre is open seven days a week, from 7 am to 9 pm.

Finding Your Feet

First Two Hours

New Zealand's three main international airports are at Auckland, Wellington and Christchurch. Some flights from Australia also land at Queenstown, Dunedin, Hamilton and Palmerston North.

Ground Transport Fares
£ under NZ$10 ££ NZ$11–$20 £££ NZ$21–$30 ££££ over NZ$30

Travelling by air

■ All passengers arriving on international flights have to clear customs and immigration and undergo **biosecurity checks**. On your plane, you'll fill in an arrival card and a declaration form for any biosecurity risk goods (meat, dairy products, fruit, plant and animal material) you may be carrying. Sniffer dogs work at the baggage claim area, monitoring luggage for **animal and vegetable products**. Officers from the Ministry of Agriculture and Forestry will check your declaration form and luggage if necessary. Packaged foods are usually acceptable, but if you're unsure it is best to declare what you are bringing in and **check with the MAF officers**. Fines for knowingly or accidentally bringing in undeclared biosecurity-risk goods can be up to NZ$10,000, plus an instant fine of NZ$200.
■ Travellers leaving New Zealand on international flights must pay an **international departure charge**. Payments can be made in cash or with a credit card at the airport, but sometimes travel agents will add the fee to your ticket price.

Arriving in Auckland

■ About 80 per cent of flights into New Zealand arrive at the **international terminal** of the **Auckland International Airport**, 23 km from the city.
■ **Once you exit customs** on the ground floor, there are information and foreign exchange desks, luggage storage facilities, a domestic transfer check-in counter and car-hire desks.
■ The best way to get to downtown is on the **Airbus** (tel: 0800 247 287, ££), which leaves from the forecourt of the arrivals area (to your left as you exit the terminal). It departs every 20 minutes from 6 am to 10 pm and takes about 50 minutes to get to the city, stopping at all major hotels and landmarks along the way. It may make extra stops on request if they are *en route*. Buy your ticket on the bus.
■ Some hotels have **free shuttle services**, so check with your accommodation.
■ Small **door-to-door shuttle buses** (£££; **Supershuttle:** tel: 0800 748 885, toll-free), which wait for passengers outside the terminal, are only slightly more expensive than the Airbus but can often be faster.
■ **Taxis** (££££) are the most expensive means of transport. Both taxis and shuttle buses leave from a bay to your left as you leave the terminal.
■ If you are **transferring to a domestic flight**, the domestic terminal is about 800m away. Follow the blue lines painted on the pavement outside the international terminal, or catch the free inter-terminal bus, which departs every 20 minutes from the arrivals end of the forecourt.
■ Any of the transport options from the airport to the city will drop you off where you need to go, but **orientation is straightforward**. The airport is to the south of the city, overlooking Manukau Harbour. The main artery downtown is Queen Street, which stretches from Quay Street at the waterfront to the junction of the city's main motorways.

Auckland Visitor Information Centres

■ The centre at the international terminal is **open daily** while flights are arriving or leaving. The office at the domestic terminal is open 7–7.

■ The inner city information centres (287 Queen Street and at the Viaduct Basin, corner of Quay and Hobson streets; tel: (09) 979 2333; reservations@aucklandnz.com; www.aucklandnz.com) are open 9–5:30, with extended hours during peak seasons.

■ The centres offer **free maps, brochures and up-to-date timetables**.

Arriving in Wellington

■ **Wellington International Airport** is about 10km from the inner city on the edge of the Miramar peninsula. The **international and domestic terminals** are housed within the same building.

■ International passengers arrive on the **ground floor of the terminal building**. Car-hire desks and luggage storage facilities are near the baggage claim carousels, and an information desk, shops and cafés are on the first floor, near the check-in counters.

■ The best way to get to the city is on the **Flyer** (£), which connects the airport with central Wellington and the Hutt Valley. The bus departs from a bay on the right of the arrivals area, every 30 minutes on weekdays (7:20 am–8:20 pm) and at weekends and public holidays (7:50 am– 8:50 pm; hourly before 8:50 am and after 6:50 pm).

■ **Taxis** (£££) and **shuttles** (££) depart from bays opposite the main exit.

■ **Wellington's inner city** stretches along the waterfront, between Mount Victoria (overlooking Oriental Parade) and the Parliament complex. The main arteries through downtown are The Terrace, with several offices, and Lambton Quay, with shopping arcades and cafés.

■ Wellington can be **confusing for drivers** because the streets don't follow a regular grid and the inner city is circumnavigated by a one-way system. The motorway runs through Wellington. Beyond the city centre it forks into SH1, going north to the Kapiti Coast, and SH2, to the Hutt Valley.

Wellington Visitor Information Centre

■ The **main centre** is on 110 Wakefield Street, at the corner of Civic Square (tel: (04) 802 4860; bookings@wellingtonnz.com; www.wellingtonnz.com). The centre has free maps and information about attractions, accommodation, and regional buses and trains. Open Mon–Fri 8:30–5:30, Sat–Sun 9:30–5:30.

Arriving in Christchurch

■ International flights arrive at **Christchurch International Airport**, about 12km northwest of the city centre. The **international and domestic terminals** are close together. There are information and car-hire desks at both.

■ The **Canride Airport Bus** (£; tel: (03) 366 8855) departs from a bay just outside the international terminal, on weekdays every 30 minutes from 6:45 am to 6:15 pm and then hourly to 9:15 pm; at weekends and public holidays every hour from 8 am to 9 pm (8 am to 7 pm on Sundays), with additional services at 2:30 pm and 3:30 pm.

■ **Taxis** (££) and **shuttles** (£) depart from a lane beginning outside the domestic and international terminals.

■ Christchurch is laid out in a **grid pattern**, with Colombo Street as the main north–south thoroughfare, going though Cathedral Square and ending at the Port Hills in the south. Hagley Park is a dominant feature, separating the inner city from the western suburbs.

Getting Around

City Transport Fares
£ under NZ$5 **££** NZ$6–$10 **£££** NZ$11–$15 **££££** NZ$16–$20

Intercity Transport Fares
£ under NZ$30 **££** NZ$31–$50 **£££** NZ$51–$100 **££££** over NZ$100

Most telephone numbers beginning 0800 are free within New Zealand only.

In Auckland

- Auckland has an integrated public transport system that comprises buses, trains and ferries. Contact **Rideline** (tel: (09) 366 6400; www.rideline.co.nz) for all routes and timetables.
- **Buses** (£) depart from various city centre streets.
- At Visitor Information Centres you can get the **Auckland Busabout Guide**, which lists all destinations, their bus route number and departure point.
- The **Link Bus** (£) travels clockwise and anticlockwise around a loop that includes most of the inner-city attractions. The bus runs about every ten minutes (6 am–10:30 pm Mon–Thu; 6 am–11:30 pm Fri; 7 am–11:30 pm Sat; 7 am–11 pm Sun). During the America's Cup, there is also a free bus that runs between the waterfont and inner-city attractions.
- The Link and other buses often connect with **ferries** across to Auckland's northern suburbs (££) and to the Hauraki Gulf islands (£££). Ferries depart from the berth between Princes and Queens Wharf. The most frequent ferry connections are to Devonport (every 30 minutes, 6:15 am–11 pm), Birkenhead (every 1–2 hours, 7:20 am–8:40 pm Mon–Fri) and Bayswater (about hourly, 6:55 am–9:10 pm Mon–Fri) in the north, and to Waiheke Island (every 30 minutes or hourly, 5:30 am–11:30 pm). Contact **Fullers** (tel: (09) 367 9111; www.fullers.co.nz/main.html) for timetables.
- The metropolitan **commuter train service** (£–££; Tranz Metro, tel: (09) 366 6400) runs west to Waitakere and south to Papakura.

In Wellington

- Wellington has an **excellent public transport network**, with buses running frequently and late into the night. Almost 30 per cent of those who commute into central Wellington use public transport. The visitor information centre has maps of the capital's bus network; or contact Ridewell (tel: (04) 801 7000, 0800 801 7000 toll-free; www.wrc.g.ovt.nz/timetables) for route and timetable details.
- **Buses** connect the inner city with all suburbs, including the Hutt Valley.
- The **Stadium Shuttle** (£) is a special service linking the central city with the WestpacTrust Stadium. For most major events, services commence approximately two hours prior to the start and continue to leave from the stadium about every 15 minutes until the crowd has dispersed.
- The **City Circular** (£) takes in all major inner-city attractions and destinations. The distinctive yellow buses travel the circuit every ten minutes (weekdays 7:30–6, Sat 9–6, Sun and public holidays 9:50–6).
- **Tranz Metro** also operates a metropolitan commuter train service (£–££) in Wellington, connecting the inner city with Upper Hutt in the Hutt Valley and Paraparaumu on the Kapiti Coast north of the capital.

In Christchurch

- Most **buses** (£) depart from the Bus Exchange in Lichfield Street, where the Businfo kiosk (tel: (03) 366 8855) has all route plans and timetables. Staff members are exceptionally helpful and will book door-to-door **shuttle buses** (£) to destinations not covered by the bus network (such as the railway station).
- The **Shuttle** (free) is a bus service that runs along a loop between the town hall and convention centre, through the central city to a shopping mall south of the city. The bus runs every 10–15 minutes (Mon–Thu 8 am–10:30 pm; Fri 8 am–midnight; Sat 9 am–midnight; Sun and public holidays 10 am–8 pm).

Visitor Information Network

There are more than 100 official visitor information centres in New Zealand, indicated by the green "i" logo. Most of them are open seven days a week, with opening hours depending on the season. The centres offer free maps and help with information and bookings. Ask for the Visitor Information Network directory, which lists all centres and includes their address, phone and email details.

Intercity Connections

Domestic Flights

- **Air New Zealand** (0800 737 000 toll-free; www.airnz.com) is the country's international and main domestic airline, providing daily domestic connections between 26 destinations. The main hubs are Auckland, Wellington, Christchurch and Queenstown, and flights are available to most cities in New Zealand. Special fares are available on most sectors, usually involving advance bookings and payments (three weeks prior to departure). These special fares can be booked only in New Zealand, but cheaper fares may be available in connection with an international flight (ask your travel agent).
- **Freedom Air** (part of the Air New Zealand group, 0800 600 500 toll-free; www.freedom.co.nz) offers flights along the main trunk between Auckland, Wellington and Christchurch.
- **Qantas** (0800 808 767 toll-free; www.qantas.com) also operates services along the main trunk.
- **Origin Pacific** (tel: (03) 547 2020, 0800 302 302 toll-free; www.originpacific.co.nz) operates flights to several national destinations, mostly in the North Island and between Wellington and Nelson.
- **Soundsair** (0800 505 005 toll-free) flies between Wellington and Picton.

Buses

- Long-distance buses travel along all major routes (£–££). The main company is **Intercity** (tel: (09) 913 6100; info@coachnet.co.nz; www.intercitycoach.co.nz), which also operates **Newmans** (tel: (09) 913 6200; info@coachnet.co.nz; www.newmanscoach.co.nz). Both bus services offer a range of travel passes, which allow for unlimited travel in a particular region.

Trains

- New Zealand's train system, operated by **Tranz Rail** (tel: (04) 498 3303, 0800 802 802 toll-free; passengerservices@tranzrail.co.nz; www.tranzrail-travel.co.nz), runs along a main trunk from Auckland to Wellington and Picton to Christchurch, with the TranzAlpine branching to Greymouth.
- Trains are comfortable, and about as fast as buses, but more expensive.

Ferries

■ Tranz Rail also operates the ferry services across Cook Strait. There are two car and passenger ferries: *The Interislander*, which takes about three hours, and *The Lynx* fast ferry, which crosses the Strait in two and a quarter hours.

Shuttles

■ Several small door-to-door shuttle bus companies offer useful **regional services**. Ask at the Visitor Information Centre or consult the local Yellow Pages under the keyword "buses".

Driving

■ **Motorways** are generally fast two-carriageway roads; numbered **State Highways** (single or dual carriageway) link major cities; **rural roads** are usually single-carriageway links between smaller centres; and you'll find **unsealed roads** in remote areas. Distances are measured in kilometres.

■ Outside the main centres, **traffic is light** and driver courtesy is reasonable.

■ The usual minimum legal age to **hire a car** in New Zealand is 21, in some cases 25. Most companies require an international drivering licence. Because hire car accidents are common in New Zealand, insurance premiums are relatively high.

■ Check with your hire company whether any roads are excluded from your **insurance policy**. Most companies don't cover the road to Skippers Canyon (➤ 168), and don't allow you to drive on Ninety Mile Beach (➤ 69).

■ For up-to-date **State Highway Reports**, call 0900 33 222 (at a charge of $1 per minute).

■ Regular road signs give the frequency for the **local tourist radio station**. Tune in to hear the hourly news bulletins, which usually end with a traffic and weather report for the area.

■ If you are a member of a motoring organisation affiliated to the Alliance Internationale de Tourisme (AIT), then you are entitled, for a period up to six months, to reciprocal services from the **New Zealand Automobile Association**. If you break down, call 0800 224 357 toll-free.

Road Rules

■ **Drive on the left**. On a motorway, keep to the left lane unless you are passing another vehicle.

■ When **turning at a junction**, give way to traffic not turning, and to all traffic crossing or approaching from your right.

■ **When turning left at a junction** and a vehicle coming from the opposite direction is turning right, you must give way (this differs to the turning rules in many other countries).

■ **Traffic signals** are red, amber and green, and you cannot turn left at a red light, unless there is a green arrow pointing left.

■ All occupants, including passengers – adults and children – in the back seats, must wear **seatbelts**.

■ The normal **maximum speed** on the open road is 100 kph
  in urban areas 50 kph
  in a Limited Speed Zone (LSZ) is 50 kph in adverse weather conditions, 100 kph in normal conditions.

■ **One-lane bridges** are common on rural roads. Approach cautiously and be prepared to give way. Watch for right-of-way signs before the bridge.

■ The **legal limit for alcohol** is 30mg alcohol per 100ml blood for drivers under 20, and 80mg alcohol per 100ml blood for licensed drivers aged 20 and over. There is no insurance cover for drivers over the legal limit.

■ All **cyclists must wear helmets**.

Accommodation

Choose between luxurious country lodges, campsite chalets, bed and breakfast in a character villa, sharing life on a farm, the privacy of a self-catering apartment or the conviviality of a backpacker hostel.

Hotels

- In smaller towns and rural areas, some **pubs** offer simple accommodation with lots of character, but they can be noisy.
- Most **hotel chains** are represented in the main cities and resorts. Rooms have tea and coffee-making facilities and some may also have hair dryers, irons and ironing boards. Many places offer non-smoking rooms.
- **Rates in city hotels** range from around NZ$100 to $700 for a double room. In business areas, hotels may offer discounted rates at weekends.
- Good hotel chains include: **Six Continents** (Crowne Plaza, Inter-Continental, Holiday Inn; tel: 0800 801 111 toll-free, www.sixcontinentshotels.com) and **Flag Choice** (Flag, Quality Hotels; tel: 0800 237 893 toll-free; www.flagchoice.com.au; www.qualityinn.com).

Lodges

- From heritage buildings furnished with antiques to exclusive sporting retreats with fishing, hunting or golf, lodges offer **top-class facilities** in beautiful surroundings, usually in the countryside and often with excellent food. They may cost from NZ$500 to $1,000 per person per night.
- The best way to contact the **New Zealand Lodge Association** is on its website: www.lodgesofnz.co.nz. Alternatively, try: Pen-y-Bryn Lodge, 41 Towey Street, Oamaru.

Motels

- Motels are popular with families and travellers who want to drive to the door of a self-contained unit and cater for themselves. They tend to be **designed for convenience** rather than charm, but are reasonably priced and generally well appointed, with phone, television, *en suite* bathroom and cooking facilities. Laundry facilities may be in a separate block.
- Most motels offer **breakfast**, delivered to the unit at an extra cost. Some complexes have swimming pools and children's playgrounds. Rates are usually around NZ$80–$150 per double room.
- Good motel chains include: **Best Western** (tel: 0800 237 893 toll-free; www.bestwestern.com) and **Golden Chain** (tel: 0800 80 465 336 toll-free; (03) 358 0821; fax: (03) 358 5012; www.goldenchain.co.nz).

Serviced Apartments

- Self-catering apartments are increasingly popular in the larger cities. **Centrally situated**, they may be in converted offices or heritage buildings and range from studios to spacious suites, at prices to match. You can pay anything from NZ$75 to $350 a night, though prices are often reduced at weekends and for stays of several days.
- They usually have **fully equipped kitchens and laundry facilities**, and are serviced daily or according to your needs. Breakfast provisions are often supplied, at least on the first day.
- Good companies for finding serviced apartments are: **Citylife Hotels** (tel: 0800 368 888 toll-free; www.dynasty.co.nz) or **Pacific Star** (tel: (0508) 737 378; www.pacificstar.co.nz).

Bed and Breakfast

- This covers **hosted accommodation** from boutique hotels to guest houses, vineyard cottages, and rooms in private homes ("homestays"). The proprietors live on the premises and you can expect a personal welcome.
- Rooms may have **private or shared bathrooms**. There is usually a guest lounge. Some places offer evening meals as well as breakfast.
- **Prices** range from NZ$80 to $200 or more, with dinner extra.
- For more details contact: **New Zealand Federation of Bed and Breakfast Hotels** (tel: (06) 358 6928; fax: (06) 355 0291; www.nzbhotels.com). Other useful organisations are **Superior Inns of New Zealand** (tel: (03) 328 7209; fax: (03) 328 7209; www.superiorinns.co.nz) and **Heritage and Character Inns of New Zealand** (www.heritageinns.co.nz).

Home and Farm Stays

- **Staying with a family** at their home or farm for a couple of days is a popular way to meet the locals. Guests share family meals and you can often join in the milking, mustering, shearing, or harvesting crops.
- The **cost** is likely to be around NZ$80 to $150 a double for bed and breakfast, with dinner extra.
- The following organisations can help you: **Friendly Connections** (tel: (03) 355 6737; fax: (03) 355 6737; www.nzhomestay.co.nz), **Rural Holidays New Zealand** (tel: (03) 355 6218; 0800 88 33 55 toll-free; fax: (03) 355 6271; www.ruralhols.co.nz), **New Zealand Farm Holidays** (tel: (09) 412 9649; fax: (09) 412 9651; www.nzaccom.co.nz).

Budget Accommodation

- **Backpacker hostels** are booming in New Zealand, with about 450 purveyors offering anything from dormitories at NZ$15 a night to double rooms with private bathrooms at around $50. There are **communal** cooking facilities and a lounge. Bed linen may be provided at an extra charge.
- **Campsites and holiday parks** are often in beautiful locations. Many have chalets which, though modestly furnished, have fully equipped kitchens and private bathrooms and sleep a family comfortably for around $50.
- Contact: **Budget Backpacker Hostels** (fax: (07) 377 1568; www.backpack.co.nz), **Hostelling International (YHA)** (tel: (03) 379 9970; 0800 278 299 toll-free; fax: (03) 365 4476; www.yha.org.nz), **Holiday Accommodation Parks New Zealand** (tel: (04) 298 3283; fax: (04) 298 9284; www.holidayparks.co.nz)

Practical Tips

- **Prices tend to be higher in the north of the North Island** and may climb steeply in the main tourist resorts during the high season.
- **Pre-book in peak season** (Dec to Apr), and in ski resorts in the winter.
- **Tourism New Zealand**'s website, www.purenz.com, is useful. **AA New Zealand Travel Guides** (PO Box 101 001 North Shore Mail Centre, Auckland; www.aaguides.co.nz), published annually, include detailed accommodation directories, especially of motels and campsites.
- The **Qualmark** rating and classification system, a joint venture by Tourism New Zealand and the NZAA, awards stars to hotels, motels, hostels and holiday parks, based on annual assessments.

The following categories are used for hotels listed in this guide, based on two people sharing a double room:

£ under NZ$150   ££ NZ$150–$300   £££ more than NZ$300

Food and Drink

Eating out has changed dramatically in the last decade. Liberated by new licensing laws, Kiwis have embraced the café society. Dining tends to be casual, compared with Europe, and award-winning chefs are as likely to be found in bustling brasseries and vineyard restaurants as in top hotels.

New Zealand Food

■ New Zealand's **European heritage** is largely British, with a farming culture strong on roast meat, baking and hearty breakfasts. You may still get this sort of food at farm and homestays and country pubs, but nowadays a family meal is more likely to be a barbecue.

■ Modern New Zealand chefs draw on influences from **Asia, the Mediterranean and the Pacific**, developing a cuisine that reflects the climate and New Zealand's position in the world, sometimes called "Pacific Rim" food. Menus often focus on regional products, such as lamb, scallops, oysters, wines and cheeses. Many vineyards have restaurants offering food to match their wines.

■ Although New Zealand is still largely a nation of meat-eaters, most restaurants offer **vegetarian** options, and there are some specialist vegetarian establishments.

Fine Dining
Fine dining in a formal sense is not common in New Zealand. The surroundings may be spectacular and the food exquisitely presented, but Kiwis are an informal lot. Meals can cost less than NZ$100 a head.

Four of the Best
■ **Vinnie's**, Herne Bay (➤ 73)
■ **Logan Brown**, Wellington (➤ 123)
■ **Herzog's**, Blenheim (➤ 123–124)
■ **Pescatore at the George**, Christchurch (➤ 147)

Cafés
Stylish and quirky, often with deli bars and a reputation for good coffee, these are popular meeting places, and good value. A main course usually costs less than $15; a coffee around $3.50.

Ethnic Restaurants and Takeaways
Informal ethnic restaurants offer some of the cheapest eating options. Japanese sushi bars and Thai, Chinese, Mexican and Indian restaurants are common, and often have takeaway services. Chinese *yum cha* (also known as *dim sum*) is popular at weekend lunchtimes – a range of Cantonese *hors d'oeuvres*, washed down with copious amounts of Chinese tea. The favourite takeaways are still meat pies, and fish and chips.

Hangi
Many places, especially in Rotorua, offer the opportunity to try a Maori *hangi*. Traditionally, this is a simple meal of meat and vegetables cooked over hot stones in an underground oven. Although a version can be tasted at some hotels, for a more authentic experience it's best to go to a *marae* (area around a meeting house) or other Maori venue, such as Tamaki Maori Village (➤ 94–95) or Whakarewarewa (➤ 85). See also ➤ 89.

Bring Your Own (BYO)

Some restaurants still allow you to bring your own wine to drink with the meal. You save the restaurant's mark-up fee, but they charge corkage.

Pubs

Cheap, hearty meals are available in many country pubs. Pubs serve a range of draught and bottled beer, spirits and a limited range of wine. Boutique breweries offering interesting local beers are increasingly popular, especially in the cities.

Practical Tips

- **Restaurant hours** are usually noon–2:30 pm for lunch, and 6:30–10:30 for dinner, although many **cafés** offer all-day dining, and **bar snacks** may be served until the early hours.
- **Service charges and government taxes** are included in menu prices. Tipping is not traditional, although it is becoming more widespread in tourist centres and upmarket restaurants.
- When travelling, **take a picnic** – there may be long distances between refreshments. Places in country towns close early and may not open at the weekend.

Ten of the Best for...

...**Location**: Duke of Marlborough Hotel, Russell (➤ 74)
...**View**: Panorama Room at the Hermitage, Aoraki/Mount Cook (➤ 147)
...**Breakfast**: 50 on Park at the George, Christchurch (➤ 147)
...**Vineyard lunch**: Twelve Trees Restaurant, Blenheim (➤ 124)
...**Afternoon tea**: The Blue Baths, Rotorua (➤ 99)
...**Seafood**: Kermadec, Auckland (➤ 73)
...**West Coast tavern**: Mahinapua Pub, Hokitika (➤ 143)
...**Heritage building**: Coronation Bath House, Queenstown (➤ 172)
...**Country café**: Colenso, Coromandel Peninsula (➤ 74)
...**People-watching**: The Strip, Christchurch (➤ 150)

Kiwi Specialities

- **Kumara**: sweet potato
- **Manuka honey**: distinctively flavoured honey, from the flowers of the manuka (the New Zealand tea tree, known for its medicinal properties)
- **Feijoas**: an egg-shaped fruit with green skin and aromatic, cream-coloured flesh. You'll find it fresh, stewed, pickled or juiced
- **Tamarillos** (tree tomatoes): egg-shaped fruit with gold or crimson skin and dark seeds. Eat fresh, as a sweet or savoury sauce, or as a chutney
- **Greenshell mussels**: native New Zealand mussels, with green-lipped shell
- **Bluff** (deep sea) **oysters**, **crayfish** rock lobster and **Nelson scallops**
- **Kina**: sea eggs, with prickly shell and edible roe. Be warned; these are usually eaten raw and are an acquired taste!
- **Paua**: abalone, with meaty black flesh, usually eaten as steaks or fritters
- **Pavlova**: meringue and fruit dessert, the subject of much friendly rivalry between New Zealand and Australia as to which country invented it
- **Hokey pokey**: honeycomb toffee
- **Milo**: a popular malted milk energy drink

The following categories are used for restaurants listed in this guide, based on the price per person for a three-course meal, excluding drinks:

£ up to NZ$45   **££** NZ$45–$60   **£££** over NZ$60

Shopping

New Zealand is fast losing the sleepy hollow reputation that caused wits to quip that they had visited, but it was closed. Liberalised trading hours mean it's now possible to shop every day in many places. You can find a range of shopping, from chic boutiques and old-fashioned department stores to factory outlets, markets, craft co-operatives and fashion retailers. In the suburbs, traditional or individual shops are being replaced by undercover one-stop shopping centres. Goods posted to overseas destinations are free of the 12.5 per cent government tax normally imposed, and many stores offer mailing and shipping services.

Arts and Crafts

- Everywhere you go, no matter how small the community, there's likely to be a **gallery** or **co-operative** selling paintings or pottery, woodcarving or jewellery. With ventures like the Nelson craft trail and Christchurch Arts Centre you can meet the artist and buy direct. In Northland, look out for items made from swamp kauri – wood up to 50,000 years old, buried after some ancient natural disaster, which is being unearthed and transformed into anything from tables to bookends.
- **Pictures of native birds**, **flowers and woods** decorate souvenirs, from mugs to ashtrays, T-shirts and corkscrews to placemats. Paua (abalone) are used to cultivate iridescent pearls, which command top prices.
- **Maori art** is unique to New Zealand: intricate wood carvings on canoes and meeting houses depict ancestors and tell traditional stories. Paua shell, used for the eyes of *tiki* (human figures), and greenstone (jade), used for weapons and symbolic gifts, are now turned into jewellery and ornaments in traditional and modern designs.
- Also popular are **bone carvings** in fish-hook and symbolic designs – you can even carve your own. Rotorua is a good place to watch Maori artists and hear explanations of their work (➤ 85).
- **Antiques shops** often turn up bargains for collectors, especially 19th-century furniture and silver brought over by early European settlers. Browse around High Street in Christchurch, George Street in Dunedin, and Cuba Street in Wellington.

Sheep Products

- With an estimated 20 sheep to every person, it's not surprising that sheepskin turns up in many guises, from hats, slippers, gloves and coats to rugs.
- The wool is made into a remarkable range of garments: handspun jerseys, rugged Swanndri bush jackets, gossamer-soft merino underwear and trans-seasonal fashion knitwear by houses like Sabatini.
- Lanolin is used in a range of skin-care products.

Clothing

- New Zealand's funky young **fashion designers** are making a splash on international catwalks with labels like Nom D, Zambesi, Zana Feuchs and Kate Sylvester. Their designs are often available here at a fraction of what you would pay overseas.
- Some designers have their own outlets in Auckland, but each of the main centres has a fashion quarter worth exploring: High Street and Merivale in Christchurch, Lambton Quay and Willis Street in Wellington,

High Street and Newmarket in Auckland.
- **Dressmart** operates multiple factory outlet shopping malls in Auckland, Wellington and Christchurch.
- **Outdoors enthusiasts** head for Christchurch, home to specialist manufacturers and importers such as Mainland, Macpac, Kathmandu and Bivouac, to stock up on high-tech sports and climbing gear. Christchurch is also home to the Canterbury brand of leisurewear, which has outlets in the main tourist centres.
- **All Black** rugby shirts and other paraphernalia associated with New Zealand's sporting heroes are available from most souvenir shops.

Wine
- New Zealand wines have a growing **international reputation**, particularly Marlborough's distinctive sauvignon blanc, but the range exported is limited, so wine-lovers will enjoy the opportunity to discover labels and grape varieties produced by the more than 300 wineries dotted around the country.
- Marlborough and Hawkes Bay are the **main wine-producing areas**, but picturesque vineyards and fine wines can also be found in the Auckland region, Martinborough, Nelson, Canterbury and Otago.
- Many wineries are open for **tastings**.
- **Dessert wines**, affectionately known as "stickies", are particularly good value compared with prices in Europe.
- Supermarkets sell wine quite cheaply, but specialist shops such as Glengarry in Auckland and Vino Fino in Christchurch have a **wider selection of top labels**. A word of warning: many wines are made in such small quantities that they are only available from the winery itself or from certain restaurants.
- For descriptions of individual wines, ➤ 14–15.
- For more details on wine trails, ➤ 46. For tours in a particular region, see the relevant Where to... Be Entertained section of this guide.

Food
- In country areas, **roadside stalls and farms** sell local produce, from organic fruit and vegetables to lavender, honey, cheese and salmon.
- **Native flower honeys** such as rata and manuka make attractive gifts. They are available prettily packaged at souvenir shops or more cheaply at supermarkets.
- **Apricots, cherries, apples** and **kiwi fruit** are turned into fruit brandies, chocolates and preserves – even kiwi fruit wine.
- Lovers of **New Zealand lamb** can take home top-quality meat packaged for export by Gourmet Direct (tel: 0800 737 800 toll-free; fax: (06) 870 6597; sales@gourmetdirect.co.nz; www.gourmetdirect.com

Shopping Hours
- **Shopping hours** are generally 9 am–5:30 pm, with a late night, usually Friday, until 9 pm.
- **In smaller towns**, shops may close at 1 pm on Saturday and all day Sunday.
- In large cities **supermarkets** are often open daily 8 am–9 pm, at least.

Methods of Payment
Most city shops are geared up for EFTPOS (Electronic Funds Transfer at Point of Sale) and accept major credit cards. Be prepared to pay cash at markets and in some rural areas. Travellers' cheques can be exchanged at most banks.

Entertainment

Outdoor Activities

- New Zealanders love the great outdoors. **All the major cities are at or near the sea** – Auckland and Wellington spectacularly so – and unspoiled countryside is never far away. Local councils and the Department of Conservation maintain a range of footpaths, and guide maps are available from visitor centres.
- The most popular swimming beaches are manned by **lifeguards** during the summer.
- **Spectator sports**, especially rugby, rugby league and cricket, command a passionate following. All the main centres have large stadiums and host national matches and international tests.
- **Horse-racing** is also a popular day out. Each racecourse has regular meetings: phone the local Harness Racing or Jockey Club for details.
- **Golf** is very popular, and many courses are in spectacular sites.
- Salmon and trout **fishing** are also popular, especially around Taupo and the South Island rivers, with guides who can supply equipment. Sea fishing trips are on offer at all seaside resorts.
- Surfing, windsurfing, sailing, parasailing, kayaking, water skiing – whatever **water sport** takes your fancy, someone will be offering to hire out the gear and teach you what to do.
- **Skiing** may be less glamorous in New Zealand than in Europe but, particularly in the South Island, it's accessible, as challenging as you want and relatively cheap. During the ski season, usually June to September, you can hire equipment on the field or from shops in town.

Adventure Sports

- To many travellers, New Zealand is synonymous with adventure sports such as bungy jumping, jet boating, sea kayaking, white-water rafting, zorbing, sky diving and ever more daring variations of such activities.
- Make sure the risks you take don't extend to your insurance – it's imperative that your policy is extended before you go to cover named "dangerous sports". The slight extra cost could save you thousands of dollars in medical bills. See also Insurance ➤ 194.

Performing Arts

- New Zealand's **national symphony orchestra and ballet company**, both based in Wellington, perform regularly, and there are plenty of theatres, opera companies, choirs and orchestras elsewhere.
- At festivals and in the long summer holidays, the **arts move outdoors**, with opera under the stars, theatre in the park, vineyard concerts, buskers in the street, and free programmes of family entertainment.

Festivals and Shows

From art deco in Napier (February) to wild foods in Hokitika (March), New Zealanders love any excuse for a festival.

- In February, you could also catch the start of the month-long **International Festival of the Arts** in Wellington, the gay and lesbian **Hero Parade** in Auckland, and **wine and food** festivals in Marlborough, Queenstown, Hawke's Bay, Nelson, Canterbury, Devonport and the Coromandel.
- Most of the main centres hold annual **literary festivals** at different times of the year.

- **Pacific Island culture** is celebrated with Pasifika in March, held in Auckland. For many, the most significant national event is **Waitangi Day**, on 6 February, when the birth of the nation is celebrated in Waitangi and on *marae* all over the country.
- **Agricultural shows** are important events in each region, with funfairs and food stalls alongside the prize cattle, sheep-shearing and wood-chopping competitions. Auckland's Royal Easter Show, and Showtime Canterbury, held in November, are among the most popular.
- New Zealand's major horticultural event, the **Ellerslie Flower Show**, is held at Auckland Regional Botanic Gardens in November.
- See also recommendations in the Where to... Be Entertained sections.

Wine Trails

- Going to a vineyard for a **wine-tasting** or lunch is a popular pastime, especially in the warmer months. Many wineries welcome visitors and have built attractive cellar-door facilities, often with a restaurant.
- **Regions have their distinctive personalities** but as a rough guide, Marlborough is the biggest, Nelson and Waiheke are the prettiest, Waipara and Martinborough are so compact you can walk between some vineyards, Hawke's Bay has the best range of reds, and Central Otago has the most spectacular sites.
- **Wine trail maps** of most regions are available from wineries or visitor centres. Wine trail tours range from small, education-orientated groups to party buses. The local visitor centre should be able to advise.

Nightspots

- Apart from the nightclubs on Auckland's **K Road** (➤ 76) and Wellington's **Courtenay Place** (➤ 126) night life in most New Zealand centres is focused on **restaurants and bars**.
- Several of the bigger cities and resorts have casinos that stay open until the early hours, or even 24 hours a day. Some, like Sky City in Auckland, are large and purpose-built, with a choice of restaurants, bars and gaming rooms; others are boutique affairs in ornate heritage buildings. Dress codes and age restrictions may be applied.

Making Reservations

Many theatres, concert halls and sporting venues use booking agencies such as Ticketek and Response Ticketing who can advise on the availability of tickets and make the bookings for you. Check the local phone book.

Some Kiwi Treats

- Hokey-pokey ice-cream
- Wine-tasting on Waiheke Island
- Coffee in a Wellington café
- Windsurfing on the Estuary in Christchurch
- Do-it-yourself bone carving
- Bush walks
- The Devonport ferry
- Queenstown at sunset
- A pie and a pint in a West Coast pub

Admission Prices: categories used in this guide:

Inexpensive up to NZ$10 **Moderate** NZ$10–$20 **Expensive** more than NZ$20

Around Auckland

Getting Your Bearings

Auckland is New Zealand's only truly big city, but size has not diminished its charms. The "City of Sails" is regularly voted one of the world's top ten cities for its cosmopolitan lifestyle and exhilarating recreational opportunities.

Set between two harbours, Auckland's heart is the waterfront, with its busy wharf, attractive marinas and an inviting café scene. In the Maori language, Auckland is known as *Tamaki Makau Rau* – "the spouse of a hundred lovers" – and Aucklanders certainly are passionate about their city. More than a million people – almost a third of all New Zealanders – call Auckland home. Many can't understand why anybody would want to live south of the Bombay Hills, which form an imaginary boundary line south of the city.

Aucklanders have good reason for their local patriotism. Their metropolis blends modern city life with an easily accessible outdoor playground. Mountain ranges, rainforests and the glistening Hauraki Gulf with its myriad islands are all within reach – and even the bustling downtown breathes easily, courtesy of countless parks that cover the city's dramatic volcanic landscape.

Apart from its metropolitan and outdoor appeal, Auckland is also home to the world's largest concentration of Polynesian people, who add an eclectic mix of languages and traditions and make the city pulsate to the rhythm of the Pacific.

For those who want to escape from city life, Auckland is the ideal gateway to subtropical Northland and the Bay of Islands, or the rugged and romantic Coromandel peninsula.

The Hole in the Rock is a highlight of a Bay of Islands visit. Page 47: Maori carvings turn up in unexpected corners of Auckland

Bay of Islands
5 **12** Swimming with dolphins
Kerikeri
Russell
Paihia
Kaikohe
Kawakawa
Hikurangi
Whangarei
Poor Knights Islands
0   50 km
0   30 miles
Dargaville
Ruakaka
Waipu
Hen and Chicken Islands
Little Barrier Island
Port Fitzroy
Great Barrier Island
Wellsford
Cape Colville
Mercury Islands
Orewa   Tiritiri Matangi Island
Colville
Coromandel
Whitianga
Gannet colony at Muriwai Beach **11**
Whangaparaoa
Devonport
4 Hauraki Gulf
Waimauku
Rangitoto Island
AUCKLAND
6 Coromandel
Tairua
Piha Beach **10**
Manukau Harbour
Firth of Thames
Waiuku
Pukekohe
Thames
L. Waikare

Life is a beach in Auckland, which basks in a mild, maritime climate and is blessed with accessible islands and regional parks. The ocean is a constant presence as you explore the subtropical north and the rugged Coromandel peninsula.

In Five Days

Day 1

Morning
From **❶ Downtown**, get your bearings from the viewing platform of the **Sky Tower** (left; ➤ 52–53), with sweeping views over Auckland's skyline and its volcanic hills. Then stroll down **Queen Street** from **Aotea Square** (➤ 52) and explore downtown Auckland. Collect brochures and bus timetables at the visitor information centre at the Viaduct Basin (➤ 54), where you can also pick up a map for the Link bus (➤ 59), which runs a circular route past most of Auckland's attractions. At the **❷ Harbour**, Viaduct Basin is the site of New Zealand's America's Cup victory (➤ 25–27), as well as the **New Zealand National Maritime Museum** (➤ 54–55). Have lunch at its café.

Afternoon
Catch the Harbour Explorer ferry or a bus from the end of Queen Street to the fascinating **Kelly Tarlton's Antarctic Encounter and Underwater World** (➤ 55) on the far side of town. Afterwards, take a short stroll along Tamaki Drive for vistas of Devonport (➤ 61) and the **❹ Hauraki Gulf** (➤ 60–61). Return to Auckland by ferry to get a good view of the **Harbour Bridge** (➤ 54) from the water.

Evening
Return to the **Sky Tower** for night views of Auckland and to try Orbit, the revolving restaurant, for dinner (➤ 53). Ponsonby Road, to the southwest of the city centre, is another good place to eat – you will be spoilt for choice with its many small ethnic restaurants.

Day 2

Morning

Plan at least two hours to explore **3** **Auckland War Memorial Museum** (➤ 57–59) and the Auckland Domain, then walk to the historic **Parnell village** (above; ➤ 75) for lunch and shopping.

Afternoon

During the afternoon, explore the **4** **Hauraki Gulf** islands (➤ 60–61). A "coffee cruise" will give you good views of many islands and look back as you leave Auckland harbour for some of the best views of the city's skyline. If you are interested in natural history, go for a walk on **Rangitoto Island**. If your tastes are more for arts, fine food and wine, explore **Waiheke Island** (➤ 61). On your way back from the Hauraki Gulf, catch a ferry that stops at Devonport (➤ 61) for a walk and your evening meal.

Day 3

Get up early to fly to Kerikeri. Then hire a car or catch a shuttle for the short distance to Paihia, to start your visit of the **5** **Bay of Islands** (➤ 62–64). Join a boat cruise to see or **12** **swim with dolphins** (➤ 68–69), and in the afternoon visit historic **Waitangi National Reserve** (➤ 63–64) and explore its historic grounds, the Treaty House and the meeting house.

Day 4

Take a day cruise of the sun-drenched Bay of Islands and the spectacular Hole in the Rock. Explore the historic township of **Russell** (➤ 63) in the afternoon and evening.

Day 5

Fly back to Auckland and then drive to the **6** **Coromandel peninsula** (➤ 65–66) where you can explore Hot Water Beach, sandy bays (such as the one pictured right), rugged hills and charming seaside towns.

❶ Downtown Auckland

When the first Europeans arrived in New Zealand, Auckland was smaller than Wellington, Christchurch and Dunedin, but its mild climate and scenic maritime setting soon attracted thousands of new migrants. Their vibrant mix of cultures is still obvious as you walk along Queen Street, Auckland's main artery, to the harbour.

Start your downtown explorations from **Aotea Square**, the focal point for Auckland's performance venues and civic offices. In one corner is the triangular **Town Hall**, with its Oamaru limestone façade. On the other side of the square, the low **Aotea Centre** was built at the request of locally trained opera singer Kiri Te Kanawa, and is now the country's foremost concert hall.

Auckland's skyline is dominated by the **Sky Tower**. Completed in 1997, it's part of a complex called Sky City that also includes a casino, restaurants, cafés, a hotel and a theatre. At 328m, the Sky Tower is the highest structure in New Zealand, beating France's Eiffel Tower by almost 30m. It was designed to survive once-in-a-millennium storms and a magnitude 8 earthquake 20km away.

The four observation decks all offer stunning views of Auckland's urban sprawl. If you're scared of heights, beware: the glass panels in the floor of the main observation deck (the second stop on the way up, before the outdoor deck and the top deck) are rather scary to walk across, and the breeze on the outdoor deck certainly adds some drama.

The map that comes with your entry ticket points out all the landmarks you can see from the top, and there are also explanation panels on the observation deck itself. Look for the Harbour Bridge (► 54) and the Westhaven marina, with its hundreds of yachts, and then survey Auckland's

A bird's perspective from the Sky Tower

Leap for the Stars

In October 1998, the irrepressible A J Hackett (► 26) used the Sky Tower to set a new height record for bungy jumping from a fixed structure. Leaping from the observation deck, he fell 180m at 130 kph, breaking his own record, set (illegally) the year before at the Eiffel Tower. It makes the 102m fall at Shotover River (► 168) seem positively tiny, although it doesn't feel that way to nervous jumpers.

northern suburbs to Devonport (➤ 61), the Hauraki Gulf islands (➤ 60–61) and the War Memorial Museum (➤ 57–61) in the Auckland Domain. The distant rugged ranges behind the Hauraki Gulf islands belong to the Coromandel peninsula (➤ 65–66).

This is also the best way to see at least some of the 48 extinct volcanoes in the area. Mount Hobson, named after New Zealand's first governor and Auckland's founder Captain William Hobson, looks like a giant armchair, and although One Tree Hill (➤ 67) has lost its lone pine tree, it is still easily recognised by the tall obelisk. All volcanic cones are reserve land, so they stand out like green pyramids amid the suburbs.

Back on terra firma, continue on Queen Street towards the harbour, wandering down some of the narrow side streets, such as **Vulcan Lane**, **High Street** and **O'Connell Street**, to window shop for gifts and fashion.

Top left: Watch out for kiwis in unexpected places. Below: Auckland puts on a sparkling show at night

TAKING A BREAK

If, after your heady trip up the Sky Tower, you feel in need of refreshments, try **Orbit Restaurant** (for reservations, tel: (09) 363 6000) or, for a lighter snack, the **Sky Stop café and bar**.

Visitor Information Centres

➕ 196 B5 ✉ Viaduct Basin, corner Quay and Hobson streets or ➕ 196 B4 ✉ 287 Queen Street ☎ (09) 979 2333; reservations@aucklandnz.com; www.aucklandnz.com 🕐 Daily 9–5:30 (extended hours during peak seasons) ℹ Also at the airport (➤ 35)

Sky Tower

➕ 196 A4 ✉ Corner Victoria and Federal streets ☎ (09) 363 6000, 0800 759 2489 toll-free; skytower@skycity.co.nz; www.skycity.co.nz 🕐 Sun–Thu 8:30 am–11 pm; Fri, Sat 8:30 am–midnight. Last lift leaves 30 mins before closing time 🚌 Link bus (➤ 59) 💲 Moderate; Sky Deck (top public level): expensive

DOWNTOWN AUCKLAND: INSIDE INFO

Top tips The Sky Tower is open late and the **night views** are particularly spectacular.

Hidden gem Albert Park, accessible from Kitchener Street or Wellesley Street Easl, is an oasis of calm in the hustle and bustle of the city centre.

2 Auckland Harbour

Every fifth Aucklander owns a boat, so the waterfront is where it's all happening. Walk along Quay Street, between Queens Wharf and the Viaduct Basin, to see luxury yachts, tall ships, steam boats, ferries, fishing dinghies and enormous cruise liners all plying the waters of the Waitemata Harbour.

Flung across the narrow Tamaki isthmus, Auckland is surrounded by the sea: the Waitemata Harbour and Hauraki Gulf to the east and the Manukau Harbour and Tasman Sea to the west. The largest of Auckland's six marinas, Westhaven marina, at the southern end of the Harbour Bridge, bobs with more than 2,000 masts, most metamorphosing into full sail every summer weekend.

The Harbour Bridge connects downtown Auckland with its northern suburbs

A focal point of the waterfront is the **Viaduct Basin**, home to Auckland's fishing fleet since the 1930s but extensively rebuilt for New Zealand's defence of the America's Cup in 2000 (▶ 25–27). The basin is a short walk downhill from the Sky Tower (▶ 52–53), and only a few metres from the historic ferry building opposite the harbour end of Queen Street.

The cup races will bring the basin alive again in early 2003 but between races, and without the big syndicates, fantastic vessels and thousands of fans, the Viaduct Basin is somewhat less glamorous. But you can still get a taste of cup-fever: as you walk towards the basin, you will see the *KZ1*, the boat that sailed for New Zealand during the 1988 America's Cup challenge, strung up across the entrance. And you can book a two-hour turn around the harbour on the winning 1995 America's Cup boat *NZL40*.

The history of the America's Cup – told from a New Zealand perspective – takes up a whole gallery in the **New Zealand**

National Maritime Museum, whose entrance is just below the *KZ1*. You can see the darker side of the sea in the first of the museum's 14 galleries, where there is a collection of photographs and eye-witness reports about New Zealand's worst maritime disaster: the 1968 sinking of

The suspended *KZ1* challenger yacht marks the Viaduct Basin

the inter-island ferry *Wahine*, which capsized in a storm after hitting a reef just outside Wellington harbour, killing 51 people. Further in, the Hawaiki gallery features a number of original vessels, from Pacific Island dugouts to a twin-masted outrigger canoe. These are fittingly installed in a room beautifully decorated with traditional Maori woven wall panels and built with rough-sawn timber lashed together with ropes.

Even more impressive are the displays about early settlement. The 300,000 immigrants who embarked on the journey from Europe during the first wave of settlement in the 1840s faced three to six months at sea, travelling in cramped quarters without seeing daylight and with only a pint of drinking water per day. The museum has recreated one such gloomy bunk cabin, peopled with lifesize dummies; moving floors give an instant sensation of being at sea.

Up close with Maori carving traditions

The museum is just beside the passenger terminals at **Princes Wharf**. You may see some of the world's largest cruise ships berthed here, but this area is also the starting point for ferries sailing across the harbour and to the islands of the Hauraki Gulf (➤ 60–61). From here, you can catch the Harbour Explorer ferry, or a bus from the end of Queen Street, to **Kelly Tarlton's Antarctic Encounter and Underwater World**, about 6km from downtown on Tamaki Drive. Kelly Tarlton was an avid diver and treasure-hunter, and his idea of showing marine life is the reverse of the usual aquarium experience: here animals get most of the space while humans watch from a confined hide. There are two main sections: in the Antarctic Experience, you can visit a recreation of Captain Scott's 1911 South Pole hut then board a snowmobile to drive through a vast, authentic Antarctic landscape to see thriving colonies of king and gentoo penguins. Afterwards, you can move through a plexiglass tunnel to Underwater World and watch sharks and stingrays roam freely overhead. Several marine habitats are represented, and you can see some of the thousands of sea creatures that thrive in New Zealand's waters.

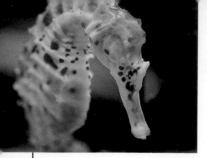

The **café at the maritime museum** offers a range of reasonably priced drinks and snacks, and there are several bars and restaurants on Princes Wharf.

Seahorses are a children's favourite at Kelly Tarlton's Antarctic Encounter and Underwater World

NZL40
⊞ 196 B5 ✉ Booking booth next to maritime museum, Viaduct Basin
☎ (09) 359 5987, 0800 724 569 toll-free; nzl40@sailnewzealand.co.nz
🕐 Daily; up to five two-hour sailings in peak season, depending on demand
💷 Moderate

New Zealand Maritime Museum
⊞ 196 B5 ✉ Corner Quay and Hobson streets, Viaduct Basin
☎ (09) 373 0800, 0800 725 897 toll-free; museum@nzmaritime.org; www.nzmaritime.org
🕐 Daily 9–6, Oct–Easter; 9–5, Easter–Sep; closed 25 Dec
💷 Moderate

Kelly Tarlton's Antarctic Encounter and Underwater World
⊞ 196 C5 ✉ 23 Tamaki Drive, Orakei, Auckland ☎ (09) 528 0603; ktinfo@kellytarltons.co.nz; www.kellytarltons.co.nz
🕐 Daily 9 am–9 pm, Nov–Feb; 9 am–6 pm, Mar–Oct; last entry an hour before closing time
🍴 Jacques' Café (£) 🚌 746, 756, 767, 769 depart from downtown bus terminal on Commerce Street
💷 Expensive

Inside out: visitors in a tank and fish free to roam

AUCKLAND HARBOUR: INSIDE INFO

Top tips Tamaki Drive offers the best views of Devonport, a Victorian suburb on the North Shore, and its two volcanic cones, Mount Victoria and North Head.

Hidden gems Several historic vessels are berthed in sheltered moorings at the museum's marina, including a 1926 steam floating crane and the *Eliza Hobson*, a replica 1900 water taxi that still takes people on short harbour cruises.

In more depth Ask at the visitor information centre about guided walks to the top arch of the Harbour Bridge.
• Opened in 1985, Kelly Tarlton's Antarctic Encounter and Underwater World was built into disused sewage holding tanks. The interesting story of its construction is detailed in a photographic display there.

3 Auckland War Memorial Museum

This superb museum houses one of the best collections of Maori treasures and ethnic crafts from the Pacific, and provides a compelling introduction to the country's history and culture. Built as a memorial to Aucklanders who died at war, the museum also chronicles New Zealand's involvement in global conflicts, from the 1800s to the present day.

Sad and proud memories of war at Auckland's War Memorial Museum

Set in the Auckland Domain, one of the city's oldest volcanic cones, the Auckland War Memorial Museum is a landmark building with sweeping views across the waterfront. At the entrance a cenotaph, modelled on the one in Whitehall, London, is a reminder of the building's origins as a memorial to the country's war heroes. The museum's three architects, who had all served in World War I, chose a Greek neo-classical style to recreate the view of Greek temples they had seen from warships in the Mediterranean Sea.

Once you step inside, you will encounter a Maori warrior blowing a conch shell to draw people to the exhibition of Maori treasures. You could easily spend an hour in this part of the museum alone, and it's a good idea to allow two hours for your visit if you want to see other exhibitions.

The best way to start your museum visit, particularly if you're new to Maori culture, is by watching a 20-minute **cultural performance**, which includes several Maori action songs, traditional stick games, weaponry displays and a *haka*, the fierce Maori war dance.

The Maori treasures are on display on the ground floor – the most impressive being the carved meeting house and the war canoe. Built around 1836 to transport people across Manukau Harbour, the canoe (known as *Te Toki a Tapiri* or "Tapiri's Battle Axe") is the **last of the great Maori war canoes**. One hundred warriors fit inside the 25m hull, which was carved by hand from a single Totara tree.

The **meeting house** is a magnificent example of traditional Maori carving and weaving crafts, both ancient methods of story-telling. Each carved beam and woven panel depicts the stories of a tribe or an ancestor, and was crafted to transmit

Left: A Fijian sailing canoe is one of many Pacific relics
Second left: Musical instruments from a bygone era

history from generation to generation. The house on display was a wedding gift, exchanged when one tribal chief's daughter married into another chief's tribe. The building was completed in 1875 and you can see that the Maori had already started combining traditional carvings with modern materials such as corrugated iron, paint and milled timber. Inside you will find elaborate carvings of Hotonui, the ancestor after whom the house was named, as well as other, mythical figures.

The building follows the typical architectural plan for meeting houses, or *whare nui* (meaning "big house"), which represent a god-like guardian who watches over the people gathered within. At the apex of the roof is the guardian's head, the ridgepole is the backbone, the bargeboards the arms, outstretched in a welcoming gesture and, inside, the rafters represent the guardian's ribs.

Next to the large meeting house is the much smaller, but equally intricately carved **storage house**. These were erected on stilts to stop animals and water from damaging the precious food reserves inside. Take your time to explore the nearby collection of carved paddles, weapons, garments and objects used during rituals, notably some beautifully carved gourds intended to hold placenta.

Right: In memory: images of war
Far right: Live collections such as these locusts are always a hit with kids

Getting Around

The Link Bus travels clockwise and anticlockwise on a loop that includes most of Auckland's inner-city attractions (Sky City, Queen Street, War Memorial Museum, Auckland Domain and Parnell). It also stops at the railway station, hospital, University of Auckland, Auckland University of Technology, and the Sheraton. The bus runs about every 10 minutes (6 am–10:30 pm Mon–Thu; 6 am–11:30 pm Fri; 7 am–10:30 pm Sat; 7 am–11 pm Sun) and tickets cost $1. They're easy to recognise from their blue and yellow Link logo.

Upstairs, the emphasis moves away from Maori culture. The **first floor** has displays on natural history and two discovery centres, and the **second floor** focusses on war-related exhibits (Scars of the Heart, World War II Hall of Memories, Holocaust Gallery, World War I Sanctuary, Spitfire Gallery).

TAKING A BREAK

Try the museum café, **BB's Coffee and Bake**, which is on the ground floor, in the foyer.

Auckland War Memorial Museum
✚ 196 C3 ✉ The Domain, Auckland ☎ (09) 309 0443, (09) 306 7067 recorded infoline, 0800 256 873 toll-free; www.akmuseum.org.nz ◷ Daily 10 am–5 pm, except 25 Dec, 25 Apr (Anzac Day) morning; Maori cultural performance, daily 11 am, noon, 1:30 pm 🚌 Link bus (see panel)
🎫 Donation: inexpensive; temporary exhibitions may incur extra charge

---

AUCKLAND WAR MEMORIAL MUSEUM: INSIDE INFO

Top tips Focus on the Maori treasures and the war-related displays – the natural history exhibits are excellent, but you'll find similar ones in museums throughout the country.

Hidden gems The Auckland Domain's winter gardens and fernery are less than five minutes from the museum. The Domain is the city's oldest park and this is a beautiful spot to relax.

In more depth On the same floor as the Maori treasures, the **"City" exhibition** charts the growth of Auckland, from its founding days under New Zealand's first governor, William Hobson, to the present-day multicultural metropolis.

4 Hauraki Gulf

The balmy seas and enchanting islands of the Hauraki Gulf are only 30 minutes from downtown Auckland. More than 50 islands provide a refuge for both endangered wildlife and city-weary humans.

The Hauraki Gulf is a protected marine area stretching from Auckland to the Coromandel peninsula (➤ 65–66). Several outer islands are nature reserves, off limits to people. However, the inner gulf islands are public reserves and visitors are free to explore. Ferry services leave Auckland's waterfront each day for Rangitoto and Waiheke, and there are several sailings each week to some of the other islands.

Rangitoto Island, which guards the entrance to the Waitemata Harbour, is Auckland's largest and youngest volcanic cone. Its last eruption was only 600 years ago, and its volcanic landscape is clearly unfinished, almost alien, with eerie lava caves, rugged rock formations and primeval vegetation. The hardened lava hasn't had time to break down into soil, and the lower reaches of the island are covered in pohutukawa trees, growing straight from the fissured rock. There are no rivers, no lakes and no fresh water; any rainfall trickles straight through the rocks and accumulates in underground reservoirs, feeding the roots of the trees and about 200 other plant varieties that are establishing under the canopy.

The strange landscapes alone are worth the visit, but if you walk to the island's summit, you will be rewarded with spectacular views of the Hauraki Gulf, the Harbour Bridge and Auckland's skyline. Guided tours cover the entire island on a

Rangitoto's volcanic embrace of Auckland's harbour

canopied trailer towed by a 4WD tractor, which takes you to the start of a boardwalk, 900m from the summit. At the top, you'll find parts of a bunker and viewing post – remnants of the island's military past.

Waiheke Island is a complete contrast: perfect for relaxing on white sandy beaches and enjoying fine food, arts and crafts. Covering 93sq km, it is the second largest of the gulf islands after Great Barrier Island, and it is also the most accessible (by ferry, car ferry or plane). In the past, it attracted mostly alternative lifestylers, but has since developed into a genteel suburb of Auckland, with a commuting population making the 17km journey across the water to the city each day. About 8,000 people live on Waiheke; but the population swells to more than 30,000 during summer weekends and holidays.

As you arrive at the small port of Matiatia, buses, taxis, shuttles and trikes will be waiting to take you uphill to the main settlement of Oneroa, 2km away. You can also hire a car at Matiatia, but make sure to book early during summer. On the way to Oneroa is the Artworks Centre, with several galleries, businesses, community groups and the local visitor information centre. From there you can explore the white beaches between the Oneroa and Onetangi bays and the tidal southern coastline, visit the vineyards or join a tour of art galleries and studios.

Arriving at Waiheke Island – a perfect place to relax

TAKING A BREAK

A **"Coffee Cruise"** provides magnificent views and short stops at Devonport and Rangitoto Island.

Fullers Cruise Centre
🔂 196 B5 ✉ Ferry Building, Quay Street ☎ (09) 367 9111 for reservations, (09) 367 9102 for timetables; enquiries@fullersakl.co.nz; www.fullers.co.nz 🕐 Office: daily 8:30–5. Phone reservation line: daily 7:30–5:30

Waiheke Visitor Information Centre
🔂 off 196 B5 ✉ 2 Korora Road, Oneroa ☎ (09) 372 9999; info@waihekenz.co.nz; www.ki-wi.co.nz/vin; www.gotowaiheke.com 🕐 Daily 9–5, summer; 9–4, winter

HAURAKI GULF: INSIDE INFO

Top tips If you are planning to visit **Rangitoto Island**, bring sturdy footwear, sun protection and drinking water.
• On your return to Auckland, disembark at **Devonport** for your evening meal and a walk among the suburb's Victorian architecture. Regular ferry services connect Devonport with Auckland.

Hidden gem Tiritiri Matangi is an open sanctuary where you can see endangered birds in their natural habitat.

In more depth Four times a week, ferries and small planes depart for **Great Barrier Island**, a rugged, mountainous island 80km from Auckland. It's a popular destination for visitors looking for activity – you can hike or ride a horse along the island's network of tracks, or enjoy water sports off the coast.

5 Bay of Islands

The Bay of Islands is one of New Zealand's most popular destinations and a boat-lover's paradise. What you see from the beach is a mere hint of the turquoise and blue wonders further offshore. Sprinkled with almost 150 mostly uninhabited islands, the bay is a subtropical haven of secluded coves, forest-clad hills and unspoilt sandy beaches.

As the site of the first permanent English settlement in New Zealand, the area is also of immense historic significance. **Paihia**, a small resort that grew from one of New Zealand's first Christian mission stations, established in 1823, is the base for most operators. It's a rather functional town but has plenty of amenities and is a good starting point for explorations.

The most popular cruises are the dolphin-watching trips (► 68–69) or all-day excursions to the **Hole in the Rock**, an impressive natural arch at the tip of **Cape Brett**. The rugged tunnel cuts through **Piercy Island**, at the entrance to the Bay of Islands, and is just wide enough for a catamaran to travel through on a calm day. The cruise catamarans double as goods-delivery boats and make brief stops at most inhabited islands. Only the farm managers are permitted to build here, and the houses nestle in palm groves or pockets of native forest. It's often impossible to tell whether anybody lives there at all until an excited farm dog bursts forth to meet the boat at the jetty.

Sheltered **Otehei Bay**, on **Urupukapuka Island**, is a popular lunch stop for cruise ships and private yachts. American writer Zane Grey camped here in the 1920s and used the island for his fishing expeditions, but today people come to swim in the clear water or to scrutinise the depths from the glass-bottom boat *Nautilus*. Urupukapuka is the largest island in the bay and from its summit, about 15 minutes from the beach, there are panoramic views of the surrounding islands and the

Perfect hideaway: sun-spoiled beaches and a sparkling ocean in the Bay of Islands

Border: Maori designs are used frequently, as in this jetty decoration

A Sense of History

At the end of the waterfront café strip you'll find a historic gem: Pompallier. This French colonial building still houses the printing works for the Roman Catholic mission founded by French missionary Bishop Pompallier in 1841. Inside, missionaries would tan leather and print and bind books in the Maori language, crafts continued today for the benefit of visitors.

deeply fissured coastline leading to Cape Brett. The bumpy ride through the Hole in the Rock is an imposing finale, within view of the cape's lighthouse and with the entire bay unfolding before you.

On your return, you can disembark at **Russell**, the first European settlement in the area. Today it's a small seaside town with whitewashed weatherboard houses enclosed by white picket fences and cottage gardens. The waterfront is dotted with cafés and restaurants, which spill out onto the sunny promenade. The town's present tranquillity belies its turbulent past as the "hell-hole of the Pacific". It started out as a destination for 19th-century sailors, whalers and traders looking for provisions, rum and fun after months at sea. The first Europeans to settle were not usually idealists hoping for a new life but largely ship deserters and time-expired convicts from New South Wales, who did nothing to enhance the town's reputation.

It's a short ferry ride back to the bustle of Paihia and from there to one of New Zealand's most significant historic sites. It was in the Bay of Islands that 46 Maori chiefs gathered in February 1840, to discuss and sign the **Treaty of Waitangi**, a document that remains the lynchpin of race relations in New Zealand (► 10). So you shouldn't miss the **Waitangi National Reserve**, about 2km from Paihia. The Waitangi grounds include the Georgian-style Treaty House, originally built as the home of James Busby, whose job it was to protect British commerce in the embryonic colony, and a magnificent Maori meeting house, Whare Runanga. Completed in 1940 to commemorate the

Below: Rowdy Russell has turned into a tranquil town
Bottom: The Waitangi meeting house hosts the treaty commemorations every year

centenary of the treaty, 14 carved panels in the meeting house represent all major Maori tribes. This symbolises the unity of the tribes under the treaty, as meeting houses usually show carvings that relate only to a particular tribe or region. Walk across the sweeping lawns to see two war canoes, launched every year on 6 February for the Waitangi Day celebrations.

TAKING A BREAK

If you want to avoid the buzzing activity of Paihia, there are several cafés along the waterfront at Russell. The **Waikokopu café** at Waitangi is also pleasant.

Fitting finale for a Bay of Islands cruise

Bay of Islands Visitor Information Centre
➕ 202 B4 ✉ The Wharf, Marsden Road, Paihia ☎ (09) 402 7345; visitorinfo@fndc.govt.nz ⏰ Daily 8–6

Fullers Bay of Islands
➕ 202 B4 ✉ Maritime building on waterfront, Paihia ☎ (09) 402 7421; reservations@fullers-bay-of-islands.co.nz ⏰ Daily 8 am–6 pm; 7 am–9 pm for phone reservations

Waitangi National Reserve
➕ 202 B4 ✉ Waitangi ☎ (09) 402 7437 ⏰ Daily 9–5 🍴 Tea rooms (£) 💲 Inexpensive

Pompallier
➕ 202 B4 ✉ The Strand, Russell ☎ (09) 403 7861; pompallier@historic.org.nz ⏰ Daily 10–5, Dec–Apr, school holidays; other times, guided tours only: daily 10:15, 11:15, 1:15, 2:15, 3:15 💲 Inexpensive

---

BAY OF ISLANDS: INSIDE INFO

Top tip Don't forget to **protect yourself from the sun**, especially if you are going out on a cruise.

Hidden gems Kerikeri, a charming town surrounded by citrus orchards, is worth exploring for its historic buildings and a replica Maori village.
• When in Russell, wander through the graveyard around **Christ Church**, the country's oldest, still scarred with bullet holes – legacies of a clash between a group of Maori and the British navy.

In more depth Explore the Bay of Islands by kayak, on a chartered sailing boat or aboard a replica tall ship modelled on an old schooner. **To hire a kayak** in Paihia, try New Zealand Sea Kayak Adventures (at the waterfront, tel: (09) 402 8596) or Coastal Kayakers (tel: (09) 402 8105; coastalkayakers@nzinfo.com; www.seakayakingadventuresnz.com). **To charter a boat**, One Stop Booking Shop (tel: (09) 402 7127) offers boats, fishing charters, yachting, water taxis, tours and cruises as well as dives to several sites, including the wreck of the *Rainbow Warrior*, the Greenpeace flagship that was destroyed in 1985.

6 Coromandel

Escape from the city to the Coromandel peninsula, with its dramatic coastline and forested mountains. With a history of relentless logging and gold-mining, the peninsula has become the cradle of New Zealand's environmental movement, and inspires those seeking an alternative lifestyle.

On a clear day, you can see the Coromandel's mountains from the Hauraki Gulf islands (▶ 60–61). Much of the peninsula's spine is covered with pockets of regenerating bush and remnants of kauri trees, which were logged almost to extinction during the pioneer period. Its rugged interior is fringed with fine surfing beaches, sheltered inlets and estuaries, with the most scenic coastal scenery on the eastern side.

The gateway to the Coromandel is its main town, **Thames**, on the shallow Firth of Thames about 90 minutes from Auckland, where rich saltwater shallows and mud flats provide a habitat for migratory and wading birds. Thames is small and sleepy, its streets lined with old wooden houses, some built in the town's 19th-century Gold Rush heyday. Its main attraction is the gold mine and the rock crushing stamper battery at its northern end.

The road between Thames and **Coromandel town** hugs the coastline, offering exquisite views over pretty bays, small settlements and calm beaches. The 55km journey is particularly scenic during December and January when the pohutukawa trees lining the road burst into crimson flower. Coromandel town also showcases its gold-mining history – it was just north of here, at Driving Creek, that New Zealand's first gold discovery was made in 1852.

From Coromandel, you can cross to the east coast by either taking the longer (46km) but more scenic SH25, or the 32km unsealed "309 Road", which passes a waterfall and a grove of Kauri trees. The state highway winds around estuaries, through holiday towns and past beautiful beaches, offering stunning views of the **Mercury Islands** offshore, before it reaches **Whitianga**. This is the peninsula's main holiday resort and a pleasant town from which to explore **Mercury Bay** – named by Captain Cook, who anchored there to watch the transit of the planet Mercury in 1769.

The Coromandel's most popular beaches are south of Whitianga, near **Hahei**. Just north of Hahei is **Cathedral Cove**, a gigantic, arched limestone cavern that connects two white beaches but is accessible only at low tide. To the south of Hahei

Digging in for a soak at Hot Water Beach

COROMANDEL: INSIDE INFO

Top tips Be careful if you want to take a cooling swim in the ocean at Hot Water Beach. There are **dangerous currents** and several tourists have drowned. Consider bringing a bucket to sluice yourself down after the hot soak.

Hidden gem At Driving Creek, local potter Barry Brickell has built a 2.5km **narrow-gauge railway**, originally to transport clay from one end of his property to his kiln. The railway travels up steep grades, across trestle bridges, along two spirals and through two tunnels.

is **Hot Water Beach**, where thermal waters boil up just below the surface and people gather at low tide to dig private natural spa pools.

Cathedral Cove is a magnet for nature lovers

TAKING A BREAK
Café Nina (20 Victoria Street, Whitianga, tel: (07) 866 5440) offers good coffee and home-cooked food in a 100-year-old cottage.

✚ 202 C3
Thames Visitor Information Centre
✉ 206 Pollen Street, Thames
☎ (07) 868 7284; thames@ihug.co.nz;
www.thames-info.co.nz
🕓 Mon–Fri 8:30–5, Sat–Sun 9–4

Coromandel Information Centre
✉ Kapanga Road, Coromandel
☎ (07) 866 8598; coroinfo@ihug.co.nz
🕓 Mon–Fri 9–5, Sat–Sun 10–1

Whitianga Information Centre
✉ Albert Street, Whitianga ☎ (07) 866 5555;
whitvin@ihug.co.nz
🕓 Mon–Fri 9–5, Sat–Sun 9–1

Thames Gold Mine and Stamper Battery
✉ Main Road (SH25), Thames, PO Box 278
☎ /fax (07) 868 8514
🕓 Daily 8–6, 26 Dec–Mar, 10–4, Apr–24 Dec
💲 Inexpensive

Driving Creek Railway and Pottery
✉ About 3km north of Coromandel town
☎ (07) 866 8703; barry@drivingcreekrailway.
co.nz; www.webtrails.co.nz/coromandel/
coromandeltown/dcrailway/Index.cfm
🕓 Hour-long round trip:
daily at 10, noon, 2 and 4 in summer; 10 and
noon in winter
💲 Moderate

At Your Leisure

7 Auckland Art Gallery

This gallery's extensive collection of New Zealand's paintings ranges from classic Maori portraits by Charles Goldie and Lindauer to more contemporary works by Colin McCahon and Frances Hodgkins. The earliest works are in the permanent exhibition "Divine Inspiration", which features paintings based on religious themes, dating from the 12th to the 17th century. The "Pavilioned in Splendour" exhibition features European art from the late 16th to early 20th century.

Auckland Art Gallery is a chest of classic and contemporary art treasures

🚹 196 B4 ⊠ Corner Wellesley and Kitchener streets ☎ (09) 379 1349 (info line); www.akcity.govt. nz/around/places/artgallery/ index.html 🕙 Daily 10–5 💷 Free; exhibitions: inexpensive

8 One Tree Hill

This (along with Mount Eden) is the place to come for fantastic views of Auckland, but it also has an eventful history. Many of the volcanic

The Story of One Tree Hill

The summit of One Tree Hill (also known by its Maori name Maungakiekie) was once marked by its single sacred totara tree. After settler vandals cut it down in 1852, Sir John Logan Campbell (a founder and mayor of Auckland) planted a pine to make amends. But in the early 1990s, his choice of an exotic tree over a native totara provoked some local Maori to attack it with a chainsaw. The tree has now been removed.

cones dotted around Auckland were once occupied by Maori, and One Tree Hill has some impressive remnants of their *pa*, or fortified villages. Terracing and dugout storage pits are still visible. The eponymous tree, however, is gone (see panel) and only an obelisk tops the summit. On the fringe of the hill is the Auckland Observatory, with a 360° planetarium called the Stardome.

Auckland Observatory and Stardome
🚹 196 B1 ⊠ Near gates to One Tree Hill domain ☎ (09) 624 1246; www. stardome.org.nz 🕙 Tue–Fri 9–5, 7:30–10, Sat 1–4, 7:30–10:30, summer; Tue–Fri 9–5, 6:30–9:30, Sat 1–4, 7:30– 10:30, winter; Sun 12:30–4 🚌 30, 31 from Victoria Street 💷 Inexpensive

9 Mount Eden

Mount Eden (Maungawhau) is Auckland's highest volcanic scoria cone, and from its 196m summit there are panoramic views of Auckland and the bay. Several quarries once produced dressed stone from here for the city's older buildings and the basalt kerbstones that line its streets. One quarry on the flanks of Mount Eden has since been rehabilitated as Eden Garden, known for its camellias and rhododendrons. July and August are the best times to see the camellias in flower.

🔠 196 B1 ✉ Omana Avenue. Road access to a car park near the summit off Mount Eden Road; pedestrian access from Clive Road and Owens Road (steep path). Access to the Eden Garden is via Mountain Road to Omana Avenue ☎ (09) 638 8395; eden@edengarden.co.nz; www.edengarden.co.nz 🏵 Garden daily 9–4:30 🍴 Café (£) daily 10–4 🚌 274, 275 from Commerce Street 💲 Inexpensive

Mount Eden's volcanic origins are still clearly visible

10 Piha Beach

About an hour's drive from central Auckland, the city's western coastline is dramatic and rugged, with many iron-sand beaches. Piha Beach is one of the most popular black beaches and comes alive in summer with surf competitions, horse-races and beach parties. Jutting several metres into the ocean is windswept Lion Rock, which has a short, steep track leading to its 101m summit (a one-hour return trip). Beware: west coast beaches have powerful currents and heavy surf and you should always stay between the flags. Keep children under supervision, and if in doubt, ask a lifeguard.

🔠 202 B3

Steep cliffs provide perfect flight conditions for Australasian gannets

11 Gannet colony at Muriwai Beach

The colony of Australasian gannets was once confined to a small rock stack offshore, but has now spilled over to several cliffs along Muriwai Beach. An easy walking track skirts the cliffs, providing excellent views of the elegant seabirds as they nest on the rocks or dive for fish (binoculars are useful here). The first birds begin nesting in late July and their numbers peak by mid-November. Chicks fly when they are 15 weeks old and migrate to the east and south coasts of Australia. Several years later they return to Muriwai Beach to breed. The road to Muriwai Beach is signposted from Waimauku on SH16.

🔠 202 B3

12 Swimming with dolphins

The experience of seeing hundreds of dolphins swirling in the water with you is unforgettable, particularly as the water in the Bay of Islands is relatively warm, reaching 23°C in January and February. Operators supply wetsuits, masks, snorkels and fins, and will generally take you on another free trip if you don't see any dolphins or whales. Visitor information centres in Auckland and Paihia list operators but two reputable companies are detailed below.

Dolphin Discoveries

➕ 202 B5 ✉ Corner Marsden and Williams roads, Paihia ☎ (09) 402 8234; dolphin@igrin.co.nz; www.dolphinz.co.nz 📷 Nature tours, snorkelling, swimming with dolphins, kayaking

King's Dolphin Cruises & Tours

➕ 202 B5 ✉ Maritime Building, Paihia ☎ (09) 402 8288; enquiries@kings-tours.co.nz; www.kings-tours.co.nz 📷 Cruises, swimming with dolphins, dolphin and whale watching

🔟 Ninety Mile Beach

If you want to go north as far as Cape Reinga (see below) and Ninety Mile Beach, take a morning flight from Auckland to Kaitaia, and set aside a day to drive to the northern tip of New Zealand. Ninety Mile Beach is the western portal through which sands have been blown to create the

Ninety Mile Beach and the most northern tip of Northland look spectacular from the air

Aupouri peninsula, a skein of land connecting Kaitaia with North Cape and Cape Reinga, which were once islands. The sand came from the volcanic eruptions of the central North Island and was carried north by the Waikato River, ocean

currents and the wind. Much of the dune landscapes are now covered by forests, but almost the entire western coast is flanked by Ninety Mile Beach (actually only 90km long). The beach is so hardened that you can drive on it, but most hire cars are not insured for this. Three roads lead from the main road to the beach, sometimes negotiable only by 4WD vehicles. Daily bus tours and scenic flights are available, but just walking along the beach for a while is evocative enough.

Information Far North

➕ 202 A5 ✉ Jaycee Park, South Road, Kaitaia ☎ (09) 408 0879; visitorinfo@fndc.govt.nz 🕐 Daily 8:30–5; Sat–Sun, 8:30–1, winter

🔟 Cape Reinga

In Maori legend, Cape Reinga is the departure point for spirits of the dead, which travel north to the mythical homeland of Hawaiki-a-nui. The gnarled branches of an 800-year-old pohutukawa tree, seen hanging off the cliff-face at Cape Reinga, form the entrance to the underworld.

The cape is often referred to as New Zealand's northernmost point, but that title is actually taken by a cliff-face at North Cape, 30km to the east. Nevertheless, it's invigorating to walk on windswept Cape Reinga. It's the convergence zone of the Tasman Sea and the Pacific Ocean, and on a stormy day 10m waves swirl around the maelstrom at Columbia Bank below Cape Reinga lighthouse. There is a network of tracks leading to the beaches on either side of Cape Reinga and to Cape Maria van Diemen.

➕ 202 A5

Best for kids
• Feeding times at **Kelly Tarlton's Antarctic Encounter and Underwater World** (► 55). Divers jump into the water with the stingrays and sharks every afternoon to feed them by hand. The moray eels, turtles and seahorses also get a meal, usually in the morning. Phone for exact feeding times before your visit.
• Both **Kelly Tarlton's** and the **Auckland War Memorial Museum** (► 57–59) have excellent hands-on discovery centres for children.

Stingrays are unperturbed by visitors walking through the viewing tunnel

15 Te Paki sand dunes

Most of the northern sand dunes are now covered with forests, but where the wind blows unfettered, the sand has formed landscapes of rare elemental beauty, such as the giant, shifting dunelands that have built up at Te Paki stream. The turn-off to Te Paki stream is about 15km from Cape Reinga. A picnic area is set aside at the road end, immediately below towering 30m sand hills. A brief walk into the dunes seems to take you to the middle of a desert. Watch out for signs warning about areas of quicksand in the stream.

✚ 202 A5

16 Waipoua Forest and Tane Mahuta

Waipoua Forest is the largest remaining tract of native forest in Northland, once dominated by giant, ancient kauri trees. Most were felled for their timber during the years of early settlement. However, pockets of kauri, such as Waipoua forest, remain along the western coast of Northland.

It's not so much the height of kauri trees that is impressive as their girth and age. Tane Mahuta is the largest living kauri tree, a "mere" 50m but with a girth of more than 13m and an estimated age of 2,000 years. It stands in the northern reaches of Waipoua Forest (look for the road signs), and is only a short walk from SH12, which runs through the forest and along the west coast of Northland. About 2km further south is another turn-off and car park; a 10-minute track leads to The Four Sisters, a rare stand of four tall and graceful trees. Both tracks are suitable for wheelchairs.

Watch out for kauri trees whenever you turn a corner along SH12. No kauri was felled when the road was cut through the forest, so it has to wind its way around the giant trees.

✚ 202 B4

Where to... Stay

Prices
Expect to pay for two people sharing a double room
£ under NZ$150 ££ NZ$150–$300 £££ more than NZ$300

AUCKLAND

Aachen House Boutique Hotel ££–£££

This early 20th-century house in the chic suburb of Remuera has been restored and turned into a luxurious bed and breakfast hotel with lofty ceilings, grand fireplaces and elegant furnishings. Rooms are decorated in period style, with king-size or twin beds and private bathrooms. There's also a conservatory in tranquil gardens. The motorway is near by.

🚹 off 196 C1 ☒ 39 Market Road,
Remuera, Auckland ☎ (09) 520 2329;
fax: (09) 524 2898;
www.aachenhouse.co.nz

Brooks' Longwood £

In 1880, this was an original farmhouse of Remuera. The fields are now streets, but the house retains its character, with wide verandahs, polished wood and country furnishings. Rambling roses and other plants surround the house, and steps lead down to a swimming pool. There are two guest bedrooms – one twin, and one "queen" with a day bed. You live in the family home and order breakfast to suit – healthy or hearty. The shops and restaurants of Newmarket and Parnell are close by.

🚹 off 196 C1 ☒ 4 Seaview Road,
Remuera, Auckland ☎ (09) 523 3746;
fax: (09) 523 3742; www.brooksnz.co.nz

The Heritage ££

Formerly an art deco department store, The Heritage is in a convenient downtown location near the Viaduct Basin. It's the largest hotel in New Zealand, with 467 rooms and suites straddling two sites. The complex has a tennis court, ballroom, swimming pools, health clubs, restaurants, bar and shops. Suites have a separate bedroom, living and dining area, and full kitchen. Some suites also have a washing machine and dryer, CD player and balcony.

🚹 196 A5 ☒ 35 Hobson Street,
Auckland ☎ (09) 379 8553; fax: (09)
379 8554; www.heritagehotels.co.nz

Karaka Lodge ££

Tom and Sheryl Brownlee are keen golfers and have built a ranch-style six-suite lodge next to Pukekohe Golf Course. It's a 35-minute drive south of Auckland, but they can collect you from the airport. Sheryl is a noted cook and food writer and offers dinners featuring local produce. Golf tuition is available, or Sheryl can arrange tours of the area, famous for its market gardens.

🚹 off 196 C1 ☒ Bream Revel Way,
Karaka, Pukekohe ☎ (09) 292 7516;
fax: (09) 292 7440;
www.karakalodge.co.nz

Sheraton Auckland Hotel £ Towers ££–£££

Recently refurbished, the Sheraton is one of Auckland's best-equipped hotels, with 411 rooms, three restaurants, a bar, a fitness centre and a swimming pool. In the luxurious Towers section, a butler is at your disposal to unpack, press your clothes and polish your shoes. Nice touches include fresh fruit, mineral water and coffee in your room, and a private lounge offers complimentary cocktails and breakfast. The hotel is near the motorway and the Karangahape Road club district and not far from the Domain. There's a free shuttle to the city centre.

🚹 196 B3 ☒ 83 Symonds Street,
Auckland ☎ (09) 379 5132; fax: (09)
377 9367; www.sheraton.com/auckland

Abri Apartments ££

Nestling in native bush, these self-catering chalets feel secluded even though Paihia is only a few minutes' walk away. From the deck and the living area there are views of the bush and a fine panorama of the Bay of Islands. The apartments are not large, but are modern and tastefully furnished, with air-conditioning, a kitchen, and a luxurious bathroom with a double spa bath. Breakfast is complimentary on the first day.

✚ 202 B3 ✉ 10 Bayview Road, Paihia ☎ (09) 402 8003; fax: (09) 402 8035; www.abri-accom.co.nz

Ludbrook House ££

Ludbrook house is set on a 420ha sheep and cattle property, halfway between Paihia and the Kauri Coast, The Ludbrook family has been farming here since 1860. The homestead, built in the 1920s, has commanding views and is surrounded by mature gardens. Decorated in period style, it is a gallery for work by local artists. Although there's a formal lounge, owner Christine Ludbrook finds that most guests gravitate to the kitchen to chat as meals are prepared. The four guest rooms are simply but comfortably furnished and have private bathrooms. The tariff includes dinner, bed and breakfast.

✚ 202 B4 ✉ SH1 Ohaeawai, RD2 Kaikohe ☎ (09) 405 9846; fax: (09) 405 9846; www.ludbrook.co.nz

Orongo Bay Homestead ££–£££

Originally the home of the first American Consul in New Zealand, this homestead on the road to Russell is set in spacious grounds, with a pond among mature trees and native bush. Michael Hooper and Chris Wharehinga Swannell have turned it into a luxurious bed and breakfast retreat, with a guest lounge and rooms in the original house as well as in lodges in the grounds. Dinner is available by arrangement: Michael is a food and wine writer and both owners are keen cooks.

Produce from the garden and oysters from the bay are their specialities.

✚ 202 B4 ✉ Aucks Road, RD1 Russell ☎ (09) 403 7527; fax: (09) 403 7675; www.thehomestead.co.nz

The Summer House ££

Christine and Rod Brown have built their French-inspired bed and breakfast in a former citrus orchard on the outskirts of Kerikeri. Though some trees have been replaced with a lush subtropical garden, there are still plenty to provide juice for breakfast. Lodgings include one "queen" room, another with an antique French bed, and a self-contained super-king suite with a Pacific theme. All are en suite.

✚ 202 B4 ✉ Kerikeri Road, Kerikeri ☎ (09) 407 4294; fax: (09) 407 4297; www.thesummerhouse.co.nz

Kuaotunu Bay Lodge £

This purpose-built lodge is set in 5ha of pasture and native bush overlooking Kuaotunu beach, with views of the Coromandel Peninsula and nearby islands. Guest rooms have private bathrooms and fine views view, with French windows leading onto a private deck. Dinner is by arrangement – a good idea in this remote spot. There's a comfortable lounge, and a conservatory where breakfast is served.

✚ 202 C3 ✉ SH25, RD2, Whitianga ☎ (07) 866 4396; fax: (07) 866 4396; www.kuaotunubay.co.nz

Villa Toscana Lodge £££

Giorgio and Margherita Allemano built a grand Tuscan villa in the hills above Whitianga, with spectacular views. The lower level is a lavish, self-contained, two-bedroomed suite. Breakfast is provided and you can choose to dine with the Allemanos, who are lovers of gourmet Italian food and wine. They also own a game-fishing boat, which guests can charter.

✚ 202 C3 ✉ Ohuka Park, Whitianga ☎ (07) 866 2293; fax: (07) 866 2269; www.villatoscana.co.nz

Where to...
Eat and Drink

Prices
Expect to pay for a three-course meal, excluding drinks
£ up to NZ$45 ££ NZ$45–$60 £££ more than NZ$60

Kermadec ££–£££
Seafood is the theme of this first-floor complex in the Viaduct Basin. One part is a casual brasserie and bar, which spills out onto a balcony. The upmarket restaurant next door carries the sea theme into its dramatic décor, with bright tapa-cloth sails slung from the ceiling and Japanese tatami rooms with a water wall and stone garden. As well as traditional Japanese *nigiri* and *maki sushi*, you can order seafood platters to share and also fusion dishes like chargrilled swordfish served with turmeric potatoes and an olive and pinenut reduction.

➕ 196 A5 ⊠ Viaduct Quay, Auckland ☎ Brasserie: (09) 309 0413; restaurant: (09) 309 0412 ⊚ Brasserie: daily 11 am–11:30 pm; restaurant: Mon–Fri noon–3, 6 pm–11 pm, Sat–Sun 6 pm–11 pm

Prego £
One of the longest-standing restaurants on Ponsonby Road's "munchy mile", this stylish Italian café offers good food at reasonable prices. Dining is in an enclosed front courtyard. Pizzas and roasts are on offer, including lamb and whole fish, cooked in the wood-fired oven. They don't take bookings, but you can always drink at the bar while you wait for a table.

➕ off 196 A4 ⊠ 226 Ponsonby Road, Auckland ☎ (09) 376 3095 ⊚ Daily noon–11 pm; closed 25 and 26 Dec

Vinnies £££
Prue Barton and David Griffiths have spent years developing this Herne Bay restaurant, frequently voted Auckland's best. Influenced by the traditional style they experienced in Europe, the food revels in French-Italian cooking with a New Zealand twist. Indulge in classics like caviare with champagne, or try more individual dishes like grilled quail with Vietnamese green papaya salad. There's often a themed menu inspired by the produce of a region, and most dishes are offered with a wine match. You'll need to book.

➕ off 196 A4 ⊠ 166 Jervois Road, Herne Bay, Auckland ☎ (09) 376 5597 ⊚ Daily from 6:30 pm; closed Good Fri, 25 Dec

Mudbrick Vineyard and Restaurant ££
Built in French provincial style from hand-made earth bricks, Mudbrick Vineyard has spectacular views over the Hauraki Gulf. The upmarket restaurant offers an à la carte menu of French and rural vineyard dishes, such as venison paté, and chicken breast stuffed with wild mushrooms. Vegetables come from the vineyard's landscaped organic potager. The vineyard produces distinctive red and white wines, and also offers tours and tastings.

➕ off 196 B5 ⊠ Church Bay Road, Oneroa, Waiheke Island ☎ (09) 372 9050 ⊚ Daily 11 am–5 pm, 6 pm–1 am; closed 25 Dec

Hotel du Vin £££
About 45 minutes' drive south of Auckland on the way to the Coromandel Peninsula, Hotel du Vin

is a luxury vineyard retreat at De Redcliffe Winery. The restaurant specialises in French cuisine, using local ingredients such as crayfish, duck and greenshell mussels. On Sundays you can combine a fixed-price four-course lunch with leisure activities such as tennis, swimming and wine-tasting. Bookings are necessary. The hotel, picturesquely set among the vines, is also recommended.

🚹 **202 C3** ⊠ **Lyons Road, Mangatawhiri Valley, Pokeno** ☎ **(09) 233 6314** 🕐 **Daily noon–2:30 pm, 6–10 pm**

COROMANDEL PENINSULA

Colenso Café £

This café and country shop on the main highway between Whitianga and Tairua is a delightful place to stop for lunch or a snack. Set in an old-fashioned herb garden, it has shady verandahs where you can sit among the flowers, and also tables indoors, where the rooms are crammed with local crafts. The blackboard menu features home baked lunch dishes using herbs from the garden. There's also a selection of New Zealand wines, teas and coffee. Freshly squeezed citrus juice from the café's organic orchard is a speciality. Juices and other orchard produce are also for sale at the road-side stall.

🚹 **202 C3** ⊠ **Main Road, Whenuakite** ☎ **(07) 866 3725** 🕐 **Daily 10–5, Sep–Jul; closed Aug, 25 Dec**

The Fireplace ££

A massive fireplace greets visitors to this rustic restaurant and bar on the waterfront overlooking Whitianga inlet, and the theme is carried on inside. The menu features traditional pizzas from the wood-fired oven, beef from the chargrill and chicken and lamb from the rôtisserie. There's also a selection of chef's specials, including pasta, curry and Coromandel oysters.

🚹 **202 C3** ⊠ **9 The Esplanade, Whitianga** ☎ **(07) 866 4828** 🕐 **Daily from 5 pm; closed 26 Dec, 1 Jan**

Only Seafood £–££

Seafood is an obvious choice in the Bay of Islands, an area famous for its game fishing. At Only Seafood, on the Paihia waterfront, you don't only get seafood – you also get a view. Oysters farmed locally at Orongo Bay are a speciality. So is game fish, served lightly seared with Asian seasonings, and hapuka. The restaurant is on the upper level of a weather-board building, the bottom part of which is a bistro run by the same owners for meat-lovers.

🚹 **202 B4** ⊠ **40 Marsden Road, Paihia** ☎ **(09) 402 6066** 🕐 **Daily from 5 pm; closed 25 Dec**

Sommerset Restaurant, Duke of Marlborough Hotel ££

It's hard to think of a more romantic place than this old waterfront hotel in Russell. The site of so many dramatic goings-on in New Zealand history (► 63), it's now a peaceful spot, looking onto the sparkling water and bobbing boats of the bay so get a table on the verandah. Local seafood is a speciality but the menu also includes a range of grills. The hotel has a verandah bar with an equally good view, and guest rooms.

🚹 **202 B4** ⊠ **35 The Strand, Russell** ☎ **(09) 403 7829** 🕐 **Daily 7:30–10 am, noon–2:30 pm, 6:30 pm–late**

Marsden Estate £

Named after Samuel Marsden, who planted New Zealand's first grapevines in Kerikeri in 1819, Marsden Estate is one of several vineyards that are bringing wine-making back to Northland. The informal restaurant is a pleasant place to have lunch. There's seating inside, where wine tasting takes place, and outdoors on a patio over-looking the vines. The menu ranges from antipasto platters and salads to pasta and desserts such as pecan pie.

🚹 **202 B4** ⊠ **Wiroa Road, Kerikeri** ☎ **(09) 407 9398** 🕐 **Daily 1 am–5 pm, Oct–Jun; Wed–Sun 10 am–4 pm, Jul–Sep**

Where to...
Shop

Shopping Centres

Near the waterfront, the **Downtown Shopping Centre** (11–19 Customs Street, tel: (09) 379 5068) has 70 speciality shops. **DFS Galleria**, in the restored 1880s Customhouse (cnr Customs and Albert Streets, tel: 0800 388 9373 toll-free) specialises in designer fashions and the usual duty free items. Down Queen Street, take in the **BNZ Tower Shopping Centre**, with its rooftop views, the 1880s department store **Smith and Caughey and Queens Arcade**. In the suburbs, **Westfield Shopping-town St Lukes** (80 St Lukes Road, Mt Albert; tel: (09) 678 6011) is the largest in New Zealand, with around 130 shops. For bargains, **Dressmart**

(151 Arthur Street, Onehunga, tel: (09) 622 2400) has more than 60 factory outlet shops.

Fashion

Head for High Street, with its leading New Zealand designers such as **Kate Sylvester** (47 High Street, tel: (09) 307 3282) and **Karen Walker** (15 O'Connell Street, tel: (09) 309 6299), as well as international labels like **Versace** (40 Courthouse Lane, tel: (09) 359 1108). Many fashion houses have stores in the chic suburb of Newmarket. Try **Zambesi** (2 Teed Street, tel: (09) 523 1000), **Workshop** (4 Teed Street, tel: (09) 524 6844) and **Saks** (254 Broadway, tel: (09) 520 7630).

Parnell

A picturesque cluster of heritage villas is now a village of boutiques, galleries and cafés, linked by rustic courtyards. For crafts, browse at **The Elephant House** (237 Parnell Road, tel: (09) 309 5277), a co-operative of 300 craftspeople.

Markets

Recognisable by its 42m high chimney, **Victoria Park Market** has 60 shops around a cobbled courtyard. On Fridays and Saturdays, stalls in **Aotea Square** sell produce, crafts and fashion. Visit the **Otara Market** in Newsbury Street on Saturday mornings, where you'll find Pacific Island food, crafts and bric-a-brac.

Food and Wine

Downtown, the **New Zealand Winemakers Centre** (National Bank Centre, Elliott Street, tel: (09) 379 5858) offers wine-tasting, retail and tour advice. In Newmarket, gather a picnic at **Zarbo** deli-café (24 Morrow Street, tel: (09) 520 2721).

Roadside signs advertise potters' and painters' studios, orchard produce and craft shops.

The Cabbage Tree (Williams Road and Maritime Building, tel: (09) 402 7318) has two shops in

Paihia selling crafts and leisure wear. In Kerikeri, pick up a guide to its **Art and Craft Trail** from the visitor centre (Pahia Wharf, tel: (09) 402 7345). **Living Nature** (SH10, Kerikeri, tel: (09) 407 7895) sells natural skincare products.

Buy cheese from **Mahoe Farmhouse Cheese** (SH10, Oromahoe, tel: (09) 405 961), chocolates from **Makana Confections** (Kerikeri Road, tel: (09) 407 6800) and local **Bay of Islands Ice Cream** (Main Road, Kerikeri, tel: (09) 407 8136).

At the **Ancient Kauri Kingdom** (SH1, Far North Road, Awanui, tel: (09) 406 7172) ancient logs are converted into furniture. Smaller items include bowls and bookends.

Pick up a copy of the Coromandel Craft Trail from a visitor information centre. Shop for a picnic at **Matatoki Farm** (SH26, Thames–Paeroa Highway, tel: (07) 868 1284) cheese factory and delicatessen.

Where to...
Be Entertained

AUCKLAND

The "TimeOut" section in Saturday's *New Zealand Herald* lists what's on.

Nightspots

Karangahape Road ("K Road") is the centre of Auckland's club scene. Tune in to Radio bFM's gig guide for recommendations. **Sky City Casino** (cmr Federal and Victoria Streets, tel: (09) 363 6000) is open 24 hours.

Performing Arts

The **Aotea Centre** (Mayoral Drive, tel: (09) 307 5000) is Auckland's premier classical concert venue. The Auckland Theatre Company performs at the University's **Maidment Theatre** (cmr Princes and Alfred Streets, tel: (09) 308 2383).

Sports

Boat charters in Waitemata Harbour are offered by almost 100 companies, from big game fishing to crewing an America's Cup yacht. There are popular **windsurfing** beaches at Bayswater, Mission Bay, Takapuna and Point Chevalier. Over 40 golf courses are near by, including New Zealand's longest, the **Formosa Country Club** (11 Jack Lachlan Drive, Beachlands, tel: (09) 536 5895). Auckland has three stadiums, hosting rugby union, rugby league or test cricket. Call **Ticketek**, tel: (09) 307 5000. Watch the tennis at the **ASB Bank Tennis Centre** (72 Stanley Street, tel: (09) 373 3623), or have a flutter at **Ellerslie Race Course** (Greenlane Road, tel: (09) 524 4069).

Wine Trail

Auckland wine-makers produce a **wine trail map**. Enquire about tours at the visitor centre (Viaduct Harbour, tel: (09) 979 2333).

Festivals

The Aotearoa **WOMAD** (world music arts and dance) and the **Pasifika Pacific Island** cultural festival are held in March. See also ▶ 45–46.

COROMANDEL PENINSULA

Sports

Whangamata has a famous surfing beach and charter operators offer fishing, diving, kayaking and scenic cruises. Take a wilderness walk with **Kiwi Dundee Adventures** (tel: (07) 865 8809). Golf courses include **Mercury Bay Golf Club** (Golf Road, Whitianga, tel: (07) 866 5479).

Festivals

The crimson-flowered **pohutukawa tree** is celebrated in December. January brings a popular **Celtic Fair**.

NORTHLAND

Sports

The Bay of Islands is famous for its game fishing and you'll find plenty of charter operators at Paihia Wharf. The region also has some spectacular golf courses. Try the **Waitangi Golf Club**, near the Treaty House (tel: (09) 402 7713).

Wine Trails

Several wineries in Northland are open to visitors. Get a **wine trail map** from the visitor information centre in Paihia (Marsden Road, tel: (09) 402 7345).

Festivals

The region's most famous celebration is **Waitangi Day** (▶ 10), on 6 February. The **Russell Oyster Festival** is held in September and the **Bay of Islands Taste Experience** wine and food festival in November. May brings the **Bay of Islands Country Rock Festival** and August the **Jazz and Blues Festival**.

Central Plateau

Getting Your Bearings

The volcanic plateau in the central North Island is New Zealand's hotspot of angry natural forces – one of the world's most active geothermal areas. Towering geysers, hissing steam, boiling mud and evil smells are constant companions as you travel along the Thermal Explorer Highway from Rotorua to Taupo, exploring New Zealand's contribution to the Pacific Ring of Fire.

The Taupo Volcanic Zone stretches 250km, right through the central North Island. This band of thermal activity varies in width from 30km to 80km and is anchored by White Island in the north and the three Tongariro volcanoes in the south. These four remaining active volcanoes enclose a huge field of dormant mountains and vast craters formed by earlier eruptions.

In this area, the earth is constantly on the move, spewing fiery bad breath wherever toxic fumes find an escape route through the thin crust. Nature is at her rawest – her face pockmarked with festering boils and oozing craters – but also at her most impressive and beautiful.

The region's original inhabitants, Maori belonging to the Te Arawa tribe, learned to harness the region's tremendous natural energy, cooking their food in hot springs and relaxing in mineral-rich warm pools. They were also the country's first tour guides, back in the 1870s, as the area gained a reputation for its natural spectacles and began drawing British visitors, inspiring New Zealand's first commercial tourism ventures.

But in 1886 Mount Tarawera erupted, destroying several villages and popular tourist attractions. The region recovered only slowly. Rotorua finally rediscovered its heritage as a spa town and several of the original mock-Tudor buildings

Top: A Maori challenge to test peaceful intentions of visitors
Left: Safe above boiling mud pools and hissing fumaroles

have been restored to their former glory, adding charm and contrast to the city. Today, many of the modern tourist guides are young Maori, proudly continuing their ancestors' tradition of hospitality.

Greenstone, a sacred resource for Maori, is often carved into jewellery

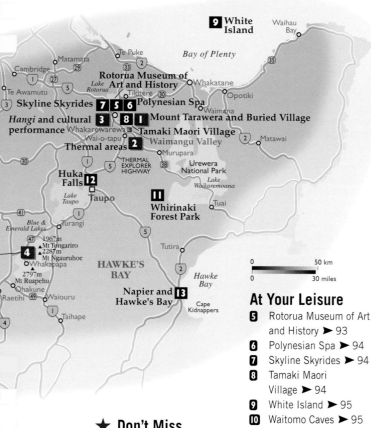

9 White Island

7 **5** **6** Rotorua Museum of Art and History

Polynesian Spa

3 Skyline Skyrides

Hangi and cultural performance

3 **8** **1** Mount Tarawera and Buried Village

Tamaki Maori Village

2 Thermal areas

Waimangu Valley

12 Huka Falls

4

11 Whirinaki Forest Park

13 Napier and Hawke's Bay

| 0 | | 50 km |
| 0 | | 30 miles |

★ Don't Miss

1 Mount Tarawera and Buried Village ➤ 82

2 Thermal areas ➤ 85

3 *Hangi* and cultural performance ➤ 89

4 Tongariro National Park ➤ 90

Page 77: Spitting fury at the Whakare-warewa thermal area

At Your Leisure

Further Afield

This is one of the few areas in the world where you can get up close and personal with the volatile forces of nature and still enjoy the comforts of civilisation. The thermal areas are also steeped in history and Maori culture.

In Four Days

Day 1

Morning

Check out the visitor information centre in downtown Rotorua to make bookings for your **3** *hangi* and **cultural performance** (➤ 89). Walk to the Government Gardens om the shores of Lake Rotorua and take your time to explore the **5 Rotorua Museum of Art and History** (➤ 93), which has excellent exhibits about the devastating eruption of Mount Tarawera. Take tea at the Blue Baths (➤ 99) or drive 20km to Lake Tarawera for lunch at the Landing Café (➤ 100).

Afternoon

Walk along the shore of Lake Tarawera or join a cruise on Lake Rotomahana (right) past the former site of the Pink and White Terraces. Then drive back 1km to visit the fascinating **1 Te Wairoa, the Buried Village** (➤ 82–84), which was devastated by the volcanic explosion. Return to Rotorua to relax in the hot pools at the **6 Polynesian Spa** (➤ 94).

Day 2

Morning

Spend another day in Rotorua, this time exploring **2 Whakarewarewa**

(➤ 85–86), where most of the survivors from the Buried Village moved after the volcanic eruption. This thermal resort also offers excellent performances of Maori culture and is next to the New Zealand Maori Arts and Crafts Institute (left). Have lunch at the coffee shop there.

Afternoon

Return to the lake's western shore on the other side of Rotorua and take a ride on the **7** **Skyline Skyrides** (► 94) for sweeping views across the city, Lake Rotorua, Mount Tarawera and the steaming thermal areas in between. Spend the rest of the day exploring the **Agrodome** or **Rainbow Springs** animal park (► 102), and enjoy a traditional **3** *Hangi* **and cultural performance** (► 89) in the evening.

Day 3

Morning

Drive 19km south along SH5 to the stunning Waimangu Valley **2** **thermal area** (► 86–88), which was created by Mount Tarawera's eruption. Spend the morning exploring the startling landscapes and springs, and take lunch at the coffee shop.

Afternoon

Continue for another 10km further south to visit the colourful Wai-o-tapu **2** **thermal area** (► 88) to see its rainbow-coloured silica terraces and hot pools. Continue south towards **Taupo** (► 90). You can take a detour through **11** **Whirinaki Forest Park** (► 96) or stop to see **12** **Huka Falls** (► 96).

Day 4

Morning

Stroll along the shores of **Lake Taupo** (the rock carvings pictured above are only accessible by boat) or explore any of the water-based activities on offer. Then drive along the lake towards Turangi and Whakapapa in magnificent

4 **Tongariro National Park** (► 90–92). Take the chair lift up Mount Ruapehu for a view across the park's other two volcanoes and have lunch at the top.

Afternoon

Walk or take the chair lift down the mountain. Explore the visitor information centre and some of the short walks at **Whakapapa** (► 91).

▯ Mount Tarawera and Buried Village

Mount Tarawera is sacred to the Maori tribe that first settled this area. It isn't one of New Zealand's highest mountains, but its many jagged peaks and long, deep crater are reminders that it is one of the most volatile. One winter night in 1886, the volcano exploded, burying the surrounding area under a layer of mud and obliterating its famous silica terraces.

The violence of the 1886 eruption is still evident even from a distance. One of the best places for a good view of Mount Tarawera is the **Landing Café at Lake Tarawera** (▶ 100). The mountain's base is wide, running along most of the opposite shoreline. Its summit is nonexistent – instead, Mount Tarawera has a giant, gaping crater. When it blew, the mountain opened and ripped a 17km fissure into the land below, creating a new lake and the thermal Waimangu Valley (▶ 86–88) and ejecting enough material to blanket 16,000sq km around it.

The spectacular walk along Mount Tarawera's crater rim

Boat cruises are available on Lake Tarawera, and 4WD vehicles or helicopters can take you all the way to Mount Tarawera's crater rim (at a high price) to see the eruption's devastating effect on the landscape.

However, the most haunting sight of the mayhem that followed the eruption can be found at **Te Wairoa, the Buried Village**, about 1km from Lake Tarawera. Several smaller settlements once flourished at the foot of the mountain, but they were too close for anybody to survive. Te Wairoa was just far away enough for some of the villagers to escape before their houses disappeared under mud and ash.

The village was the hub of tourism and home to several guides who took visitors to the famous **Pink and White Terraces** during the 1870s, the biggest tourist attraction of the time. These huge, buttressed silica terraces once poured hot water into nearby Lake Rotomahana, which was less than half its current size before the eruption.

The magnitude of the 1886 eruption becomes clear from the top of Mount Tarawera

A small museum at the entrance to the Buried Village provides an excellent introduction to the area. Photographs recount the development of Te Wairoa from a quiet settlement to a thriving staging post for travellers. Eyewitness accounts describe the chaos and tragedy of the rescue effort that followed the eruption. There is also the chilling story of the warnings that preceded it. According to several witnesses, a

Sleeping Dragon
Today, Mount Tarawera looks peaceful and is thought to be dormant. But people who live in its shadow believe the volcano's sleep to be restless and expect it to erupt again, perhaps with equally devastating effect.

One of the many carvings at the Buried Village

group of tourists was crossing Lake Tarawera shortly before the eruption with Guide Sophia, one of the most popular guides, when they saw a phantom Maori canoe; the warriors paddling towards the mountain had the faces of dogs. The village sage, Tuhoto Ariki, interpreted the sighting as a warning of imminent destruction. Soon after, the entire village disappeared under debris and more than 150 people were killed. The last photograph of the 100-year-old sage is also displayed at the museum.

Excavations of Te Wairoa began in the 1930s and have revealed a number of small dwellings and hundreds of artefacts, among them the blacksmith's tools, millstones and gears from the village mill, the baker's large oven and full bottles from the tavern. The excavated huts and workshops remain in situ and are accessible to visitors. Even when the grounds are busy, there is a respectful silence around the dwellings, particularly at the house of the old sage (see box, ➤ 84).

MOUNT TARAWERA AND BURIED VILLAGE: INSIDE INFO

Top tips Join a **guided tour** through the museum and the excavation sites. Some of Guide Sophia's descendants now work as guides and their personal connection with the area brings the stories to life. Plan to spend up to two hours: 30 minutes at the museum and the rest walking around the excavated houses and displays.

Hidden gems Traditional Maori villages used to have communal storehouses to keep food for winter. During excavations of the storehouse at Te Wairoa, archaeologists discovered some rare **Maori stone carvings**, and two of these precious relics are now on display in their original position at the storehouse entrance.

In more depth Take a little more time to follow the **meandering path** that connects all excavation sites to a trout stream, where you can feed rainbow trout, and further to a waterfall about 10 minutes from the main village.

Left: Several houses have been excavated from the mud
Below: A restored fireplace

TAKING A BREAK

There are **tea rooms** at the entrance to the Buried Village, but if the weather's good, have a **picnic** under the tall aspen poplars that have grown from the original fence posts since the eruption.

The Price of Wisdom

An eerie atmosphere surrounds Tuhoto Ariki's house. He had warned villagers that they would be punished for their greed in encouraging tourism. When his predictions came true, villagers blamed him for the disaster and refused to dig him out. He was finally rescued four days later but died within a week.

✚ 201 D4
Visitor Information Centre
✉ 1167 Fenton Street, Rotorua ☎ (07) 348 5179; marketing@tourism.rdc.govt.nz; www.rotoruanz.co.nz
🕐 Daily 8–6

Te Wairoa – the Buried Village
✉ Tarawera Road, RD5, Rotorua ☎ (07) 362 8287; discover@buriedvillage.co.nz; www.buriedvillage.co.nz
🕐 Daily 9 am till dark 🎟 Moderate

Lake Tarawera Launch Services
✉ The Landing Café, Lake Tarawera ☎ (07) 362 8995; jill@purerotorua.com; www.purerotorua.com 🕐 Daily, Eruption Trail, departs 10:30 am; 45-min scenic cruises depart 1:30, 2:30; bookings essential 🎟 Inexpensive

2 Thermal areas

Rotorua is the centre of a thermal wonderland of bubbling mud pools, kaleidoscopic silica terraces and spouting geysers. The odour of hydrogen sulphide pervades the city day and night, and has earned it the nickname Sulphur City.

Bubbling Over

Wai-o-tapu is home to the Lady Knox geyser, which erupts at 10:15 every morning – with a little help. As the story goes, prisoners were brought here in the 1900s to wash their clothes in the hot pools. A warden noticed that the water started boiling as it became soapy, so he had the prisoners build a rock cairn over the pool to confine the water and drive up a fountain. Today, silica has coated the cairn and it acts as a natural geyser, but still has to be triggered with soap.

Three of the most stunning spectacles are along the **Thermal Explorer Highway** (State Highway 5) between Rotorua and Taupo. Although they're all within 30km of Rotorua, plan to spend at least two hours at Whakarewarewa thermal reserve and a day at lush Waimangu Valley and the Wai-o-tapu thermal area.

Whakarewarewa is closest to downtown Rotorua, at the southern end of the city, and most locals simply call it Whaka. Uniquely, it combines an extensive geothermal park, featuring several geysers and mud pools, with Maori culture. Whakarewarewa village became the new home for those displaced by the 1886 eruption of Mount Tarawera (▶ 82–84), and some of their descendants now work here. Villagers still use the hot pools for bathing and cooking, and you may be able to taste a cob of corn cooked in one of the mineral pools.

Whakarewarewa's main attraction is the geyser flat, a moonscape silica terrace of about 1ha pierced by seven active geysers. Two are very reliable: the **Prince of Wales Feathers** geyser regularly spouts hot fountains about 12m high and heralds the awakening of **Pohutu** ("Big Splash") geyser, at 30m New Zealand's largest. It erupts every hour or so and while you wait you can stroll through a bizarre landscape of burping mud puddles, bubbling hot pools and steaming vents.

Glorious mud: bubbling mud pools fed by steam

Most people come to see the earth forces, but you shouldn't miss the **meeting house** and the **New Zealand Maori Arts and Crafts Institute**, established in 1963 to preserve Maori heritage and now a respected training school for carvers and weavers. You can watch Maori artisans instructing young craftspeople, and browse the galleries for souvenirs. The ornately sculpted meeting house near by is

used for daily midday concerts, which are included in the entrance fee.

South of Whakarewarewa, 19km along SH5, you'll see a sign for **Waimangu Valley**, which is about 6km from the turn-off. This narrow, gently sloping valley was created by the eruption of Mount Tarawera, which tore a gash into the land around its base. The valley has since filled with regenerating bush, creating splendid landscapes. Before you enter the valley, spend a few minutes at the visitor information centre browsing through the photographs taken before and after Mount Tarawera exploded, and pick up a self-guided trail map.

Just a few metres from the start of the walkway, the valley opens up for a panoramic view across its steaming beauty, with the tortured crater of the restlessly sleeping Mount Tarawera in

Inset top: Minerals give pools their iridescent colour. Left: A moment of calm before the geyser's outburst. Right: Colourful algae hang over the Warbrick Terrace at Waimangu

Inset top: Some hot pools are still used to cook food
Left: The beautiful Champagne Pool is 2,000sq km of bubbling water. Right: The Prince of Wales Feathers geyser in full swing

the background. From here the path winds its way past cool, algae-covered **Emerald Pool** to **Frying Pan Lake**. This is the world's largest hot spring, fed by boiling water and toxic fumes and producing incredibly eerie sounds. Continue past smaller fizzing pools and a steaming rock face to a hot stream and a barren basin, whose rim is marked with a white cross. Here, in 1903, four people were killed by the **Waimangu geyser**, the largest known hot fountain. The geyser used to spit muddy water 400m high for a short time in the early 20th century, but it is dormant at the moment.

A few minutes further into the valley, the constantly gurgling **Inferno Crater** gives a performance that befits its name every month or so. Closer to **Lake Rotomahana**, the magnificent **Marble and Warbrick terraces** channel hot water

THERMAL AREAS: INSIDE INFO

Top tips You'll need **at least an hour** to walk to the end of the valley at the shore of Lake Rotomahana, where you can join a cruise to view volcanic features inaccessible from the paths. Alternatively, a shuttle bus makes a regular loop around the valley's thermal sites to the lake.
• Don't dress up – the odour of sulphur tends to stick to clothes for some time.

Hidden gems Visit the **Waikite thermal valley**, a small pocket of forested hills and pastures, and the tiny public pool fed by a hot stream running through the valley. Turn into Waikite Valley Road at the Wai-o-tapu Tavern on SH5.
• Whakarewarewa contains a **kiwi house**, providing an opportunity to see these flightless birds, which are now rarely spotted in the wild. One wall of the hut is made of glass, providing visitors with clear views of kiwi activity although, as the birds are night-active, lights are dimmed.

In more depth If you want to see more fumaroles and mud pools, **Hell's Gate** on is about 15 minutes from Rotorua. Travel north on SH30 past Rotorua airport, continuing right towards Whakatane. After about 4km you will come to Tikitere and Hell's Gate, on the left.

down a maze of scalloped sinter flats and cascading buttresses. The lake cruise is a very tranquil journey, past scarred and steaming cliffs and smaller geysers to the former site of the Pink and White Terraces.

From Waimangu, it's another 10km along SH5 to the awesome thermal wonders of **Wai-o-tapu**. Here, the water flows over landscapes rich in silica. As it cools, the mineral forms sinter. This thermal area is most notable for the silica-encrusted **Champagne Pool**, delicately tinged with all the colours of the spectrum, and the **Primrose Terraces**, which have formed over more than 900 years and are the largest in the Southern Hemisphere. There are also several large caves, whose overhanging ceilings are decorated with filigreed formations of crystallised sulphur.

TAKING A BREAK

Both Waimangu Valley and Wai-o-tapu have excellent **coffee shops**, which offer a range of light meals and snacks.

Whakarewarewa Thermal Reserve
✚ 201 D4 ✉ Hemo Road, Rotorua ☎ (07) 348 9047; 0800 494 252 toll-free;
information@maci.co.nz; www.nzmaori.co.nz ⏰ Daily 8–6, Oct–Mar; 8–5, Apr–Sep; concert daily
12:15 pm; 3hr cultural performance: 6:15 pm, Oct–Mar; 5:15 pm, Apr–Sep 💲 Moderate

Waimangu Volcanic Valley
✉ 587 Waimangu Road, Rotorua ☎ (07) 366 6137; waimangu@voyager.co.nz;
http://rotoruanz.com/sub/waimangu.html ⏰ Daily 8:30–5 💲 Moderate

Wai-o-tapu Thermal Wonderland
✚ 201 D4 ✉ Wai-o-tapu Loop Road, off SH5, Rotorua ☎ (07) 366 6333; info@geyserland.co.nz;
www.geyserland.co.nz ⏰ Daily 8:30–5, later during summer 💲 Moderate

Hell's Gate
✚ 201 D4 ✉ Tikitere ☎ (07) 345 3151, bryan@hellsgaterotorua.co.nz ;
www.hellsgaterotorua.co.nz ⏰ Daily 9–5 💲 Moderate

3 *Hangi* and cultural performance

After decades of assimilation, Maori language, culture and crafts are experiencing a renaissance among both Maori and *Pakeha* (New Zealanders descended from European settlers).

Digging the pit for a *hangi*

The best way to experience Maori culture is to attend a performance at a venue such as Tamaki Maori Village (➤ 94–95) or Whakarewarewa Thermal Reserve (➤ 85). Both sites include a traditional Maori village with a *whare nui* (large meeting house), smaller dwellings and storehouses, and combine a *hangi* with a performance of action songs and dances.

Hospitality is essential to Maori culture. You will receive a traditional welcome, when a warrior will perform mock attacks and lay out a small branch as a challenge. The elected "chief" of your group picks up the branch to signal a peaceful visit. The women will then call you onto the *marae* (area outside the meeting house), where hosts and guests exchange speeches and songs. Maori songs and dances are an integral part of oral history and are accompanied by actions to illustrate the story. A *hangi* is traditionally prepared in an earth oven by steaming vegetables and a range of meats together over hot boulders.

Tamaki Tours
✉ Meet at corner of Pukaki and Fenton streets, Rotorua ☎ (07) 346 2823; tamaki@wave.co.nz; www.maoriculture.co.nz 🕐 Daily, bookings required 💲 Moderate

HANGI AND CULTURAL PERFORMANCE: INSIDE INFO

Top tips Catch the **courtesy bus** to your venue rather than driving there yourself. The bus drivers often use the journey to explain the protocol of visiting a *marae*.
• Be prepared to **exchange songs** with your Maori hosts. It doesn't have to be anything elaborate – a popular song will do. It's better to sing something badly than not to sing at all!

4 Tongariro National Park

Few views are as striking as the first glimpse of the three volcanoes of the Tongariro National Park. Rising starkly from a surrounding plateau of tussocklands and near-desert, the peaks mark one of the country's most popular national parks.

Tongariro was New Zealand's first national park, the vision of a Maori tribal chief who gave the mountains to the nation to ensure their protection (► 11). Volcanic forces and weather continue to mould this area, which is one of a handful of places worldwide with dual World Heritage status in recognition of its natural and cultural value. It's also a magnet for outdoor enthusiasts, who come to walk its tracks in summer and to ski the slopes of **Mount Ruapehu** (at 2,797m the North Island's highest mountain) in winter.

The most scenic approach is from **Taupo**, at the northern end of **Lake Taupo**. The huddled peaks first come into view across the water as you drive along the lakefront. The lake's calm, deep blue water belies its violent creation from one of the world's biggest volcanic eruptions. The Taupo explosion in 186 AD is believed to have darkened skies and caused blood-red sunsets as far away as Italy and China, and pumice now forms a thick layer over much of the North Island. The lake, which fills several of the craters carved by the eruption, is the country's

Tongariro National Park is a popular winter playground

largest and is a trout-angler's paradise. Rainbow trout are hooked by the tonne each day and you are likely to spot lines of anglers sitting on the lake's banks as you drive south for about 50km along its eastern shores.

Even from a distance, it is clear that the volcanoes of Tongariro National Park are anything but dormant. **Mount Ngauruhoe**, an almost perfect cone with a clearly recognisable volcanic crater at the 2,287m summit, smoulders and occasionally belches steam and gas into the sky. **Mount Tongariro**, at 1,967m the lowest of the volcanic trio, is a maze of volcanic craters and spouts the cascading Ketetahi hot spring from one of its flanks. **Mount Ruapehu**, the only peak that is constantly snow-capped, erupts every few years. During the last eruption, in September 1995, Ruapehu sprayed rocks down its slopes and spewed out clouds of fine ash, then continued to hiss and groan threateningly for another year after that.

The national park's main access is through the small settlement called **Whakapapa**, itself worth a visit, not least to see one of New Zealand's best known hotels, Grand Chateau (➤ 98–99). The Department of Conservation, which administers all protected lands, runs a visitor centre at Whakapapa with excellent displays on the region's geology and history, as well as information about walks and weather forecasts. At the entrance, you are greeted by a bust of **Horonuku Te Heu Heu Tukino** (➤ 11), the far-sighted paramount chief of the local Ngati Tuwharetoa

The Emerald Lakes are a striking feature of the Tongariro Crossing walk

people, who realised in 1887 that the only way to preserve an area of cultural significance was to give it away. The mountains remain sacred to the tribe's descendants. Just outside the centre, a commemorative rock is a reminder of the peaks' special status for Maori.

To explore the park, you can take the ski field chair lift and on a clear day the views from the top terminal are stunning – just sit outside and take in the majestic atmosphere. Scenic plane and helicopter flights are available from a small airfield a few minutes from Whakapapa, and there are myriad short walks and nature trails starting from the village.

TAKING A BREAK

Take tea at **Grand Chateau** or eat at **Knoll Ridge Chalet** (open 9:30 am–4 pm), which, at about 2,000m above sea-level, is New Zealand's highest restaurant. Out of the ski season, these – and other amenities – may be closed, but nearby **Lorenz's Bar and Café** at Top o' the Bruce often stays open.

Frequently and atmospherically, Tongariro disappears in the clouds

Whakapapa Visitor Information Centre
🞦 200 C3 ✉ SH48, Whakapapa; mailing address: Private Bag, Mount Ruapehu 2650 ☎ (07) 892 3729; whakapapavc@doc.govt.nz; www.doc.govt.nz 🕓 Daily 9–6 ℹ Free leaflets and brochures, maps: inexpensive; organise scenic flights from here

Mount Ruapehu
🞦 200 C3 ✉ Guided walks and chair lift from Top o' the Bruce, road end SH48, Whakapapa ski area ☎ (07) 892 3738; info@mtruapehu.com; www.whakapapa.co.nz 🕓 Chair lift services to ski field: 9–4:30, last ride up 3:30, Dec–Apr 💷 Moderate

Mountain Air
Offers scenic plane and helicopter flights over Tongariro National Park
☎ (07) 892 2812, 0800 922 812 toll-free; mountain.air@xtra.co.nz; www.mountainair.co.nz

Helistar Helicopters Limited
Offers scenic flights over the entire Central Plateau
☎ (07) 374-8405; fly@helistar.co.nz; www.helistar.co.nz

TONGARIRO NATIONAL PARK: INSIDE INFO

Top tips Take time to explore the **Whakapapa Visitor Information Centre** and its small museum of skiing fashions and equipment.
• Be aware that out of the **skiing season** (approximately November to March), most of Whakapapa's amenities are likely to be closed.

One to Miss It is possible to **climb to the top of Mount Ruapehu**, but the track is not well marked and a return trip can take up to six hours, so it is only for experienced walkers with a guide who knows the area. The weather can change very quickly and clouds can close in around the peaks within a few minutes, so if you're not a confident hiker save your energy and stay close to the top station of the chair lift to enjoy the views.

In more depth The **Tongariro Crossing** is one of the most popular day walks in New Zealand. The track makes its way over the saddle between Mounts Ngauruhoe and Tongariro through volcanic landscapes of craters, steaming valleys, hot springs, and the tantalisingly named Emerald and Blue Lakes, in stark contrast to the lush forests into which it descends at the northern end of the park. It takes about eight hours. Buy maps from the Whakapapa Visitor Centre.

At Your Leisure

5 Rotorua Museum of Art and History

Come here for more on Rotorua's thermal activity, the area's significance to local Maori tribes, and the town's past as a spa resort. The museum itself is housed in the Bath House, a beautiful Tudor-style building with gables, towers and a grand staircase, surrounded by the Government

The regional museum is one of Rotorua's historic gems

Gardens. Bath House was the government's first major commitment to the region's tourist industry, which was thriving by the time the "Great South Seas Spa" opened in 1908. The rich and famous came to soak in the hot mineral waters that still bubble up near Lake Rotorua. They even took baths in tubs connected to electrical currents – all in the name of health. The old treatment rooms and bathtubs have been restored and are now permanent exhibits at the museum. Another display features ancient carvings of the Te Arawa, the local Maori tribe. You can witness the violent eruption of Mount Tarawera (➤ 82–84) in a brief film, before exploring the

Happily Ever After

The love story of Hinemoa and Tutanekai is retold in the popular Maori song "Pokarekare Ana". Both lovers were of high birth in their respective subtribes, but as Tutanekai was an illegitimate son, Hinemoa's family was not in favour of a marriage. Hinemoa lived on the western shore of Lake Rotorua, while Tutanekai lived on the lake's Mokoia Island, where he liked to play his flute. The wind would carry the music to Hinemoa – until one night she couldn't resist and swam across to him. When the families heard of her feat, they celebrated the couple's union. You can see the lovers embracing at the main gates to the Whakarewarewa thermal reserve.

museum's display on the tragedy. Next to the museum are the Blue Baths, which were designed during the 1930s for recreational rather than medicinal bathing and one of the first public pools where people could indulge in mixed bathing.

Rotorua Museum of Art and History
🔲 201 D4 ✉ Government Gardens
☎ (07) 349 4350; rotoruamuseum@rdc.govt.nz; www.rotoruamuseum.co.nz
🕐 Daily, 9:30–6, Oct–Mar; 9:30–5, Apr–Sep 🍴 Bath House Café (£)
✋ Inexpensive

Pick a temperature to suit your mood at the Polynesian Spa

Polynesian Spa

After a hard day's sightseeing, treat yourself to an evening soak in the hot mineral pools and elegant atmosphere of the Polynesian spa. The facility has integrated elements of a spa house built on the same site during the 1930s. You can choose between warm, invigorating acidic pools, set in rocks at a sheltered part of Lake Rotorua's shoreline, and soothing alkaline pools that are fed by a boiling spring beside the complex. Follow up your soak with massages, skin treatments and mud baths – all with a view out to the lake. If you're looking for privacy, a number of small, enclosed pools can be locked.

Polynesian Spa
201 D4 ⊠ Hinemoa Street, Government Gardens, Rotorua ☎ (07) 348 1328; info@polynesianspa.co.nz; www.polynesianspa.co.nz Daily 6:30 am–11 pm; therapies and treatments 9–9 Treatment: expensive; pools: inexpensive

Skyline Skyrides

For those with energy to spare, this family entertainment area combines a gondola ride with several luge tracks and bush walks. The gondola climbs the side of Mount Ngongotaha to almost 500m above sea level, opening up panoramic views of Rotorua, the lake and the surrounding district. At the top you can choose different activities, including a flight simulator, flying fox (aerial cableway) and luge tracks, ranging from scenic to advanced. You can also walk downhill following easy paths.

Skyline Skyrides
201 D4 ⊠ Fairy Springs Road, Rotorua ☎ (07) 347 0027; enquiries@skylineskyrides.co.nz; www.skylineskyrides.co.nz Daily 9 am–late Licensed restaurant (££), Pavilion Food Court (£) Moderate

Tamaki Maori Village

If you want to see how Maori people lived before Europeans arrived in New Zealand, visit this re-created village. It was built into a sheltered forest, complete with a market place, meeting house, sleeping houses, store houses for *kumara* (sweet potatoes) and a fortified entrance and lookout tower. Maori performers bring the

village alive as they go about their daily business, such as weaving and carving. A highlight is the evening cultural performance and *hangi* feast (➤ 89). Visitors receive a formal welcome onto the village, and then enjoy a traditional concert before sharing a dinner cooked in an earth oven over hot boulders.

Tamaki Maori Village
201 D4 ✉ 14km south on SH5 towards Taupo. Tamaki Tours: meet at corner Pukaki & Fenton streets, Rotorua ☎ (07) 346 2823; tamaki@wave.co.nz ⏲ Daily 9–4, bookings required 🚌 Courtesy transport from and to accommodation, with introduction to Maori protocol Moderate; access to craft shops free

History comes alive at the Maori village outside Rotorua

9 White Island

The plume of smoke rising from White Island can be seen from the coastline of the Bay of Plenty. New Zealand's most active cone volcano is about 50km offshore, near the towns of Whakatane and Opotiki and accessible only by pre-booked boat or helicopter. The volcano had a sulphur mine within its crater in the late 19th and early 20th centuries, until an eruption in 1914 killed all 12 of the miners who were working there. The island's wide crater floor is littered with fumaroles, and hot water and steam constantly escape from these sulphur-encrusted vents. There is no jetty; boats land on the beach, so trips are weather-dependent.

White Island Tours
201 E4 ✉ PeeJay Charters ☎ (07) 308 9588; 0800 733 529 toll-free; info@whiteisland.co.nz 🚌 Courtesy transport available Expensive

10 Waitomo Caves

Waitomo is a sleepy settlement famous for its limestone caves. The region is riddled with more than 50km of cave passages, part of a karst limestone landscape that has been sculpted by water into blind valleys, sinkholes, arches and fluted outcrops. About two to three hours' drive west of Rotorua, the village is 8km off SH3, between the towns of Te Kuiti and Otorohanga. It consists of not much more than the main road, but over half a million visitors come every year to see the caves. You could easily spend a day exploring the activities on offer. Most people come to walk through the glow-worm caves to see the stalactites and stalagmites; other options range from four-hour cave tubing expeditions (navigating an underground river on a tyre inner tube), to all-day abseiling and climbing. A shuttle bus runs daily return trips between Rotorua and Waitomo (tel: (07) 873 7559).

Visitor Information Centre
200 C4 ✉ Museum of Caves ☎ (07) 878 7640; waitomomuseum@xtra.co.nz; www.waitomo-museum.co.nz ⏲ Daily 9–5

Wrap yourself in rubber and ride through the caves

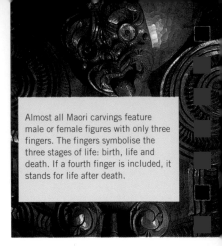

🔟 Whirinaki Forest Park

Towering and graceful native trees, including the forest giants kahikatea and totara, form an almost impenetrable temperate jungle in Whirinaki Forest Park. The park, about 100km southeast of Rotorua on SH38, is a rare enclave noted for the sheer majesty and density of its native podocarp forests. It forms the boundary between the exotic pine plantations in the west, and wild Te Urewera National Park in the east. The 609sq-km park harbours 1,000-year-old tree giants and supports rare birds such as the kaka (forest parrot) and the endangered New Zealand falcon. There are walking tracks, scenic drives, lookouts and waterfalls.

➕ 201 D3 🕙 Open 24 hours ✋ Free

> Almost all Maori carvings feature male or female figures with only three fingers. The fingers symbolise the three stages of life: birth, life and death. If a fourth finger is included, it stands for life after death.

Graceful and protected: tall native trees in Whirinaki Forest Park

🔟 Huka Falls

Just a few minutes north of Taupo, the Waikato, New Zealand's longest river and normally 100m wide and 4m deep, is forced through a narrow granite cleft that's only 15m wide and 10m deep. The blue water surges through the channel and bursts out in a foaming waterfall, plunging over an 11m shelf. There is a footbridge across the channel and a walking track to the falls, but you can also take a jetboat or a 1907 paddlewheeler to view them from the water.

The Waikato is New Zealand's most highly developed river for electricity generation, with eight hydroelectric stations producing 25 per cent of New Zealand's hydropower.

From Huka Falls it's a short drive to the Aratiatia Rapids. The rapids and the beautiful narrow gorge dried up after a dam was installed on the Waikato, but the dam is opened for half an hour several times a day so that people can still see the majesty of the rapids.

Huka Falls, Aratiatia Rapids

➕ 201 D3 🕙 Rapids: 10 am, noon, 2 pm, 4 pm, Oct–Mar; 10 am, noon, 2 pm, Apr–Sep ✋ Free access

Huka Falls Paddlewheeler

✉ Departs from Aratiatia dam
☎ (07) 378 5828; 0800 278 336 toll-free; rapids@xtra.co.nz
🕙 Daily ✋ Moderate

Hukajet

✉ Wairakei Tourist Park, SH1, 6km north of Taupo
☎ (07) 374 8572; 0800 4852 538 toll-free; info@hukajet.co.nz; www.hukajet.co.nz
🕙 Bookings essential
✋ Moderate

Further Afield

🔢 Napier and Hawke's Bay

Blessed with a Mediterranean-like climate and fertile soil, Hawke's Bay is New Zealand's prime wine-growing and fruit-producing area. Its main appeal, however, is the unmatched collection of art deco buildings in the city of Napier.

On 3 February, 1931, a massive 7.9-rated earthquake struck Hawke's Bay. Virtually every building in Napier and Hastings collapsed, and subsequent fires destroyed the city's commercial heart. Aftershocks continued for ten days and over 250 people died. But locals refused to be beaten: Napier found itself 40sq km larger, when the quake lifted what has become the port area of Ahuriri above sea level and the city was rebuilt in the styles fashionable at the time – Spanish Mission, Stripped Classical and, above all, art deco. Today, Napier has one of the world's highest concentrations of art deco architecture.

The best examples of this pastel-coloured, geometric style are on Emerson, Dalton and Tennyson streets, all within the inner city and close to Marine Parade. Some of the shop fronts on Emerson Street have

Napier rose from the rubble as a monument to 1930s architecture and design

been modernised and you'll have to look up to see the fine art deco detail. Excellent examples include the Taylor Building and the former Hawke's Bay Chambers, which were built in 1932 and now house Charlie's Art Deco Restaurant. On Tennyson Street, the Daily Telegraph building still houses the city's newspaper offices. Also interesting is the ASB Bank building, near the Marine Parade, with its decoration based on authentic Maori carving designs.

Take at least half a day to stroll through the city centre and along Marine Parade, with its trademark palms and angular Norfolk pines.

➕ 201 D3

Visitor Information Centre
✉ 100 Marine Parade, Napier ☎ (06) 834 1911; info@napiervic.co.nz
🕐 Daily 9–6 💷 Inexpensive

Art Deco Shop
✉ Desco Centre, 163 Tennyson Street, Napier (opposite Clive Square) ☎ (06) 835 0022; shop@artdeconapier.com; www.hb.co.nz/artdeco/shop
🕐 Daily 9–6

Where to... Stay

Prices

Expect to pay for two people sharing a double room
£ under NZ$150 ££ NZ$150–$300 £££ more than NZ$300

ROTORUA

Gwendoline Court Motor Lodge £

On the main road, close to Whakarewarewa, this motel offers reasonably priced self-catering accommodation near downtown Rotorua. Each of the 16 units has its own parking area, spa pool, kitchen, upstairs bedroom and separate lounge, with extra beds for families. Guests also have free use of the facilities at the nearby Heritage Motor Inn, including the heated swimming pool, mini-golf and tennis courts.

➕ 201 D4 ⊠ 361–363 Fenton Street, Rotorua ☎ (07) 347 9630; fax: (07) 346 1331

Kawaha Point Lodge £££

Set in beautiful gardens on the edge of Lake Rotorua, this lodge has the feel of a luxury hideaway, although it's close to Rotorua city. Hosts Tony and Margaret Seavill have restored the 1930s villa and its romantic stone grotto and rose gardens, and furnished the eight suites simply but elegantly in '30s period style. The lodge has a private jetty, swimming pool and croquet lawn. Menus are discussed with guests, who can either join a communal dining table or eat al fresco.

➕ 201 D4 ⊠ 171 Kawaha Point Road, Rotorua ☎ (07) 346 3602; fax: (07) 346 3671; www.kawahalodge.co.nz

Rydges Rotorua £–££

Five minutes from the city centre, on the main road next to Arawa Racecourse, this modern hotel has 135 rooms, and is reckoned to be the most spacious in Rotorua. The 91 de luxe rooms have spa baths and balconies with views across the city to the lake and the Redwood Forest. The hotel is designed around a four-storey central court with an atrium restaurant and mezzanine bar. There's a covered roof-top pool, gym and sauna, and guests have access to the golf course near by.

➕ 201 D4 ⊠ 272 Fenton Street, Rotorua ☎ (07) 349 0099; fax: (07) 349 0900; www.rydges.com.au

The Springs Fine Accommodation ££

Colleen and Murray Ward have designed this luxury bed and breakfast to blend in with the 1930s bungalows in their quiet residential street. Photos of old Rotorua line the hallway, heavy drapes, plump sofas, heavy drapes, and objets d'art decorate the library, where guests are offered refreshments on arrival. The four bedrooms have kingsize beds, en suite rooms, walk-in wardrobes and a private terrace. Colleen is a bubbly hostess and a fund of information on Rotorua's attractions. The hearty brunches feature dishes like buttermilk pancakes and lamb cutlets.

➕ 201 D4 ⊠ 16 Devon Street, Rotorua ☎ (07) 348 9922; fax: (07) 348 9964; www.thesprings.co.nz

TONGARIRO NATIONAL PARK

The Grand Chateau £–££

Perched on the slopes of Mount Ruapehu, the Grand Chateau was built in 1929 for skiers. Its glory may have faded, but it's still worth coming for the elegant atmosphere and spectacular views. Bathrooms have been modernised and the most appealing rooms look directly onto Ngauruhoe's volcanic cone. There are also self-contained family chalets. The hotel has a summer programme of walks, a golf course,

Where to...
Eat and Drink

Prices
Expect to pay for a three-course meal, excluding drinks
£ up to NZ$45 ££ NZ$45–$60 £££ more than NZ$60

ROTORUA

Bistro 1284 ££

The atmosphere is welcoming and the décor is simple but elegant, with dining on two levels. The menu offers New Zealand twists on Italian food. Roast lamb rump comes on garlic polenta; roast chicken breast comes on artichoke risotto. Home-churned ice-cream is a speciality. There's a largely New Zealand wine list, but you can also bring your own.

➕ 201 D4 ⊠ 1284 Eruera Street, Rotorua ☎ (07) 346 1284
🕑 Tue–Sat from 6 pm, open Sun on hol weekends; closed 25 and 26 Dec

Blue Baths Tearooms £

Taking tea at the renovated Blue Baths is a delightful way of reliving Rotorua's spa-resort past as 1930s music plays among the potted palms. Views extend over the croquet lawns on one side and thermal pools on the other. Dainty sandwiches, scones and cakes are served on tiered cake stands. Teas include Darjeeling and Russian caravan, and ice-cream sodas for the child-at-heart. Lunches are also available.

➕ 201 D4 ⊠ Government Gardens, Rotorua ☎ (07) 350 2119 🕑 Daily 10–4.30 summer; 10–4 winter; closed 25 Dec

---

indoor pool, sauna and tennis courts. There's a choice of dining, from *à la carte* in the elegant Ruapehu restaurant to casual in the café and pizzeria.

➕ 200 C3 ⊠ SH48, Mount Ruapehu, Tongariro National Park ☎ (07) 892 3809; fax: (07) 892 3704; www.chateau.co.nz

HAWKE'S BAY

McHardy House £££

Once the hilltop residence of a pioneering farming family, McHardy House has been restored to its former grandeur by Markus Burkhard and Brenda Robins, who have made it a luxury boutique hotel. The house has panoramic views of the Pacific Ocean, gleaming timber floors, plasterwork ceilings and ornate stained glass. Each of the six *en suite* rooms is furnished in a different theme, using opulent fabrics and antiques. Markus, a German-trained chef, makes his own bread and preserves, and the garden provides herbs and

vegetables for dinner. Guests can use the swimming pool, library, and billiard room.

➕ 201 D3 ⊠ 11 Bracken Street, Napier ☎ (06) 835 0605; fax: (06) 834 0902; www.mchardyhouse.com

Hawthorne Country House ££

Expect a relaxed atmosphere at Susan Brook's property just south of Hastings: you might be greeted by the smell of home-baking as you drive up to the old country residence. The five *en suite* rooms are comfortably furnished in period style. The guest living room has an open fire, complimentary drinks and a fridge to chill your own. Wander round the mature gardens or, for even more relaxation, you can try your hand at croquet or petanque. Breakfast is usually a convivial affair with other guests in the dining room. Dinner and barbecues can be arranged if you wish.

➕ 201 D3 ⊠ 420 SH2, Hastings ☎ (06) 878 0035; fax: (06) 878 0035; www.hawthorne.co.nz

The Landing Café £–££

An idyllic location overlooking Lake Tarawera makes this simple café worth a special trip. Drink in the Old Trout Bar, or eat on the verandah (but protect yourself from the sandflies). The brunch/lunch menu is strong on open sandwiches overflowing with salad. The evening menu is more sophisticated, and bookings are essential. Chicken supreme is a signature dish, roasted with sweet chilli jam, golden kumara and green olive tapenade.

🚹 201 D4 ⊠ Spencer Road, The Landing, Lake Tarawera ☎ (07) 362 8502 ⏲ Daily 9–3, 6 pm–late; closed 25 Dec

The Pig and Whistle City Bar £

Housed in an imposing 1940s building that used to be the police station, this bar has a lot of fun exploiting the joke. Micro-brewed beers have names like Verdict Bitter and Swine Dark Ale. The bar menu ranges from burgers and kumara (sweet potato) chips to mussel chowder and Thai chicken curry. There's a leafy garden at the back. Live bands play on Friday and Saturday nights.

🚹 201 D4 ⊠ 1182 Tuatanekai Street, Rotorua ☎ (07) 347 3025 ⏲ Daily 11:30am–late (kitchen closes 9.30 pm)

Poppy's Villa ££

Built in 1905 as a holiday home, Poppy's Villa still has the air of a private house, half-hidden by shrubbery. Its intimate atmosphere is enhanced by period décor, cane furniture and floral drapes. The meat-based menu features beef and lamb. Try fillet of grain-fed beef with wild mushrooms, sweetbreads in a walnut brioche or salmon with basil beurre blanc. If you caught a trout on your fishing trip, they will cook it for you. Bookings are necessary.

🚹 201 D4 ⊠ 4 Marguerita Street, Rotorua ☎ (07) 347 1700 ⏲ Daily 6–10 pm; closed 25 Dec

Sirocco £

You can drop in for a coffee, a glass of wine or a meal at almost any time of day at this casual bar and café. Sit in the rambling villa or the garden courtyard fronting the street. The Mediterranean menu ranges from Italian pasta to Turkish mezze and Greek roast meat. There's also a selection of snacks and salads. Warm sandwiches are a speciality during the day. Lunch specials, including a main course, wine and coffee, are excellent value.

🚹 201 D4 ⊠ 1280 Eruera Street, Rotorua ☎ (07) 347 3388 ⏲ Mon–Fri 10.30 am–11 pm; Sat, Sun, public hols 10 am–10.30 pm; closed 25 Dec

Replete Café £

A combined café, delicatessen, kitchenware shop and cooking school, Replete is a Taupo institution. The café serves breakfast, brunch and lunch, with good coffee. Dishes range from toasted panini to Thai chicken curry or smoked salmon and brie flan. It's the sort of casual place where you can browse through the magazines or pick up the ingredients for a picnic.

🚹 201 D3 ⊠ 45 Heu Heu Street, Taupo ☎ (07) 378 0606 ⏲ Mon–Fri 8:45–5; Sat and Sun 8:45–3:30

Shed 2 £–££

Shed 2 is a cleverly converted 19th-century wool store on the Ahuriri quayside. Head for the bar, with its harbourside tables, during the day; or retreat from its big-screen TV to the restaurant at night, where the atmosphere is less casual but the food is the same. The menu ranges from wood-fired pizza to Asian and Middle Eastern-inspired dishes, as well as seasonal offerings. Hawke's Bay produce features strongly on the wine list. Bookings are necessary for the restaurant.

🚹 201 D3 ⊠ West Quay, Ahuriri, Napier ☎ (06) 835 0029 ⏲ Bar: Mon–Thu 2–late, Fri and Sat noon–2 am, Sun noon–10. Restaurant: Mon–Sat 6:30 pm–late

Where to...
Shop

In Rotorua, speciality shops are clustered around Tutanekai Street. The **Outdoorsman Headquarters** (Tarawera Road, tel: (07) 345 9333) has outdoor clothes and equipment. **Finns** (1225 Tutanekai Street, tel: (07) 348 7682), sells women's wear. For men's wear, try **Pollards** (1239 Hinemoa Street, tel: (07) 347 7139).

The government-owned **New Zealand Maori Arts and Crafts Institute** at Whakarewarewa (tel: (07) 348 9047) preserves the arts of wood carving (*whakairo*) and weaving (*raranga*). Walk round the carving school, visit a greenstone jeweller's studio and watch women weaving flax. At the **Tribal Marketplace** in Tamaki Maori Village (tel: (07) 346 2823), artists make and sell wood, bone and

greenstone-carving, flax-weaving, foods, Maori medicines and tribal clothing. The **Buried Village** (tel: (07) 362 8287) has Maori crafts not available elsewhere. Downtown, at the **Jade Factory** (1288 Fenton Street, tel: (07) 349 3968) carvers produce jewellery, sculptures and bowls, many in symbolic designs. Its gift centre also sells woollen products and clothing. The gift shop at the **Rotorua Museum** (tel: (07) 349 4350) is also a good place to find crafts, cards, posters, and books on local history. The **Fletcher Challenge Forests Visitor Centre**, (Long Mile Road, tel: (07) 346 2082) in Whakarewarewa Forest, sells giftware in native and exotic woods, made by local woodturners.

In Taupo, crafts can be found along the **Lake Taupo Arts Trail** – leaflets from the visitor centre. Unexpectedly, the town also has a major independent wine merchant, **Scenic Cellars** (32 Roberts Street, tel: (07) 378 5704), offering more than 2,000 different labels.

Where to...
Be Entertained

Thermalair, the weekly visitors' guide published in Rotorua on Fridays, lists concerts, exhibitions, and sporting fixtures.

Arts and Culture

Maori concert parties perform daily in Rotorua at the **New Zealand Maori Arts and Crafts Institute** (see left), **Tamaki Maori Village** (▶ 89, 94–95), local *marae* and in many hotels. To hear live bands, check out **Fuze** (1122 Tutanekai Street, tel: (07) 349 6306) on Friday and Saturday nights. Rotorua also hosts several musical events, including **Opera in the Pa** in January at Rotowhio Marae. There are regular exhibitions at the **Rotorua Museum of Art and History** (▶ 93).

Adventure and Watersports

You can swim in all the lakes in the Rotorua region except the Green Lake, which is sacred to Maori.

Whether you want to go jet boating, kayaking, white-water rafting, parasailing or water skiing, operators abound. From sky diving to aerial acrobatics, bungy jumping and luging to off-road driving, the region can satisfy most thrill-seekers.

Zorbing is a local invention – you roll downhill in an inflated ball, either harnessed inside the Dry Zorb or loose in the Wet Zorb ("the Wash Cycle"). Mountain biking is popular in Whakarewarewa Forest, and horse treks can be taken over farmland or forest trails. **Foxwood Park** (tel: (07) 345 7003) and **Paradise Valley Horse Riding** (tel: (07) 348 8195) are reputable centres.

Fishing

The Rotorua Trout Fishing Guide, produced by the local Anglers' Association, is available from **Tourism Rotorua** (1167 Fenton Street, tel: (07) 348 5179), and visitor centres have details of professional guides who can supply boats, rods and tackle. You'll need a licence, available from sports stores, guides and some petrol stations.

Lake Cruises

The **Tarawera Steamboat Excursion** (tel: (07) 362 8698) and **MV Reremoana** (tel: (07) 362 8595) visit historic sites on Lake Tarawera. On Lake Rotorua the paddleboat **Lakeland Queen** (tel: (07) 348 6634) offers breakfast, lunch and dine-and-dance cruises. The **Delta Queen** (tel: (07) 386 6445) explores the delta wetlands of Lake Taupo, home to 40 species of birds.

Walking

Well-maintained walking tracks explore native forest in the Rotorua lakes region and the volcanic terrain of Tongariro National Park. In addition to the 17km **Tongariro Crossing** (▶ 92), shorter walks like the two-hour **Taranaki Falls Track** or **Silica Rapids Track** from Whakapapa Village also take in spectacular sights. For maps contact the DOC **Whakapapa Visitor Centre** (tel: (07) 892 3729) or **Tourism Rotorua** (1167 Fenton Street, Rotorua, tel: (07) 348 5179).

Skiing

Two of New Zealand's largest ski areas are on the slopes of Mount Ruapehu: **Whakapapa** and **Turoa** (both tel: (07) 892 3738). Equipment can be hired.

Golf

There are eight golf courses within 30 minutes' drive of Taupo, and four around Rotorua. **The Rotorua Golf Club** (399 Fenton Street, tel: (07) 348 4051) promises unusual hazards – sulphur pits, boiling mudpools, and steaming lakes.

Country Life

The show at the **Agrodome** (Riverdale Park, Ngongotaha, tel: (07) 357 1050), near Rotorua, involves 19 breeds of sheep, shearing and dog-handling. Try your hand at milking a cow and feeding lambs. The show is followed by a tour of a working farm and orchard. The complex also includes a souvenir shop, restaurant, woollen mill, chocolate factory and adventure park. **Rainbow Springs** (Fairy Springs Road, Rotorua, tel: (07) 347 9031) offers a similar show and you can visit trout springs at the wildlife park and Paradise Valley. In Taupo, you can do a tour of the geothermal **Prawn Park** (Huka Falls Road, Wairakei Park, tel: (07) 374 8474), and eat the prawns at the restaurant.

HAWKE'S BAY

Wine and Food Trails

New Zealand's first winery, **Mission Estate** (198 Church Road, Greenmeadows, tel: (06) 844 2259), was established in Hawke's Bay by French missionaries in 1851. The region is now one of the country's leading producers, with more than 40 wineries, most of which welcome visitors. **Church Road Winery** (150 Church Road, Taradale, tel: (06) 844 2053), for example, runs daily tours and has a winemaker's museum, restaurant and gift shop. Get a wine trail leaflet from the **Napier Visitor Centre** (Marine Parade, Napier, tel: (06) 834 1911), or enquire about wine tours there. The annual wine festival, **Harvest Hawke's Bay**, is held in February.

You can also follow a food trail produced by the **Hawke's Bay Food Group** (tel: (06) 877 1001), which includes farms, wineries, orchards, artisans, markets, cafés and restaurants. **Sileni Estates Epicurean Centre and Cellar** (2016 Maraekakaho Road, RD1 Hastings, tel: (06) 879 8768) runs on-site winery tours, wine education courses, a culinary school, two restaurants and a gourmet food store.

Around
Wellington

Getting Your Bearings

By international standards Wellington is a small capital city, but its embassies and visitors endow it with a cosmopolitan atmosphere. A vibrant cultural scene is heightened by its attractive coastal location, buzzing cafés and good restaurants.

Defined by a magnificent harbour and hemmed in by steep forested hills, Wellington's downtown stretches across a narrow lip of flat land. Tall wooden houses cling to the hillsides, beyond the green belt of parks and reserves around the central core. The inner city is linked to the suburbs by steps, walkways and New Zealand's only public "cable car" (actually a funicular railway).

Wellington is only about a third of the size of Auckland, but in attitude, atmosphere and scenic appeal the two cities are equals. Their friendly rivalry for the title of New Zealand's best place to live keeps city planners on their toes. Redevelopment of the city centre and waterfront has spruced up arts and performance venues and confirmed the city's reputation as New Zealand's cultural capital. This is epitomised by the national museum, Te Papa, whose inspired mix of traditional and interactive exhibits draws more than a million visitors each year.

The capital's main function is the business of government,

**Previous page:
Traditional
motifs are
recreated by
contemporary
carvers at the
modern *marae*
at Te Papa**

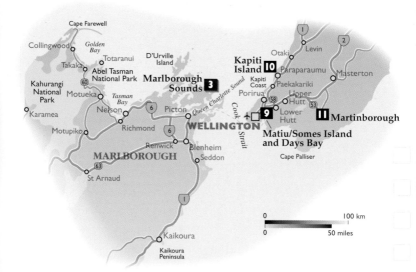

and the beautifully restored Parliament complex makes for a fascinating visit. Away from urban development, the North Island's southernmost city is the gateway to the scenic splendour of Cook Strait and the Marlborough Sounds.

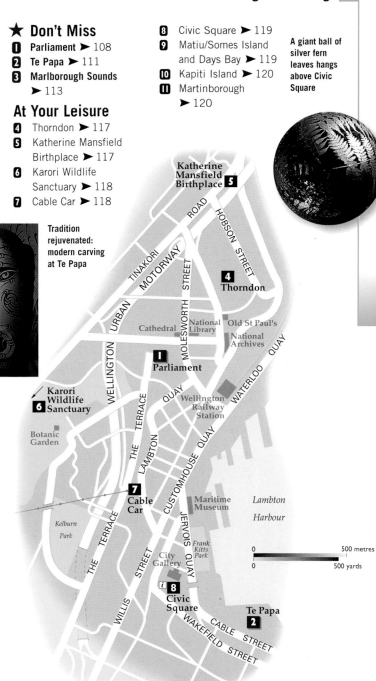

A giant ball of
silver fern
leaves hangs
above Civic
Square

Tradition
rejuvenated:
modern carving
at Te Papa

Katherine
Mansfield
Birthplace **5**

4
Thorndon

Cathedral

National
Library

Old St Paul's

National
Archives

1
Parliament

Karori
Wildlife
6 Sanctuary

Wellington
Railway
Station

Botanic
Garden

7
Cable
Car

Maritime
Museum

Lambton
Harbour

Kelburn
Park

Frank
Kitts
Park

City
Gallery

i **8**
Civic
Square

Te Papa
2

TINAKORI

URBAN MOTORWAY

ROAD

HOBSON STREET

STREET

MOLESWORTH STREET

WELLINGTON

THE TERRACE

LAMBTON

QUAY

CUSTOMHOUSE QUAY

WATERLOO QUAY

JERVOIS QUAY

THE TERRACE

STREET

WILLIS STREET

WAKEFIELD STREET

CABLE STREET

| 0 | | 500 metres |
| 0 | | 500 yards |

Wellington is a far cry from the stereotypical political capital full of grey bureaucrats. The city's wall-to-wall cafés, exquisite galleries and state-of-the-art performance venues give it a dynamic and vibrant atmosphere. Cafés spill out onto the waterfront whenever the weather in "Windy Wellington" allows for alfresco dining.

In Four Days

Day 1

Morning
Pick up bus timetables and an events calendar at the **visitor information centre** (► 110) to check for any performances and exhibitions you may wish to see during your visit. Wellington is the site of New Zealand's government, so the best way to start your visit is to explore the refurbished ❶**Parliament complex** (► 108–110), including the Beehive (pictured above) and Parliament House, and watch the politicians debate. From Parliament, head north to wander through the historic suburb of ❹**Thorndon** (► 117) and have lunch at one of the cafés there.

Afternoon
Stroll along Tinakori Road (left; ► 117), one of the capital's oldest thoroughfares, and explore some of the charming galleries, boutiques and second-hand shops. At the northern end of the road, you'll find the ❺Katherine Mansfield Birthplace (► 117) and its gardens.

Evening
Have dinner in town then take the Cable Car to the Botanic Garden for spectacular views of the city by night. If it's Friday, there may be a night walk through ❻**Karori Wildlife Sanctuary** (► 118), where you can hear the endangered kiwi call after dark, just minutes from the bustle of downtown.

Day 2

Morning

Spend the morning at **2 Te Papa** national museum (its modern *marae* is pictured right; ► 111–112), then walk to **8 Civic Square** (► 119). If you are travelling with children, explore the shows and activities at Capital E. You can also check out exhibitions at the City Gallery. Have lunch at one of the many restaurants in the inner city or Cuba Mall or take the **7 Cable Car** (► 118) to the Botanic Garden and have lunch at the rose garden.

Afternoon

Walk downhill from the gardens back to the Civic Square and stroll past the boat sheds on the waterfront to the **9 Matiu/Somes Island** (► 119) ferry terminal. Catch the afternoon boat to the island or all the way to Days Bay, on the other side of Wellington's harbour. Return to have dinner in the city and to make the most of its lively arts scene by attending a show or concert.

Day 3

If you want to see rare birds, take a day trip to **10 Kapiti Island** (► 120), one of the most accessible of New Zealand's many offshore wildlife sanctuaries. If your tastes are more for fine food and wine, visit charming **11 Martinborough** (► 120) in the Wairarapa wine-growing region. In the late afternoon, drive back or catch the train back to Wellington to catch The Interislander (left) or The Lynx fast ferry to the small South Island port of **Picton** (► 114) and have dinner there.

Day 4

Morning

Explore Picton in the morning and take a cruise around **Queen Charlotte Sound** (► 114) and to Ship Cove. This must have been Captain Cook's favourite place – he visited it five times during his voyages to the southern Pacific.

Afternoon

From Picton, drive to **Nelson** along the scenic route. Take Queen Charlotte Drive along the coast to Havelock, then follow SH6 inland, through Mount Richmond Forest Park and the Bryant Range. In Nelson, explore some of the town's many arts and crafts studios (► 125).

Parliament

It's the architecture of New Zealand's Parliament that grabs the attention. Of the three buildings in the complex at the northern end of Wellington's centre, the most distinctive is the modern Executive Wing – known as the Beehive. Beside it, the older, beautifully refurbished Parliament House and its library embody national heritage and pride.

The **Beehive** lives up to its name. Its dome rises from a broad base through layers of increasingly smaller circles of offices. A feature of Wellington since the 1970s, the building certainly stands out, some would say like a sore thumb, but others see it as a powerful example of modern architecture.

The rings of ministerial windows certainly suggest a hive of coordinated activity, but it is imposing **Parliament House**, next to the Beehive, that has been the country's political centre since Wellington was declared capital in 1865. This is where politicians convene for debates (see panel). Parliament House was built in an Edwardian neo-classical style from granite and marble between 1911 and 1922 after a disastrous fire in 1907 destroyed the wooden General Assembly Building.

If you want to see more than a live performance of politics, take a guided tour of the complex. Your first stop will be in the basement of Parliament House, where part of its foundations have been exposed to demonstrate its earthquake protection. Wellington straddles one of the South Pacific's most threatening fault lines and masonry buildings with only

The Parliament complex boasts some of Wellington's finest architectual treasures, old and new

minimal lateral movement, such as this one, were at risk from collapse. So when the complex underwent a major facelift during a three-year refurbishment project in 1992, making the building earthquake-proof was a priority. The entire building now sits on 400 round rubber bearings, isolators that allow the building to sway and roll, should the earth move below. The same technology – invented by a Wellington engineer – protects the national museum Te Papa (► 111–112).

A highlight of the tour is the ornately decorated **Maori Affairs Select Committee Room**, where Members of Parliament meet to discuss proposed law changes relating to Maori issues and race relations. The walls are covered with woven panels and intricate carvings recalling Maori legends.

Stunning suspended three-dimensional **multimedia installations** grace the **Galleria**, a glass-covered open space, formerly an open courtyard in the original Parliament House, which was roofed over during the refurbishment. To match the Edwardian style of the original, later extensions to the building had to be faced in the same materials: some of the quarries that had supplied the marble 80 years earlier were reopened especially for this one project.

Parliament's debating chamber is often the stage for high drama

One of the most beautiful areas within the parliamentary complex is the **Gothic Parliamentary Library**. Thanks to the skill of 19th-century architects, who included in their designs an early version of fire-resistant doors, the library's collection survived two fires, including the 1907 disaster. For the most

Political Drama

Parliament House debates are open: you can watch them from the public gallery above the debating chamber. Sessions start with formal opening ceremonies, including the placing of a golden mace on the central table and the recital of a prayer by the Speaker of the House; then they often turn into heated arguments. Members of the governing and opposition parties sit about four musket-lengths apart, and like politicians elsewhere, frequently fire salvoes of insults at each other.

part, the library's resources are only available to students and political researchers but it's worth having a look a its halls and corridors, which are exquisitely decorated with plaster mouldings and stained-glass windows and doors. The National Library, just around the corner, is available to the public. By law, a copy of everything published in New Zealand is sent here, and it also contains numerous periodicals and documents, some dating back to the 18th century.

TAKING A BREAK

The **Short Black Café** at the National Library (tel: (04) 474 3000) is open from 9:30 to 4, Monday to Friday, and offers light meals, though its canteen atmosphere may not entice. The **Single File Café** in the foyer of Archives New Zealand (10 Mulgrave Street, tel: (04) 495 6216) has a good selection of coffees, and its high ceilings make a welcome change from cramped downtown bars. While you're there, take a look at the original Treaty of Waitangi (► 10), which is on display at Archives New Zealand.

The Galleria is used to display art installations

Visitor Information Centre
➕ 197 B2 ✉ Corner of Wakefield Street and Civic Square ☎ (04) 802 4860;
bookings@wellingtonnz.com; www.wellingtonnz.com 🕐 Mon–Fri 8:30–5:30, Sat–Sun 9:30–5:30

Parliament Visitor Centre
➕ 197 B4 ✉ Ground floor of Parliament House, left and below the main stairs leading up to the entrance ☎ (04) 471 9999, (04) 471 9503 for groups of more than ten, which require prior bookings; www.parliament.govt.nz 🕐 Mon–Fri 9–5, Sat, public holidays 10–4, Sun 1–4, closed 25 and 26 Dec, 1 and 2 Jan, 6 Feb, Good Friday. Tours leave on the hour and take about an hour. Last tour Mon–Fri 4 pm; Sat, Sun, public holidays 3 pm 🎟 Free

National Library
➕ 197 B4 ✉ 58–78 Molesworth Street; corner of Aitken Street ☎ (04) 474 3000;
visitors@natlib.gov.nz; www.natlib.govt.nz 🕐 Mon–Fri 9–5; some collections open Sat 9–1
🎟 Free

PARLIAMENT: INSIDE INFO

Top tips Parliament usually sits on **Tuesdays**, **Wednesdays** and **Thursdays**. The most heated and entertaining debates occur during question time (2 pm– 3 pm). Check sitting schedules with the visitor centre at parliament.

Hidden gem The **grounds** surrounding the parliament complex are beautifully maintained and include several tranquil corners.

In more depth Opposite the Beehive you'll find the **Old Government Building**, one of the world's largest wooden buildings, with timber columns and slab wooden planking. You'll have to look twice to convince yourself that the building is not made of stone.

2 Te Papa

Te Papa's full name is Te Papa Tongarewa Museum of New Zealand – the Maori words mean "a treasure trove" in free translation. Bold, sometimes provocative and often imaginative, national treasures of all kinds chart the special character of New Zealand and its people.

The museum is New Zealand's most ambitious cultural project, built at a cost of NZ$317 million to tell the stories of the country's environment, arts, history and culture. Its intriguing mix of conventional museum exhibits with interactive virtual experiences can be overwhelming at first, but it's a hit with millions of visitors (see box). You will need at least two hours to see the main galleries, but you could easily spend a day exploring everything.

The building itself covers the space of three rugby fields and contains enough steel to stretch from Wellington to Sydney. Set on the waterfront, it's a prominent and enticing landmark: two wings stretch from the glass façade of its entrance lobby as if welcoming visitors with an embrace.

Start on Level 4 with the undoubted highlight of the museum – a modern *marae* (Maori meeting place). The Maori master carver Dr Cliff Whiting has created a magnificent *whare nui* (meeting house), whose symbols encompass New Zealand's ethnic groups, conveying a sense of peace and unity between cultures. The inside walls are decorated with colourful carvings symbolising historic events that set New Zealand apart. From the floor design to the wall decorations and a painted glass door, every element in this hall tells a story.

A National Winner

When Te Papa opened in February 1998, it copped a fair amount of criticism for its interactive displays and focus on learning through fun rather than scholarly discourse, but its success in attracting first-time museum visitors has since silenced many of the critics. It attracted 3.5 million visitors in its first two years, and Wellington residents are said to make three to four visits each year.

Te Papa's fingerprint logo symbolises New Zealand's unique identity

Stories from many cultures come together at Te Papa

The popular **Golden Days** object theatre is also on Level 4. Instead of displaying photographs and artefacts, the gallery is set up as a walk-in theatre. The stage is a junk shop full of *Kiwiana* (everyday things that describe national identity). The audience, seated in old armchairs and garden seats, watches a film portraying nationally significant moments as well as ordinary events: New Zealanders at work and play but also images of larger events such as Kiwi soldiers returning home from war. As the film screens a particular event, items in the junk shop move or make noises. Though it's most evocative for native New Zealanders, this is an opportunity for overseas visitors to grasp something of the national pysche.

Move downwards through **temporary exhibitions** to more interactive exhibits Level 2. The best, **Awesome Forces** and **Mountains to Sea**, cover natural history. The latter includes a realistic "tree" large enough for children to climb to see birds and animals.

TAKING A BREAK

The **Foodtrain** fast-food restaurant on Level 1 and the **Espresso Bar** coffee shop on Level 4 are good places to recharge before taking in the next exhibit.

➕ 197 C2 ✉ Cable Street ☎ (04) 381 7000; mail@tepapa.govt.nz; www.tepapa.govt.nz; 🕔 Fri–Wed 10–6, Thu 10–9 💲 Free; Time Warp and short-term exhibitions: inexpensive

A laser show starts Future Rush

TE PAPA MUSEUM: INSIDE INFO

Top tips If you are overwhelmed or lost, ask the museum's hosts (in uniforms with Te Papa's fingerprint logo) for directions, or pick up the **Te Papa Explorer brochure** at the information desk on Level 2. It suggests tracks grouping permanent exhibitions in themes such as nature, arts, Maori or "Te Papa for kids".

• If you are short of time, join a guided tour (at 10:15 and 2), which will take you around the main galleries in about 45 minutes.

• Children in particular will enjoy the **Time Warp** on Level 2. It features two interactive motion simulation rides: **Blastback** takes you through changing landscapes to the country's birth; while **Future Rush** pictures life in 50 years' time (one performance: inexpensive; both performances: moderate).

Hidden gem On Level 4 you'll find a **touchstone**, an enormous boulder of greenstone that has been polished on one side by the sheer number of hands touching it over time.

3 Marlborough Sounds

For many visitors, the Marlborough Sounds are the first sight of the South Island as they cross the turbulent waters of Cook Strait or fly over the area's intricate, narrow sea channels. The tranquil waterways are ideal for a boating holiday, and small towns along the coast have seaside charm and artisan traditions.

Many travellers fly directly from Wellington to Christchurch or strike out further afield as soon as they get off the inter-island ferry, but the area is worth exploring, particularly if you want to relax for a day or two.

The sea claws into the South Island's northeastern tip, creating Marlborough Sounds, a labyrinth of islands, peninsulas, sheltered bays and hidden coves. Although roads run along some of the gnarled and steep stretches of land enclosing each waterway, boats are a more practical mode of transport. They have always played a significant role in public transport in New Zealand; the country's rivers and coastline served as scenic highways before the construction of roads, and the best way to explore the Marlborough Sounds is on a water taxi or cruise launch.

The Sounds' rugged charm and beauty cannot fail to appeal

Start your voyage in style with the ferry crossing of the moody **Cook Strait**, a rewarding and scenic journey. There are two ferry services available from Wellington's harbour: *The Interislander* and the faster *Lynx* catamaran. *The Lynx* leaves from Wellington's inner-city wharf, while *The Interislander* leaves from the Wellington ferry terminal at Aotea Quay. Both services transport cars and passengers, but the slightly more expensive *Lynx* completes the journey in about two and a quarter hours while *The Interislander* takes about three.

On a clear and calm day, the Cook Strait crossing is a gentle cruise, always within sight of the mountain ranges behind Wellington or the coastal mountains of Marlborough and Kaikoura. On overcast and windy days, however, the strait heaves with strong ocean currents and the journey can become unpleasant. But for the longest part of the voyage the ferry

travels through the narrow passageways of the Marlborough Sounds and the sea calms down as soon as you pass the tight entrance to **Tory Channel**. From this point onwards the ferry weaves its way through a maze of steep, forest-covered hills and the dramatic scenery of the narrow waterways will be a welcome distraction.

Tory Channel stretches between a tongue of land from South Island and Arapawa Island, where 18th-century explorer Captain James Cook first spotted the strait now named after him. The island also marks the site where the Polynesian explorer and navigator Kupe finally caught up with the giant octopus that led him to discover New Zealand (see box).

Once the boat passes the island, the channel opens into **Queen Charlotte Sound** and a seascape of small coves, twisted inlets and sheltered bays. These are the result of sea level changes after the ice ages, when the ocean rose and drowned an elaborate network of branching valleys.

At the head of Queen Charlotte Sound is **Picton**, where passengers can transfer from the ferry to a bus or train. This small port has grown into a pleasant holiday town and a good base from which to explore the sounds – walking, fishing, sailing, kayaking or cruising. Picton's wharf, a short walk from the ferry terminal, is the departure point for charter yachts, cruise boats and water taxis.

Cruise options range from short journeys around the inner Queen Charlotte Sound to full-day trips to the neighbouring

Main picture:
Queen
Charlotte
Sound is popular for boat
cruises, scenic
drives and
walks
Inset left:
Aboard the
inter-island
ferry Arahura

Kenepuru or **Pelorus sounds**. Popular cruises are the mail runs along the Queen Charlotte and Pelorus sounds. Some of the most beautiful properties along the coastline are inaccessible by road and the mail boats will deliver anything from a small letter to livestock or building materials. Most bays along the way have holiday homes (which New Zealanders call *baches*) nestled among thriving native shrubs, boats moored on the sparkling water, and a string of boat sheds lining the coast. Local residents may row out to meet the boat or greet it on the beach.

Another popular destination for visitors is **Ship Cove**, almost at the seaward end of Queen Charlotte Sound, which Captain Cook visited repeatedly during his voyages. It was

Kupe and the Octopus

A Maori legend tells of the Polynesian explorer Kupe, who was being pestered by a giant octopus that was eating his harvest of fish. Kupe decided to kill it, but the creature fled and Kupe had to chase it across the ocean to the south Pacific, where he eventually discovered New Zealand. He finally caught the octopus at Arapawa Island in the Marlborough Sounds. There are several versions of the story but each includes intricate details of the chase along the coastline of the Marlborough Sounds. It is thought that such stories provided ancient Maori navigators with a verbal chart of the Cook Strait area.

here that he claimed the country on behalf of Britain, as well as letting loose the first sheep in New Zealand.

The cove is the starting point of the **Queen Charlotte Track**, which winds its way through 67km of native bush and coastline to Anakiwa, offering stunning views out across the sounds. You can arrange a water taxi to drop you off and pick you up at various points along the track and walk as far as you want to.

TAKING A BREAK

Both *The Interislander* and *The Lynx* have cafés and bars on board. For a good cup of coffee on solid ground, try **Le Café** in Picton (33 High Street, tel: (03) 573 5588).

Visitor Information Centre: Picton
✚ 200 B1
✉ The Foreshore
☎ (03) 573 7477; pictonvin@xtra.co.nz
🕐 Daily 8:30–8, Oct–Mar; 8:30–5, Apr–Sep

Visitor Information Centre: Nelson
✚ 200 B1
✉ Cnr Trafalgar and Halifax streets
☎ (03) 548 2304, vin@tourism-nelson.co.nz; http://nelson.net.nz
🕐 Daily 8:30–6, Oct–Mar; 8:30–5, Apr–Sep

Tranz Rail
✉ Booking agents throughout the country
☎ (04) 498 3303; 0800 802 802 toll-free; passengerservices@tranzrail.co.nz; www.tranzrailtravel.co.nz
🕐 *The Interislander* leaves Wellington for

Picton and back about 6 times daily; *The Lynx* leaves about twice daily; check current timetable for times
💶 Range of prices available

Mail Boat Cruises
✚ 200 B1
✉ The Waterfront, Picton
☎ (03) 573 6175, 0800 624 526 toll-free; beachcomber@xtra.co.nz
💶 Moderate

Edwin Fox
✚ 200 B1
✉ Dunbar Wharf, Picton
☎ (03) 573 6868; edwinfoxsoc@xtra.co.nz; http://members.nbci.com/edwin_fox
🕐 Daily 8:45–5
💶 Inexpensive

MARLBOROUGH SOUNDS: INSIDE INFO

Top tips You can **fly** from Wellington to Picton, Nelson or Blenheim and get a bird's-eye view of the intricate landscapes of the Marlborough Sounds.
• This is the country's largest **mussel-growing** area, so make sure you taste some of the seafood caught fresh from local waters. Try Marlborough Terranean or Twelve Trees Restaurant (► 124).

Hidden gem Pelorus Sound is equally intricate but even more remote. The sound is 42km long but has almost 400km of coastline, with many sheltered nooks and crannies to explore.

In more depth At Picton's foreshore is the battered clipper *Edwin Fox*, the last remaining ship of the British East India company and so an important reminder of the heady days of international seatrade. It was launched in 1853 and carried convicts to Australia, troops to the Crimean War and settlers to New Zealand. There's not much of it left, but it's being lovingly restored on a dry dock. An interpretation centre illuminates the ship's lively past.

At Your Leisure

4 Thorndon

Thorndon is Wellington's oldest suburb, extending from the Parliament complex to Hobson Street and Tinakori Road. It features some of the capital's finest historic villas, built at the turn of the 20th century and many retaining their original features. The visitor information

Politicians are regulars at the Backbencher Pub in Thorndon

centre (► 110) has a brochure describing a three-hour self-guided walk through the suburb. A highlight is Old St Paul's on 34 Mulgrave Street, a lovely church secluded in a small park, with a beautiful Early English Gothic interior in native timber: rimu, matai, totara and kauri. It was built in 1865 as a temporary cathedral, but maintained this role for a century until the Anglican Cathedral was erected on nearby Molesworth Street. It is still used as a backdrop for weddings and concerts. Tinakori Road has a cluster of shops, boutiques, galleries, cafés and hotels in lovely old buildings.

Old St Paul's

🕂 197 C4 ✉ 34 Mulgrave Street
☎ (04) 473 6722; oldstpauls@
historic.org.nz; www.historic.org.nz
🕐 Daily 10–5 or by special arrangement; closed Good Friday, 25 Dec; access subject to functions 🎟 Free

5 Katherine Mansfield Birthplace

Katherine Mansfield (1888–1923) – often known as "KM" to New Zealanders – is the country's most distinguished author, known internationally for her short stories and letters. Her childhood home (built in 1888) at 25 Tinakori Road, and the surrounding Thorndon suburb feature in many of her stories, and extracts from her work are displayed alongside contemporary photographs in the restored wooden house. There's a video portrait of the writer and a doll's house has been built using details in her short story of the same name. Her famous garden was planted by her father in the year of her birth. The "gully filled with tree ferns" KM saw from her house as a child has since been replaced with a motorway but the remaining lawn and flowerbeds have been faithfully restored to its late 19th-century appearance with the help of photographs and KM's own descriptions.

🕂 197 C5 ✉ 25 Tinakori Road
☎ (04) 473 7268;
kmbirthplace@xtra.co.nz 🕐 Daily,
Tue–Sun 10–4, Mon 10–2:30 🚌 14 to
Wilton stops at nearby Park Street
🎟 Inexpensive

6 Karori Wildlife Sanctuary

Just 3km from downtown Wellington is one of New Zealand's most ambitious private conservation projects,

Karori reservoir once provided the capital's main water supply

established in the late 1990s when a group of Wellingtonians decided to reclaim a pocket of bush near the inner city and return it to its original state. First, the steep-sided 250ha valley around the former Karori water reservoir was surrounded by a fence, specially designed to keep out predators. Then all pests – possums, stoats, mice and rats – inside the sanctuary were eradicated and, finally, endangered wildlife reintroduced. It's been a great success: the kiwi population produced chicks during the first season and other native birds are flocking here. It'll take about 500 years for the area to reach its full potential, but a variety of guided walks, including a heritage trail and a nocturnal tour (book in advance), allows visitors to appreciate the evolution of the sanctuary. The dynamic nature of the project means that access and facilities improve all the time, so check current policies and opening times before you go.

➕ off 197 A4 ✉ 31 Waiapu Road, Karori ☎ (04) 920 9200; kwst@sanctuary.org.nz; www.sanctuary.org.nz ✋ Inexpensive

7 Cable Car

The bright red Cable Car is a Wellington icon and the fastest way of getting from downtown to the Botanic Garden, Victoria University or the suburb of Kelburn. Cars run from an arcade off Lambton Quay (look for the Cable Car sign on the Quay, just north of Plimmers Steps). The Cable Car opened in 1902, linking the new hill-hugging suburbs to the city centre. It was immediately popular: soon, a million passengers rode in steam-powered wooden boxes each year. In the 1970s the track was reconstructed and new Swiss-made cars introduced. Near the top terminal you'll find the Cable Car Museum and the Carter Observatory, which offers planetarium shows, telescope viewing, and astronomy displays, though the view down over the city is also worth the ride.

➕ 197 B3 ☎ (04) 472 2199 ⏰ Every ten minutes, Mon–Fri 7 am–10 pm, Sat, Sun, pub holidays 9 am–10 pm ✋ Inexpensive

Cable Car Museum

➕ off 197 A3 ✉ Botanic Garden ☎ (04) 475 3578; admin@cablecarmuseum.co.nz; www.cablecarmuseum.co.nz ⏰ Mon–Fri 9–5:30, Nov–Easter; Mon–Fri 9–5, Easter–Oct; Sat, Sun, pub holidays 9–4:30

Carter Observatory

➕ 197 A3 ✉ Botanic Garden, near top Cable Car terminal ☎ (04) 472 8167; astronomy@carterobs.ac.nz; www.carterobs.ac.nz ⏰ Mon–Fri 9–5, Sat, Sun, pub holidays noon–5, Tue, Thu, Sat also 6:30 pm–late ✋ Inexpensive

Te Papa is a stunning landmark on Wellington's waterfront

In Civic Square, look up to see the fern fronds and palm leaves

City Gallery
🔲 197 B2 ☎ (04) 801 3952 (information), (04) 801 3021; art.gallery@wcc. govt.nz; www.city-gallery.org.nz ⏰ Daily 10–5 💲 Free; charges for exhibitions

Capital E
🔲 197 B2 ☎ (04) 384 8502; info@capitale.org.nz; www.capitale.org.nz ⏰ Daily 10–5 💲 Inexpensive; charges for exhibitions

8 Civic Square

Spacious Civic Square is an ideal place to start exploring Wellington's waterfront. Some of the capital's premier cultural centres surround Civic Square: to your left are the Michael Fowler Centre and the stately Edwardian Town Hall, both magnificent settings for concerts. Opposite is the Wellington public library and on your right you'll find the City Gallery. Walk up to the City to Sea bridge, which connects the square with the waterfront across Jervois Quay, and look back to see the visitor information centre on the corner of Wakefield Street, next to the Wellington City Council building. Below the bridge is the entrance to Capital E, a children's activity centre with a theatre, television studio, exhibition and a toy shop. At the lagoon end of the bridge you can hire paddle-boats and jet skis; walk south along the waterfront towards Te Papa (➤ 111–112) for inline skates and four-wheeled crocodile cycles, or north to Queens Wharf for kayaks.

9 Matiu/Somes Island and Days Bay

Matiu/Somes Island is a former quarantine station now administered by the Department of Conservation, which has turned it into a wildlife sanctuary. Lying in Wellington Harbour 8km from the city centre, it is one of the most accessible of New Zealand's predator-free islands and one of the few places where people can see tuatara in the wild. (Tuatara are the last representatives of reptiles that appeared 200 million years ago). Matiu/Somes Island has a network of footpaths and great views from the summit (half an hour from the jetty).

Departing from Queens Wharf, ferries continue on their 30-minute journey to Days Bay on the other side of the harbour – a pleasant area with a beach, parks and old houses.

🔲 Matiu/Somes Island: 200 C1 ✉ Ferries from Queens Wharf, waterfront off Jervois Quay ☎ (04) 499 1282, (04) 499 1273 for ferry timetables ⏰ Up to nine sailings daily to Days Bay, at least three daily trips to Matiu/Somes Island 💲 Inexpensive

Best for Kids

• **Discovery centres** and **Story Place** (above) at Te Papa (➤ 111–112)
• **Capital E** on Civic Square (➤ 119)
• **Play area** or **rollerblading** on the waterfront
• Seeing stars at the Planetarium in the **Carter Observatory** (➤ 118)

🔟 Kapiti Island

Kapiti Island is another pest-free wildlife reserve near the capital, 6km offshore from the Kapiti Coast. The 1,760ha island dominates the coast off Paraparaumu, about 50km north of Wellington. A sanctuary for kiwi, kaka, takahe and saddlebacks, the protected waters around it are a feeding ground for birds and a nursery for fish. Kapiti Island is open to the public, but visitor numbers are limited to 50 a day. You'll need to get a permit from DOC's Wellington office, where you can also book the boat trip from the Kapiti Coast. There are a number of walking tracks, some leading to the summit of Tuteremoana (521m), but no shops or cafés so bring provisions with you.

🟦 200 C1

Department of Conservation
🟦 197 B4 ✉ Old Government Buildings ☎ (04) 472 7356; www.doc.govt.nz 🕓 Mon–Fri 9–4:30, Sat and Sun 10–3 💷 Inexpensive

🔟 Martinborough

For wine fanatics, Martinborough is an ideal stopover for a vineyard visit. This once-sleepy town is now a popular weekend destination for well-off Wellingtonians: its fresh rural air is only an hour's drive from the city, at the end of SH53. The main draw is Martinborough's status as the centre of the Wairaga vine-growing region, and most wineries are eager to show visitors around. In November, the Toast Martinborough Festival celebrates that timeless trinity – food, wine and music.

Visitor Information Centre
🟦 200 C1 ✉ 18 Kitchener Street, Martinborough ☎ (06) 306 9043 🕓 Daily 10–4

Walking in Wellington

Wellington is hilly but compact and best explored on foot. Walks and heritage trails take in suburbs such as Thorndon, historic streets and the waterfront. Longer walks lead through parks and reserves, and the five-hour City to Sea walk (➤ 176–178) takes you from downtown to Island Bay. For inspiration, pick up leaflets from the visitor information centre.

Where to... Stay

Prices

Expect to pay for two people sharing a double room
£ under NZ$150 **££** NZ$150-$300 **£££** more than NZ$300

Hotel Inter-Continental Wellington ££-£££

Centrally situated, this striking, bronze-coloured building is a city landmark. Formerly the Parkroyal, it is close to the Lambton Quay shops, cafés, Parliament, the waterfront and the WestpacTrust Stadium. You're welcomed by a top-hatted doorman and the lobby gleams with marble. The 232 rooms include luxury suites, queen, twin and bureau (standard) rooms. There is a restaurant, a bar and grill, and a cocktail lounge, as well as a health and fitness centre with a gym, spa, sauna and heated pool, and a choice of restaurants and bars. It's worth checking for cheap weekend rates.
✚ 197 B3 ☒ Grey Street, Wellington ☎ (04) 472 2722; fax: (04) 472 4724; www.basshotels.com

Quality Hotel Oriental Bay £-££

The rooms may be modest but the views are stunning at this hotel, which clings to the hillside in the residential suburb of Oriental Bay. Located directly on the waterfront, the hotel is close to the city centre and other attractions. It has 113 rooms, a restaurant and bar, and a heated indoor swimming pool. Ask for a room with a harbour view and a balcony. The special weekend rates are good value.
✚ off 197 C2 ☒ 73 Roxburgh Street, Wellington ☎ (04) 385 0279; fax: (04) 384 5324; www.qualityoriental.co.nz

Shepherds Arms Hotel £-££

The Shepherds Arms claims to be New Zealand's oldest boutique hotel. Established in 1870, in the historic suburb of Thorndon, it is not far from Parliament, the railway station, the inter-island ferry terminal and the WestpacTrust Stadium. The hotel has been restored to its former glory, with 14 individually appointed guest rooms decorated to reflect their Victorian origins. Some rooms have four-poster king or queen canopy beds, and all but the most modest have spa baths or showers. There's a popular bar with a non-smoking snug and a dining room with an open fire and sunny deck.
✚ 197 A4 ☒ 285 Tinakori Road, Thorndon, Wellington ☎ (04) 472 1320; fax: (04) 472 0253; www.shepherds.co.nz

The Terrace Villas ££

Accommodation at The Terrace Villas is in eight character villas on The Terrace, close to the cable car and the Lambton Quay shopping district. The villas are divided into 42 self-contained serviced apartments, ranging in size from studios to three large bedrooms. Furnished with a mix of modern and character fittings, all have cable TV, laundry and kitchen facilities. A light breakfast is provided. Importantly in this busy part of town, there's also free off-street parking.
✚ 197 B3 ☒ 202 The Terrace, Wellington ☎ (04) 920 2020; fax: (04) 920 2030; info@terracevillas.co.nz; www.terracevillas.co.nz

Fernside £££

One of New Zealand's grand heritage homes, about an hour's drive from Wellington near the Martinborough vineyards, this Georgian-style country mansion was for a time the

American ambassador's residence. It's now a luxury lodge surrounded by park-like gardens. The four bedrooms are spacious, with *en suite* bathrooms. Two have dressing rooms. Downstairs, you can relax in the drawing room, library, sunroom or on the terrace. There's also a tennis court and croquet lawn. The tariff includes afternoon tea on arrival, pre-dinner drinks, *table d'hôte* dinner and breakfast.

✚ 200 C3 ⊠ SH2, RD1, Featherston ☎ (06) 308 8265; fax: (06) 308 9172; www.fernside.co.nz

MARLBOROUGH

Black Birch Lodge £

This vineyard homestay is set in the heart of Marlborough wine country. Hosts David and Margaret Barnsley have been growing grapes in Marlborough since 1980 and can help plan your wine trail itinerary. The rooms, all with *en suite* bathrooms, are decorated in country-cottage style and have panoramic views. There's a lounge with an open fire and library, and guests can use the pool and tennis court. Walk through the vines to the fine restaurant, Herzog's (▶ 122), next door.

✚ 200 B1 ⊠ Jeffries Road, RD3 Blenheim ☎ (03) 572 8876; fax: (03) 572 8806

Hotel d'Urville ££

The heritage Public Trust Building in Blenheim provides a grand location for this boutique hotel, named after the French explorer who charted the Marlborough Sounds. Much of the hotel is in the old bank vaults, and the nine rooms and suites have lofty ceilings, wooden floors scattered with Persian rugs, and exotic furniture. The original central vault, with its huge steel doors, has been converted into a guest lounge with books and complimentary aperitifs. Gravitate to the restaurant and bar to sample local food and wine.

✚ 200 B1 ⊠ 52 Queen Street, Blenheim ☎ (03) 577 9945; fax: (03) 577 9946; www.durville.co.nz

Punga Cove Resort £–££

Punga Cove is a remote and beautiful spot. Tucked in a sandy cove in the Marlborough Sounds, on a hillside covered in native ferns, the resort is accessible (just) by road, but most easily by boat. Accommodation ranges from individual chalets with *en suite* bathrooms to rooms for backpackers on the Queen Charlotte Track (▶ 116). There's a restaurant with a million-dollar view of the cove and Queen Charlotte Sound, and also a shop, pool and sauna. Continental breakfast baskets are delivered to your room.

✚ 200 B1 ⊠ Punga Cove, Endeavour Inlet, Marlborough Sounds ☎ (03) 579 8561; fax: (03) 579 8080

NELSON

Old Schoolhouse Vineyard Cottage £

Pam Robert and David Birt have moved the Redwood Valley school-house to their Kina Beach vineyard and turned it into a romantic retreat among the vines. It's full of memorabilia from the 1930s, an open fire in winter, a barbecue on the terrace in summer, and a well-stocked pantry for breakfast. There is just one bedroom (though there is also a day bed in a lounge alcove), from where you can watch the sun rising over the Moutere Estuary.

✚ 200 B1 ⊠ Dee Road, Kina Beach, Nelson ☎ (03) 526 6252; fax: (03) 526 6252; www.kinabeach.com

Te Puna Wai Apartment £

This early Victorian villa nestles in the hills above Nelson Port. The house has been lovingly refurbished, with *en suite* accommodation, oriental rugs and antique furnishings. The fridge is stocked with all manner of delights, from sparkling wine to home-made jams. Dinner can be cooked to order, or waterfront restaurants are near by. A minimum two-night stay is preferred.

✚ 200 B1 ⊠ 24 Richardson Street, Nelson ☎ (03) 548 7621; fax: (03) 548 7621

Where to...
Eat and Drink

Prices
Expect to pay for a three-course meal, excluding drinks
£ up to NZ$45 ££ NZ$45–$60 £££ more than NZ$60

WELLINGTON

Caffe L'affare £
Enzo Laffare is credited with introducing Wellingtonians to espresso. A roaster roars at this relaxed café in a side street off Cambridge Terrace, and L'affare coffee appears on many restaurant menus. The café is a popular meeting place, serving filled paninis, snacks, and all-day breakfast. Seafood chowder is a speciality. There's even a children's play area.

🚹 197 C1 ⊠ 27 College Street, Wellington ☎ (04) 385 9748 🕓 Mon–Fri 7–4:30, Sat 8–4; closed pub holidays

Icon £–££
The flagship restaurant at Te Papa, the national museum (▶ 111–112), Icon represents the various New Zealand regions. Under chef Peter Thornley, the menu is a New Zealand blend of French, Italian and Asian: look for dishes like Clevedon oysters with a ponzu dipping sauce, Golden Bay crab with fennel curry, and kaffir lime leaf brûlée. There's also a special children's menu. The restaurant looks over the harbour, with a balcony for sunny days.

🚹 197 C2 ⊠ Te Papa, Cable Street, Wellington ☎ (04) 801 5300 🕓 Daily noon–10 (lunch till 3, dinner from 6)

Logan Brown ££–£££
Logan Brown has taken a grand 1920s Grecian banking chamber and turned it into a gracious restaurant in the French style, with booth seating and a wine bar. It's a frequent winner of Wellington's best restaurant award. Its menu, which changes weekly, is contemporary with a seafood focus. Look for dishes like patua ravioli, and tuna tempura with seaweed salad. The three-course bistro menu, available at lunchtime and pre-theatre, is excellent value. There's live jazz on Fridays. Bookings recommended.

🚹 197 B1 ⊠ 192 Cuba Street, Wellington ☎ (04) 801 5114 🕓 Mon–Fri noon–2, daily 6 pm–3 am; closed 25 Dec

Shed 5 ££
Built in 1888 as a wool store on the wharf, Shed 5 has been cleverly transformed into an elegant restaurant and bar. The menu focuses on seafood and changes daily. It's also a pleasant place to have a coffee or a glass of wine, especially if you sit outside on the water's edge and watch the ferries. It can get crowded and noisy inside, especially at lunchtime and in the early evening. Reservations are recommended.

🚹 197 C3 ⊠ Queens Wharf, Wellington ☎ (04) 499 9069 🕓 Daily 11 am till late; closed 25 and 26 Dec

MARLBOROUGH

Herzog's £££
This is no casual winery restaurant but a gourmet destination re-created by Hans and Therese Herzog in the style of their celebrated Swiss restaurant. They brought key staff with them, including chef Louis Schindler, and their collection of fine wines. The decor is opulent, with antiques, ornate mirrors, paintings, and formal flower arrangements. The tables are set with Limoges china, crystal glasses and French silverware. There's a fixed-price, five-course menu focused on seasonal produce, fish

and game. With more than 300 wines, the wine cellar is one of the most extensive in New Zealand. Bookings are necessary.

✚ 200 B1 ☒ 81 Jeffries Road, Blenheim ☎ (03) 572 8770 🕒 Wed–Sun from 7 pm, Oct–Apr; Tue–Sun 7 pm, Dec–Mar

Marlborough Terranean ££

Tracy and Lothar Greiner were struck by the similarities between Marlborough and the Mediterranean and named their restaurant in Picton accordingly. The walls are covered in romantic pastel murals of *trompe-l'oeil* pillars, palisades and Italianate countryside and there's a courtyard at the back. The menu blends European classics such as duck liver pâté and *saltimbocca alla romana* with local produce, especially seafood, and there's a strong, long local wine list.

✚ 200 B1 ☒ 31 High Street, Picton ☎ (03) 573 7122 🕒 Daily from 6:30 pm, Dec–Apr; Wed–Sun from 6:30 pm, Oct–Nov; closed Jun–Sep

Twelve Trees Restaurant £

The restaurant at Allan Scott's striking rammed-earth winery is a popular place for lunch. Eat out on the sheltered garden terrace, or inside under the vaulted ceiling, where you can admire the artworks. The menu is simple and fresh, ranging from a vineyard platter or bread and dips to local mussels, salmon, and fresh salads. Allan Scott is a pioneer of viticulture in Marlborough and the producer of fine wines, so it's a good place to try them, too.

✚ 200 B1 ☒ Allan Scott Wines and Estates, Jackson's Road, RD3 Blenheim ☎ (03) 572 9054 🕒 Daily 9–4:30 (lunch 11:30–3:30); closed 25 and 26 Dec

NELSON

The Boat Shed Café ££

A converted boat shed, with water lapping its foundations, this restaurant not surprisingly specialises in seafood. Nelson is New Zealand's major fishing port, so the range is wide, from Nelson scallops and Golden Bay crabs to salmon and green-lipped mussels farmed in the Marlborough Sounds. Crabs and crayfish come straight from the restaurant's holding tanks – you can buy them to cook yourself, if that's your fancy. Either dine inside or brave the breeze on the deck, and admire the view.

✚ 200 B1 ☒ 350 Wakefield Quay, Nelson ☎ (03) 546 9783 🕒 Daily from 10:30 (lunch 11:30–2:30; dinner from 6 pm); closed 25 and 26 Dec

Denton Winery £

It's worth making a detour to visit this picturesque colonial-style winery, if just to sit on its shady terraces and enjoy the view over lake and gardens to the mountains beyond. The food is simple but appealing, designed to complement the Denton wines: home-made bread, boutique cheeses, local olive oils, salami and fruit desserts. The winery is also a gallery for Alex Denton's paintings, and sells local craft and food items.

✚ 200 B1 ☒ Awa Awa Road, off Marriages Road, Ruby Bay, Nelson ☎ (03) 540 3555 🕒 Daily 11–5, mid-Sep–Easter; closed 25 Dec

The Honest Lawyer £

This country pub sits in splendid isolation on a peninsula about ten minutes' drive from Nelson. Built of locally quarried stone, inside it looks like something straight out of history, with exposed brick, lace curtains, a massive stone fireplace and a ceiling hung with bric-a-brac. Outside, a beer garden overlooks the estuary. The pub has 15 beers on tap, a good wine list and hearty pub food like steak-and-Guinness pie or whole flounder. Portions are generous. You can also have breakfast, snacks and cream teas. There's accommodation on site in ten king rooms with *en suite* bathrooms.

✚ 200 B1 ☒ 1 Point Road, Monaco, Nelson ☎ (03) 547 8850 🕒 Daily 7 am–1 am

Where to...
Shop

Shopping Centres

Wellington is a compact city, with most shopping districts close together. There are several shopping centres at Lambton Quay, including **Lambton Square** (174–180 Lambton Quay, tel: (04) 472 6666), which has 27 speciality shops. Or step back in time at **Kirkaldie and Stains** (165–177 Lambton Quay, tel: (04) 472 5899), the country's oldest department store, founded in 1863.

Fashion

The Old Bank Arcade (223–237 Lambton Quay, tel (04) 922 0600) houses some top NZ fashion designers. For avant-garde labels, try **Zambesi** (107 Customhouse Quay,

tel: (04) 472 3638) and **Zambesi Man** (MLC Building, Lambton Quay, tel: (04) 473 2680). Head for Cuba Street to find designers like **Frutti** (166 Cuba Street, tel: (04) 384 6965) and **Jive Junkies** (130 Cuba Mall, (04) 801 6767). Get a **Fashion Map** from the Wellington Visitor Centre (101 Wakefield Street, tel: (04) 802 4860).

Arts and Crafts

Many dealer galleries specialise in fine and applied art. Try **New Work Studio** (147 Cuba Street, tel: (04) 801 9880), **Avid** (48 Victoria Street, tel: (04) 472 7703) and **Art Debonair** (53 Boulcott Street, tel: (04) 472 6601). For souvenirs, try the museum stores at **Te Papa** (Cable Street, tel: (04) 381 7000) and the **Museum of Wellington City and Sea** (Bond Store, Queens Wharf, tel: (04) 472 8904).

The **Dixon Street Deli** (45 Dixon Street, tel: (04) 384 2436) bake their own bread and have a selection of cheeses and other deli items.

The **Lindale Centre** (SH1, Paraparaumu, tel: (04) 297 0916) features agricultural speciality shops, including Kapiti cheese made on site, honey, olive products, sheepskins and a farm-kitchen restaurant.

Around Blenheim

The **Marlborough Art and Craft Trail** lists more than 30 craftspeople who welcome visitors. Brochures from the Blenheim Visitor Centre (High Street, tel: (03) 578 9904). At the **Alpaca Shop** (Koromiko, tel: (03) 573 7480) you can see alpaca and llamas and buy products made from their fleece. **Ponder Estate** (New Renwick Road, tel: (03) 572 8642) sells Mike Ponder's art as well as wines and olive oil. **Traditional Country Preserves** (Selmes Road, tel: (03) 570 5665) makes preserves from local produce, and also sells local crafts and wine accessories.

Prenzel Distillery (Riverlands Estate, tel: (03) 578 2809) makes liqueurs and fruit brandies. Charming **Leighvander Cottage** (SH63, tel: (03) 572 2851) has lavender-related products, such as oil, pillows and honey vinegar. Pick up some bread for a picnic from **De Brood Bakkers** (Redwood Bakery, Cleghorn Street, tel: (03) 578 3319).

Around Nelson

Around 300 full-time artists and craftspeople work in the Nelson region. At the **Weekend Market** (Montgomery Square, Nelson, tel: (03) 546 6454) there's everything from decorated toilet seats to organic produce. You can watch the glassblowers at work at **Hoglund Art Glass** (Lansdowne Road, Richmond, tel: (03) 544 6500). **Craft Habitat** (Richmond Bypass, SH6, tel: (03) 544 7481) is a collection of independent studios. **Real Crafty** (110 Tahunanui Drive, Nelson, tel: (03) 546 5450) has works by more than 130 craft artists.

Where to...
Be Entertained

WELLINGTON

For what's on, see the Thursday and Saturday editions of the *Evening Post* or the *Dominion*. Courtenay Place is the nightlife centre – its bars, clubs, cinemas, theatres and cafés are open until the early hours.

Performing Arts

Wellington calls itself the cultural capital of New Zealand. The large, modern **Michael Fowler Centre**, Wakefield Street, is home of the New Zealand Symphony Orchestra (tel: (04) 801 4242). The **town hall**, next door, hosts more intimate concerts. The New Zealand String Quartet, Chamber Music New Zealand, and the Wellington Sinfonia also give regular concerts. The Royal New Zealand Ballet (tel: (04) 381 9000) is based at the **WestpacTrust St James Theatre** (77–87 Courtenay Place, tel: (04) 802 4060), also the venue for musical shows, and the **NBR New Zealand Opera** (tel: (04) 384 4434).

For professional theatre, try **Downstage** (cnr Courtenay Place and Cambridge Terrace, tel: (04) 801 6946) or **Circa** (1 Taranaki Street, tel: (04) 801 7992). Alternative performers appear at **Bats** (1 Kent Terrace, tel: (04) 802 4175). Get an **Arts Map** from the visitor information centre (cnr Wakefield Street and Civic Square, tel: (04) 548 2304).

Festivals

The **International Festival of the Arts** is held in March in even years, overlapping with the annual **Wellington Fringe Festival**. A **Jazz Festival** is held in October.

MARLBOROUGH

In Marlborough, New Zealand's largest wine region, there are more than 40 wineries to choose from, several with restaurants. Pick up a **Wines of Marlborough map** from the Blenheim Visitor Centre (High Street, tel: (03) 578 9904).

Festivals

Wine Marlborough is the culmination of a festival week in February. **Hunter's Garden Marlborough** is held in November.

NELSON

The Suter (208 Bridge Street, tel: (03) 548 4699) is the region's public art museum, with four galleries, a craft shop and a theatre. There's often live entertainment at the city's many bars and cafés. Catch some jazz at the **Victorian Rose** (281 Trafalgar Street, tel: (03) 548 7631), or dance at the **Little Rock** (165 Bridge Street, tel: (03) 546 8800).

A number of wineries are open to visitors. Pick up a copy of the **Winemakers of Nelson guide map** from the visitor information centre (cnr Halifax and Trafalgar Streets, tel: (03) 548 2304). It's also New Zealand's major hop-growing region: sample a brew and take a tour at **Mac's** (660 Main Road, Stoke, tel: (03) 547 5357) or **Founders** (Founders Historic Park, 87 Atawhai Drive, tel: (03) 548 4638).

Festivals

Nelson's lively cultural and gastronomic life is reflected in its many festivals. The most extravagant is the **Wearable Art Awards**, held in September, a parade of fantasy costumes. There's also an annual **Winter Arts Festival**. Summer brings the annual **Jazz Festival**, **The Gathering** popular music fest, and the biennial **Chamber Music Festival**. **Taste Nelson**, the food and wine festival, is held at the end of January and the **International Beer Awards** are in April.

Christchurch and the Southern Alps

Getting Your Bearings

If you thought the scenery of the North Island was magnificent and the people too nice to be true, prepare to be surprised. In the South Island, the mountains soar even higher, the forests are more vigorous, time seems to stand still and the landscapes will astonish you.

Christchurch is the South Island's largest city and a gateway to all other destinations in the south. The city was planned as an antipodean outpost of the Church of England, but has grown into a cosmopolitan community with a thriving cultural scene. Around the city, the Canterbury Plains are New Zealand's largest stretch of flat land and one of its most important agricultural areas. Some of the country's biggest farms use the land here for anything from traditional sheep and dairy farming to boutique vineyards and olive groves.

The plains were built up over millions of years from silt carried by rivers from the Southern Alps, the South Island's mountainous backbone, which separates the drier eastern regions from the humid and lush West Coast.

Most of New Zealand's national parks are in the South Island, so whichever way you go from Christchurch you will find spectacular land- or seascapes and see amazing wildlife. If you head north to Kaikoura, you will share the ocean with hundreds of dolphins and whales; heading south to Aoraki/Mount Cook you'll walk through a wonderland of snow-capped peaks; and going west through Arthur's Pass to the rugged West Coast, you could be taking a stroll on a glacier within minutes of leaving the beach.

Previous page: Walkers can explore the icy wonderland of the Franz Josef Glacier safely during guided tours. Left: Get a hands-on history experience at Shantytown

★ Don't Miss

Aoraki/Mount Cook is New Zealand's highest peak

Denniston

Westport (6)

Charleston

Rotoroa

Murchison

Lake Rotoroa

St Arnaud

Lake Rotoiti

(63)

Inland Kaikoura Range

(1)

12 Punakaiki

Reefton (65)

Lewis Pass

Whale-watching at Kaikoura

13

Kaikoura Peninsula

Greymouth (7)

5 The West Coast

Lake Brunner

TranzAlpine Express route

Otira

14 Hanmer Springs

1834m ▲ Mt Ajax

Lake Summer

1612m ▲ Mt Tekoa

Culverden

Cheviot

Lake Kaniere

4 Arthur's Pass and Otira Viaduct

1987m ▲ Mt Crossley

(7)

2400m ▲ Mt Murchison

CANTERBURY

0 ___ 50 km

0 ___ 30 miles

11 Castle Hill and Cave Stream

Rangiora

Pegasus Bay

Lake Coleridge

(73) (72)

Darfield

Kaiapoi

6 Nga Hau E Wha – National *Marae*

Mount Hutt

(72) Methven

(1)

1 Christchurch

Port Hills 7 8 Lyttelton Timeball Station

Lake Ellesmere

(75)

2 Banks Peninsula

Akaroa

Akaroa Harbour

At Your Leisure

Make Christchurch your base to explore the spectacular beauty of the South Island's national parks and the rugged charm of its people.

In Five Days

Day 1

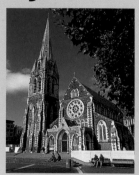

Morning

Start your exploration of **1 Christchurch** by visiting Cathedral Square and joining a tour of **Christchurch Cathedral** (right; ➤ 132). Take the tram to the Arts Centre, with its Gothic Revival buildings, and browse the galleries and craft shops (and the market, if it's the weekend). Have lunch at one of the cafés at the Arts Centre.

Afternoon

Visit the **Canterbury Museum** and check out the **Robert McDougall Gallery** (➤ 133) for interesting exhibitions. Wander through the **Botanic Gardens** and the magnificent **Hagley Park** (➤ 133). If you feel energetic after your evening meal, take a walk or drive along the summit road on the **7 Port Hills** (➤ 144) to watch the sun set behind the Southern Alps.

Day 2

Explore **2 Banks Peninsula** (left; ➤ 134–136) and its French settlement, Akaroa. On your way, stop at the Hilltop Tavern, about 60km from Christchurch, for the first panoramic view of the peninsula. Take SH75, the coastal route to Akaroa and join a harbour cruise to see some **Hector's dolphins**. Have lunch and browse the craft shops in Akaroa. Return to the hilltop via the summit road and explore some of the eastern bays of the peninsula on the way.

Day 3

Morning

Leave Christchurch early to drive to
3 Aoraki/Mount Cook (right; ➤ 137–138),
via **9 Lake Tekapo** (➤ 145) – the main roads
are SH1 and SH8 – or take an early flight
to Mount Cook airport. Explore the area and
the glaciers that flow into the valley and
join a walk or boat trip on the glacier lake.

Afternoon

Take a scenic flight over New Zealand's tallest mountain range and,
weather permitting, land on **10 Tasman Glacier** (➤ 145) for a short walk. In
the late afternoon, walk into the Hooker Valley along the glacier moraine,
and across two swing bridges, for some of the best sunset views of
Aoraki/Mount Cook.

Day 4

Morning

Fly back to Christchurch and travel to
5 the West Coast (➤ 141–143) through
4 Arthur's Pass (pictured left) and Otira
(➤ 139). Either take the **TranzAlpine
Express** (➤ 30), or drive along SH73, if
you want to stop for short walks in the Southern Alps. Explore the limestone formations at **11 Cave Stream and Castle Hill** (➤ 145–146) on the way.

Afternoon

Have lunch in Greymouth, then head south along SH6 and visit greenstone-carving and glass-blowing workshops in Hokitika.

Day 5

Continue exploring the rainforests, lakes and beaches of the West Coast
south of Hokitika. Walk to the face of either Franz Josef or Fox glacier
(➤ 142–143), and if you feel energetic, join a walking tour or a helicopter
excursion to the top of Fox Glacier, the largest on the West Coast. You can
take a scenic flight to get a bird's view of Aoraki/Mount Cook and Mount
Tasman. Alternatively, walk to **Lake Matheson** (➤ 179–181) for some of the
best views of the Aoraki/Mount Cook range, which is reflected on the lake's
surface on calm and clear days.

◗ Christchurch

Christchurch is like a lost corner of old England. Willows line the Avon River as it meanders through the city's heart, a lofty neo-Gothic cathedral rises from the central square, and many streets carry the names of English cathedral cities.

Punting on the Avon among the willows

The Arts Centre bustles with galleries and cafés

If you are arriving by air, you will see this city of gardens snuggling up against the Port Hills (► 144) and spilling out onto the largest area of flat land in New Zealand, the Canterbury Plains. Farming has always been Canterbury's economic backbone and Christchurch is hemmed in by a patchwork of fields that stretch between the wind-lashed eastern coastline and the foothills of the Southern Alps.

Start your visit at **Cathedral Square**, where there's usually some kind of street entertainment going on. The square is surrounded by numerous stately buildings and the Gothic Revival **cathedral** is worth a visit, particularly for the climb to the viewing balconies, 30m up the 63m spire.

From Cathedral Square, walk along **Worcester Street** or catch a ride on the restored tram to the **Arts Centre** and explore its historic Gothic Revival architecture, which once housed the University of Canterbury. The huddled cluster of stone buildings exudes an almost medieval atmosphere, but today it accommodates a thriving arts scene, with several galleries, craft shops, performance venues and eateries (► 149). A town crier takes guided tours of the Arts Centre, but you can also browse at your leisure.

Just across Rolleston Avenue is the **Canterbury Museum**, with its displays on the Antarctic, and the entrance to what is, arguably, the early settlers' most precious gift to the modern city – **Christchurch Botanic Gardens** and **Hagley Park**. At 161ha, Hagley Park is the largest of the city's 13 municipal parks and features a golf course and other facilities The native plants in the vast botanic gardens were gleaned from all over the country, and include everything from regenerating bush to a carefully nurtured rose garden. The gardens are particularly beautiful in evening light, when the sun's low rays shine through the trees' branches and cast reflected spotlights on the lake. Behind the museum you will find the **Robert McDougall Art Gallery**, which has over 5,000 works of all descriptions in its collection of historic and contemporary art from the Canterbury area and the rest of New Zealand.

TAKING A BREAK
You can get a fine cup of coffee on ambient **New Regent Street**, a pedestrian zone with art deco-influenced façades.

➕ 199 E4
Visitor Information Centre
✉ Old Chief Post Office, Cathedral Square West ☎ (03) 379 9629; info@christchurchnz.net; www.christchurchnz.net ◷ Mon–Fri 8:30–5, Sat–Sun 8:30–4

Christchurch Cathedral
✉ Cathedral Square, Christchurch ☎ (03) 366 0046 ◷ Mon–Sat 9–5:30; closed during services ♦ Café (£) Mon–Fri ♦ Free; balconies and spire: inexpensive

Christchurch Arts Centre
✉ 2 Worcester Boulevard ☎ (03) 363 2836; info@artscentre.org.nz ◷ Shops and galleries daily 10–6

Canterbury Museum
✉ Rolleston Avenue, at Botanic

Garden entrance ☎ (03) 366 5000; info@cantmus.govt.nz ◷ Daily 9–5:30, Sep–Apr; 9–5, May–Aug ♦ Free; discovery centre and exhibitions: inexpensive

Christchurch Botanic Gardens
✉ Rolleston Avenue ☎ (03) 366 1701 ◷ Daily 7 am–one hour before sunset; conservatories daily 10:15–4:30; information centre daily 10:15–4, Sep–Apr; 11–3, May–Aug

The Robert McDougall Art Gallery and McDougall Art Annex
☎ Main gallery: Botanic Gardens, Rolleston Avenue; Annex: arts centre ☎ (03) 365 0915; art.gallery@ccc.govt.nz, www.mcdougall.org.nz ◷ Daily 10–5:30, 23 Oct–Easter; 10–4:30, Easter to 22 Oct; guided tours 11, 1, and 2 ♦ Free

CHRISTCHURCH: INSIDE INFO

Top tips Trams travel regularly along a 2.5km loop that takes in all inner-city attractions. One-hour or day passes (inexpensive) are available from the conductor and you can hop on and off as you please.
• The region's **dry northwesterly winds** are similar to the Föhn and can cause headaches for some people.

Hidden gems Christchurch is known as **the garden city**. Visit Mona Vale gardens, or walk through Riccarton Bush, one of the last remnants of native lowland forests in Canterbury and the site of the first European settlement.

② Banks Peninsula

Banks Peninsula was once an island and, although it's been connected to the mainland for thousands of years, it has retained an independent spirit and a distinctive landscape, with many secluded bays and golden beaches.

The biggest settlement, **Akaroa,** has a distinct Gallic flavour, with street names like Rue Jolie and Rue Lavaud, the L'Aube hill as a backdrop and a romantic atmosphere reminiscent of a fishing village on the Côte d'Azur. French whaling captain Jean Langlois fell in love with the peninsula when he landed there in 1838 and promptly negotiated a land sale with the resident Maori chiefs. But when he returned with a boat of French settlers two years later, British officials had claimed sovereignty under the Treaty of Waitangi (► 10). The French stayed, nevertheless, and left an indelible mark on the town. Today's residents are proud of their short but passionate French heritage, though there are cultural overlaps with Victorian architecture and the quaint cottages.

It's fun just to walk Akaroa's narrow picturesque streets, to watch people promenade along the beach, to sample local food and wine or enjoy some of the water activities available. In summer, a catamaran cruise of the Akaroa harbour is particularly special because large pods (groups) of New Zealand's smallest dolphin, the Hector's dolphin, come into the sheltered waters to calve and will often swim alongside the boat.

Although there is public transport to Akaroa, it is worth driving the 85km from Christchurch so that you can stop for sweeping views over the peninsula and to explore some of the hidden bays. Take State Highway 75 through Taitapu to **Little River**, about halfway between Christchurch and Akaroa. This sleepy township near the head of **Lake Forsyth** is worth a

Guarding the volcanic landscapes of Banks Peninsula

Onawe
peninsula:
surfacing in
Akaroa Harbour
like a whale

brief stop for a coffee, before the road narrows and starts
winding up to the hilltop. The views from the summit in all
directions are stunning, sweeping across the entire Akaroa
harbour and the small Onawe peninsula, which juts into the
harbour like a surfacing whale. Soft, grassy hills embrace the
harbour and you can see a string of small coastal settlements
in almost every bay on the way to Akaroa. Remnants of the
once lush native forests still nestle in the humid gullies.

From this viewpoint it becomes obvious that Banks
Peninsula was born from a violent volcanic eruption. The land
flows down in all directions to the sea, which sculpted the
coastline into rocky cliffs and sandy beaches and filled the
crater to create long, narrow Akaroa harbour. The cogwheel-
shaped volcanic cone was once an island. Even Captain James
Cook originally named the peninsula Banks Island, in 1769,
because the isthmus connecting it to the mainland was too
low to be seen. It was discovered by Europeans only in 1809,
when another explorer, Captain Chase, tried to sail through
the gap. The land bridge was formed by shingle and debris,
washed down from the Southern Alps and onto the
Canterbury Plains, closing the gap about 20,000 years ago.

At the hilltop, the road forks: SH75 on the right is the
coastal route – the faster way of getting to Akaroa – and the
other route is the summit route which skirts the peninsula's
spine with turn-offs to several smaller bays. As you drop down
to the coast on SH75, the first bay you'll find is **Barrys Bay**,
where, on alternate days, you can watch cheese being
produced at the cheesemaker there, sample the finished prod-
uct and buy a range of goodies (tel: (03) 304 5809).

On the way back to Christchurch, take the **Summit Road**
and explore **Le Bons Bay**, a safe and sheltered golden beach
with a scattering of holiday homes, or secluded **Okains Bay**,
with its small museum that houses an impressive collection of
ancient Maori treasures. Take the turn-off to **Birdlings Flat**,
about 8km from Little River. You may find semi-precious

BANKS PENINSULA: INSIDE INFO

Top tips Banks Peninsula has a comprehensive network of roads for a rural area, but the Summit Road is narrow and windy, so **drive with care**. Some roads may be difficult to negotiate after rain.
• Pick up a copy of *A Historic Village Walk* from Akoaroa Information Centre on Rue Levaud. It gives details of more than 40 historic buildings in the area.

Hidden gem Hinewai Reserve is a 1,050ha conservation project southeast of Akaroa with good walking tracks through remnants of native forest. A series of 32 small reserves is scattered over the peninsula; some are easy to explore on foot. Ask for a map at the visitor information centre.

In more depth Visit the Akaroa Museum to find out more about the area's history and culture. Three historic buildings, including Langlois-Eteveneaux House, which was partly made in France, are part of the complex.

stones among the pebbles on the long and untamed beach and it's a beautiful place to watch the sunset over the ocean.

TAKING A BREAK

Turn left into the Grehan Valley as you enter Akaroa to get to **Tree Crop Farm** (Grehan Valley Road, tel: (03) 304 7158), a quirky place with extensive wild gardens crossed with footpaths. The entry charge includes a capuccino or berry juice. There's also a café that still maintains a rustic atmosphere, strewn with fur and skins, and with plenty of rough-sawn beams. Rustic cottages are also available for the night.

You may have the beach to yourself at Le Bons Bay

Visitor Information Centre
199 E4 ✉ Post shop building on corner of rues Lavaud and Balguerie ☎ (03) 304 8600
🕐 Daily 10–5 ❓ There are no ATM faciities in Akaroa so bring enough cash

Akaroa Harbour Cruises
✉ Main Wharf ☎ (03) 304 7641; info@blackcat.co.nz; www.blackcat.co.nz 🕐 Daily 11, 1:30 Dec–Mar; 1:30, Apr–Nov

Hinewai Reserve
✉ Long Bay Road, RD3, Akaroa ☎ (03) 304 8501; http://members.tripod.com/~accw/gs-eco-hinew.html 🕐 Casual walks: 24 hours; guided groups: by arrangement 💵 Free; donations to Maurice White Native Forest Trust ❓ Bring sturdy footwear for track walking. Lodge available overnight by arrangement

Akaroa Museum
✉ Corner of rue Lavaud and rue Balguerie, PO Box 35, Akaroa ☎ (03) 304 7614; akmus@xtra.co.nz 🕐 Daily 10:30–4:30 💵 Inexpensive

3 Aoraki/Mount Cook

New Zealand's highest mountain rises from the icy landscape of Aoraki/Mount Cook National Park. The pyramid of Aoraki – "cloud-piercer" – dominates all the land around it.

It's difficult to keep your eyes on the road when approaching Aoraki/Mount Cook

More than one third of the park's 700sq km is covered in permanent snow or ice. Of New Zealand's 27 peaks over 3,050m, 22 are huddled together in this area and Aoraki/Mount Cook, which towers above other peaks at 3,754m, is the centrepiece of this sparkling landscape. It might not be as high as many peaks in the European Alps, but it's a difficult mountain to climb, being exposed to ferociously rapid weather changes along the Main Divide, the mountainous chain that separates the eastern from the western coast of the South Island. It is even a difficult mountain to see: as its Maori name suggests, it often has its head in the clouds. Most visitors only get a drive-by glimpse of the giant as they travel the scenic route from Christchurch to Queenstown, but if you enjoy walks and outdoor activities, it's worth exploring the area around Mount Cook village for a day or two.

For a good view of the mountains, take a ski plane from Mount Cook airport, near Mount Cook village, or a helicopter from Glentanner Park, about 15 minutes from the village. You can choose different routes through the national park but all will give you stunning views of the massive tableau from which Aoraki rises, with the Tasman Glacier (➤ 145), the largest ice flow in the Southern Hemisphere outside Antarctica, on its side. Whichever way you go up, you can land on a glacier and go for a short walk in the snow. Once the engines are turned off, the silence can be quite eerie.

If you want to go boating on a glacial lake, join a guided sea-kayaking tour or take a trip in a small, motorised inflatable, to explore the lake at the mouth of the Mueller Glacier. The glacier flows into the Hooker Valley at Mount Cook village and forms a small lake, eventually narrowing into a river. The water is a milky azure, from the so-called glacial flour, the dust ground off the mountain as the frozen river flows over the rock faces. As the glacier slowly melts, it also breaks off large chunks of ice – "calving icebergs" – and you can explore some of these from your boat. You may also see some staggering ice avalanches crashing down from the surrounding peaks.

TAKING A BREAK

The **Coffee Shoppe** on the ground floor of The Hermitage hotel (➤ 147) offers snacks, cold drinks and coffees.

Feeling Peaky

The first people to ascend the formidable peak were the locals Jack Clark, Tom Fyfe and George Graham, who reached the summit on 25 Dec, 1894, but several famous climbers, including Sir Edmund Hillary (➤ 25), have since sharpened their skills on Aoraki/Mount Cook.

Aoraki/Mount Cook National Park Visitor Centre
✚ 198 C4 ✉ Near the Hermitage hotel, Mount Cook Village ☎ (03) 435 1818; mtcookvc@doc. govt.nz; www.doc.govt.nz/nationalparks/AorakiMountCookNationalPark.htm ⏰ Daily 8:30–6; for advice on guided tours and weather conditions

Mount Cook Ski Planes
✉ Mount Cook airport, PO Box 12, Mount Cook ☎ (03) 435 1026, 0800 800 702 toll-free; mtcook@skiplanes.co.nz; www.skiplanes.co.nz

Mount Cook Scenic Helicopter Flights
✉ Glentanner Park, PO Box 19, Mount Cook ☎ (03) 435 1801, 0800 650 651 toll-free; hlinfo@helicopter.co.nz; www.helicopter.co.nz

Glacier Sea-Kayaking
☎ Book at the Department of Conservation, YHA or Hermitage hotel; www.mtcook.com

Alan's 4WD Tours
❓ 2.5-hour trip to the flats above Tasman glacier; information or bookings at the Hermitage hotel or YHA ☎ (03) 435 1809

AORAKI/MOUNT COOK: INSIDE INFO

Top tips Mount Cook village is an excellent base for short walks. If you want to see Aoraki in the evening glow, walk along an easy track into the **Hooker Valley** for about 45 minutes, across two swing bridges, until the mountain fills the view. The setting sun tints Aoraki a deep pink.

• Check with the Department of Conservation Visitor Centre before you head off on a walk. The **weather changes quickly** and staff advise on the best options.

• There are no banking facilities and few shops in the national park, so **bring food and cash**. The Hermitage is the only hotel near by.

④ Arthur's Pass and Otira Viaduct

Just an hour and a half's drive from Christchurch, Arthur's Pass is the closest national park to any major city in New Zealand. The park straddles the Southern Alps, which form a rugged spine along the length of the South Island and separate the dry eastern coast from the temperate jungles of the west coast.

Arthur's Pass, which covers 990sq km, is a popular weekend destination for Christchurch residents, some equipped for multi-day adventures, some just keen to breathe the mountain air. Walks encompass alpine habitats, spectacular waterfalls and glacial landscapes, while the more ambitious can go skiing, tramping or mountaineering in the wilderness.

The main settlement, **Arthur's Pass village**, is 154km from Christchurch and surrounded by the soaring mountains of the Main Divide. A winter ski centre and a starting point for many short walks, nature trails and lookout points, Arthur's Pass is also a good place to have a break if you are on your way to the West Coast (► 141–143) either along State Highway 73 or aboard the TranzAlpine Express (► 30–32).

The railway line and the road run almost parallel and both are spectacularly scenic, covering a huge range of altitudes. The landscapes change as you climb almost 1km to the pass and then drop to sea level as the fertile flats and broad

Top: Mount Rolleston is the highest peak in Arthur's Pass National Park

Above: Perfect walking country

riverbeds of Canterbury gradually give way to tussocklands, scree-sloped mountains and the limestone gargoyles of Castle Hill (➤ 145), until you reach the snow-capped and glacier-scarred peaks of the **Main Divide**. At Arthur's Pass, the vegetation resembles dense rainforests, clinging to the wet western slopes. Patches of scarlet burst through the dark-green canopy, where native Rata vines have climbed up to the light on the trunks of other trees.

The road (now SH73) was cut into the hillsides in 1865 when settlers wanted a shortcut through the Alps to the burgeoning gold fields of the West Coast. Roadmen took only a year to chisel it into the rugged landscape, less than half of the time needed by modern engineers to construct the ambitous **Otira Viaduct**. It's worth stopping at the lookout point north of Arthur's Pass to see the elegant S-shaped 440m structure, before you cruise down its steep 11.7 per cent gradient. As you look down into Otira Gorge, bear in mind that, until 1999, drivers had to negotiate a steep (16 per cent), treacherous zigzag, constantly threatened by erosion, rockfall, earthquakes and floods.

TAKING A BREAK

Oscar's Haus (tel: (03) 318 9234) is a small, licensed café on the main road at Arthur's Pass, with displays of local arts and crafts.

Arthur's Pass: Department of Conservation Visitor Centre
🕂 199 D4   ✉ SH73, Arthur's Pass
☎ (03) 318 9211; www.doc.govt.nz/ ArthursPassNationalPark.htm
🕐 Daily 8–5
ℹ Information on park walks, maps and route guides; displays about Otira Viaduct and natural history of the park; up-to-date weather information

Building Otira Viaduct

Being in a national park presented challenges when building Otira Viaduct. Vehicles had to be meticulously steam-cleaned when they entered the construction site to prevent weeds from entering the park, and cleared areas had to be replanted with seeds gathered from plants near by. Physical challenges included underground rivers, large boulders with the compressive strength of steel and the proximity of the Alpine Fault (➤ 6–9).

An engineering feat in the middle of a national park

ARTHUR'S PASS AND OTIRA VIADUCT: INSIDE INFO

Top tips Birds with beautiful names thrive here – the shining cuckoo, the paradise shelduck, yellow-crowned parakeets – so bring your binoculars.
• The lookout area above Otira Viaduct is a good place to see the **kea** (alpine parrot) (➤ 16). Simply sit still and the cheeky birds will come up close.

In more depth The Department of Conservation's **visitor centre at Arthur's Pass** has a display about the viaduct, with photos of the cast-in-place cantilevers.

5 The West Coast

On a calm and sunny day, the West Coast is a magical wonderland of snowy peaks, glistening lakes and lush rainforests. But "The Coast" – as New Zealanders refer to the narrow strip of land wedged between the Tasman Sea and the South Island's mountainous spine – also experiences some ferocious weather, bringing more than 5m of rain a year and sometimes whipping the surf into a mighty ocean roar.

Exploring Franz Josef Glacier

The gold rush has slowed down, but you may be in luck

Westland could be called Wetland. The area's rainfall is surpassed only by Fiordland (▶ 158–160), New Zealand's largest national park, with which south Westland shares the honour of World Heritage status. You can often see angry clouds pressing up against the steep western side of the mountains as soon as you reach Arthur's Pass (▶ 139–140). They rarely reach the golden hills on the eastern side of the Main Divide, dissolving instead into rain as they swirl against the wall of mountains. That's not necessarily a bad thing: the rain gives the coast an exuberant freshness and vigour. And without it there wouldn't be the regions's steaming forests, juicy pastures, wild lakes and imposing glaciers.

Travelling from Christchurch, you meet the coast at **Greymouth**, a port on the River Grey. It's the region's largest town, with about 10,000 people. Founded on gold and continued on coal, it now survives on timber, fishing and tourism. It's not very exciting, but is a handy base for exploring the area. Follow SH6 south towards Hokitika, and about 8km south of Greymouth you will see the turn-off to **Shantytown**, a re-creation of a 1880 West Coast town in the gold rush, where you can still pan for gold. It's a particular favourite with children.

In **Hokitika**, about 40km south of Greymouth, Romanesque St Mary's church tower dominates the small town and there's a scattering of arts and crafts studios around the

Tramping

Fox Glacier is a short drive to the mirroring waters of Lake Matheson and the untamed beauty of Gillespies Beach (▶ 179–181).

church. Several stone- and bone-carvers and glass-blowers have opened their workshops to the public and you can watch your souvenirs evolve in their hands. This is also where the annual Wildfoods Festival (► 13–14) takes place.

Franz Josef Glacier is forever on the move

South of Hokitika the scenery becomes grander and the population smaller. The mountain ranges rise gradually as you approach the **Aoraki/Mount Cook massif** with New Zealand's highest peaks, Aoraki/Mount Cook (► 137–138) and Mount Tasman. The road moves away from the ocean to wind through pastureland, past glacier-carved lakes and along wind-battered rainforests. Trees along this coastal seam have a distinct eastward lean, their branches reaching for the mountains.

Double take of the Southern Alps' at Lake Matheson

After about 150km you'll reach the Southern Alps' glacier region, an impressive vista of ragged mountains with large snowfields and ice walls. There are more than 60 glaciers in the Westland National Park alone, and about 3,000 throughout the Southern Alps, but most are inaccessible to anybody but mountaineers. **Franz Josef and Fox glaciers**, however, stretch their icy tongues so far down the mountain ranges they could almost lick the sea.

If you have never seen a glacier up close it is worth walking for a few minutes to get a good view of the frozen pinnacles, crevasses and ice falls. Pick up information about guided walks and scenic flights at the visitor information centres at

Franz Josef Visitor Centre
✚ 198 C4 ✉ Main Road, Franz Josef ☎ (03) 752 0796 🕓 Daily 8:30–6

South Westland Visitor Centre
✚ 198 C4 ✉ Main Road, Fox Glacier ☎ (03) 751 0807 🕓 Daily 8:30–6

Franz Josef Glacier Guides
✚ 198 C4 ✉ Main Road, Franz Josef ☎ (03) 752 0763, 0800 484 337 toll-free; walks@franzjosefglacier.com; www.franzjosefglacier.com 🕓 Daily, weather-dependent

Shantytown
✚ 199 D5 ✉ 8km south of Greymouth ☎ (03) 762 6634; fax: (03) 762 6649; information@shantytown.co.nz; www.shantytown.co.nz 🍴 Everybody's Restaurant and Café (£) 🕓 Daily 8:30–5 ✋ Moderate

Alpine Guides Fox Glacier
✚ 198 C4 ✉ Main Road, Fox Glacier ☎ (03) 751 0825, 0800 111 600 toll-free; foxguides@minidata.co.nz; www.foxguides.co.nz 🕓 Daily, weather-dependent

White Heron Sanctuary Tours
✚ 198 C4 ✉ PO Box 19, Whataroa ☎ (03) 753 4120, 0800 523 456 toll-free; enquiries@whiteherontours.co.nz; www.whiteherontours.co.nz/home
🕓 Tours daily during breeding season late Oct–early Mar. Round trip from Whataroa takes about three hours and includes a short minibus ride to the Okarito River, followed by a jet boat ride to the reserve; then a 500m walk to a viewing area

Icy adventure:
Heli-walking on
top of a glacier

Franz Josef or at Fox village, 25km further south. These are
both tiny resort towns consisting of little more
than a main street lined with eateries and
tour-operators' shops. The car park for the
Franz Josef Glacier is 5km inland from the
main road, and the first lookout is a 20-
minute return walk. At the larger Fox Glacier,
you'll find a car park 4km from the main road
and similar options, from short walks to an
excursion to a one-hour excursion to the glacier's terminus.

TAKING A BREAK

The **Mahinapua Pub** (tel: (03) 755 8500) is
just south of Hokitika, on the SH6 opposite
the turnoff to Lake Mahinapua. It's a typical
old colonial building, fairly plain inside, but a
great place to drink with the locals and enjoy
some salty West Coast repartee.

WEST COAST: INSIDE INFO

Top tips Consider joining **a guided walk or helicopter flight to the glacier surface**.
No mountain experience is required and you will be equipped with a pair of
boots, instep crampons and an alpenstock.
• If you are planning a glacier excursion, or even just approaching one, bring
warm clothing. Temperatures drop noticeably as soon as you get near the ice.

Hidden gems The road between Hokitika and the glaciers passes several
glacial lakes. Lake Mahinapua, the first glacial lake on the route south from
Hokitika (from SH6, turn right to Ruatapu), is fringed by tall stands of
kahikatea. About 40km further south, SH6 runs along the shores of Lake
Ianthe, which offers picnic spots and a small campsite. Further south, about
10km before Franz Josef Glacier, is Lake Mapourika.

In more depth Visit the breeding area of the kotuku, the majestic white
herons, which nest in native bush near the Okarito lagoon. The breeding area is
accessible only for guided tours as the birds are protected. The best time to
visit is between November and February when the birds are on nests.

At Your Leisure

Above and below: The national *marae* is a showcase of Maori traditions

6 Nga Hau E Wha – National *Marae*

The *marae* is the South Island's largest Maori cultural centre and offers intro-ductions to Maori protocol, customs and history. Nga Hau E Wha stands for the four directions of the wind, signifing that the National *Marae* welcomes visitors from all corners of the world. Tours of two exquisitely carved buildings – *Wharenui* ("meeting house") and *Whare Wananga* ("house of learning") – are available, as are cultural evenings and *hangi*.

🕂 E4 199 ✉ 250 Pages Road, Christchurch ☎ (03) 388 7685, 0800 456 898 toll-free; www.marae. org.nz. Bookings essential 🚍 5, from Cathedral Square 🖐 Moderate; self-guided access free

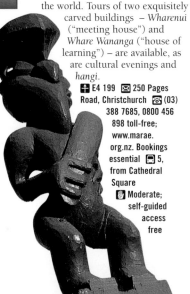

7 Port Hills

The Port Hills separate Christchurch and its seaside suburb Sumner from Lyttelton. They are the crater rim of a dead twin volcano, whose eruption created Lyttelton harbour and Banks Peninsula (► 134–136). They're the only significant elevation in Christchurch, offering breathtaking views of beaches and the Canterbury Plains from the Summit Road. Drive up Dyers Pass Road to find the Sign of the Takahe, a magnificent neo-Gothic restaurant. Built in 1948, it was the first of a string of roadhouses planned from Christchurch to Akaroa but only four were built. At the top of the pass is the second, the Sign of the Kiwi, now a tearoom. Further along Summit Road, there are sweep-ing views of the Avon-Heathcote estuary, an important feeding area for migratory birds, and of the endless New Brighton beach. Christchurch visitor information centre (► 133) has free maps of the Port Hills roads.

🕂 E4 199

8 Lyttelton Timeball Station

The picturesque port of Lyttelton is connected to Christchurch by road and rail tunnels. It's best known for its Timeball Station, built in 1876 by local prisoners. Housed in a stone castle-like building on the eastern side of town, the timeball was lowered to signal 1 pm local time each day so that sailors could check the accuracy of their chronometers to calculate longitude. It was replaced by radio time signals in 1934. During the 1970s, the station was restored and is now one of only five world-wide in working order. Once again, the ball drops at 1 pm each day.

Visitor Information Centre
🕂 199 E4 ✉ 20 Oxford Street, Lyttelton ☎ (03) 328 9093; lyttinfo@ihug.co.nz 🚍 28 from Cathedral Square

Lyttelton Timeball Station
199 E4 2 Reserve Terrace, Lyttelton (03) 328 7311; fax: (03) 328 9116 28 from Cathedral Square Daily 10–5:30, Nov–Apr; Mon–Fri 10–5:30, May–Oct (phone to check times) Inexpensive Steep steps

9 Lake Tekapo

Lake Tekapo, on SH8 between Christchurch and Aoraki/Mount Cook, is a lovely place for a break. The town has sweeping views over the glacier-fed lake; its radiant turquoise colour is thanks to minerals and dust deposited by the icy rivers from the Southern Alps. The pretty little Church of the Good Shepherd beside the lake was built in the 1930s from stone gathered near by and is a memorial to the pioneer farmers of the Mackenzie Country.
199 D4

Standing loyally beside the Good Shepherd is a bronze statue erected to commemorate the Mackenzie Country's faithful sheepdogs

10 Tasman Glacier

The Tasman Glacier is the largest ice flow in the Southern Hemisphere outside Antarctica: it stretches for 27km, is 3km wide and an incredible 600m deep. Unusually, its last few kilometres are almost flat, and are covered with debris from its higher sections. The unsealed Tasman Valley Road ends at a car park

Despite its busy port, Lyttelton harbour has many tranquil bays for recreation

about 8km from Aoraki/Mount Cook village, from where it is a 15-minute walk, past the Blue Lakes, to a look-out point over the glacier's terminus. Guided tours are available – enquire at the visitor information centre at Aoraki/Mount Cook village (➤ 138).
198 C4

11 Castle Hill and Cave Stream

If you are driving to Arthur's Pass on SH73, take a break after about 110km to explore Castle Hill and Cave Stream. Limestone formations run through the east coast of the South Island and in several places form bizarre-looking outcrops. Distinctive Castle Hill features vast gardens of sculpted limestone, often weathered into gargoyles, flutings and scallops. At Cave Stream, a small river has diverted underground and carved out a 360m tunnel. The cave is easily

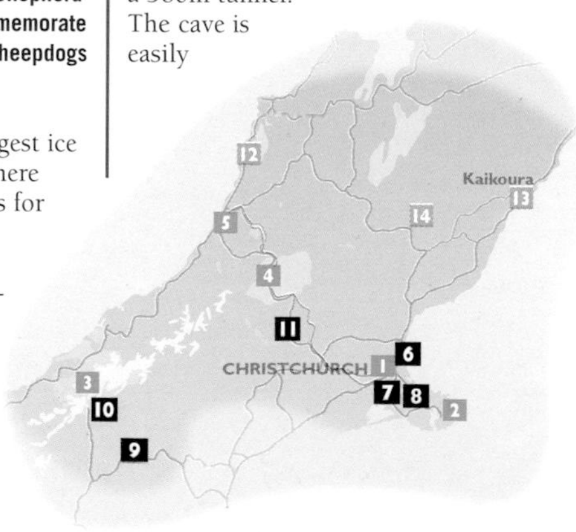

accessible, but you must go in a group with an experienced leader (tours are often organised by nearby accommodation). Don't walk into the cave after heavy rain.

➕ 199 D4 ✉ Signposted on SH73

🔢 Punakaiki

Pancake rocks are the main feature of this small settlement, about 40km north of Greymouth. Stratified limestone stacks jut from the beach, and blowholes throw up columns of hissing spray during rough weather. A ten-minute wheelchair-accessible track leads to geological forms weathered into curious shapes. From the rocks, the 15-minute Truman Track leads through a coastal forest to reach the coastline. At low tide, continue down the beach past a succession of reefs, caves and waterfalls.

➕ 199 D5

🔢 Whale-watching at Kaikoura

Groups of sperm whales come to feed offshore from the town of Kaikoura. Several boat excursions go out to see them each day, weather permitting, but it's best to go early in the morning, when the sea is calmest. The deep-diving gentle giants rise up to breathe and stay on the surface for a few minutes so you can have a good look before they disappear. Whale-watching flights are also available. While you're there, swim with dolphins, dive with sharks, visit the seal colony, or walk on Kaikoura peninsula. You can also explore colonial Fyffe House, constructed from whalebones in the mid-19th century, when the

Nature's spa: the hot pools at Hanmer will soothe your muscles after a walk

town was known for whale-hunting rather than whale-watching.

Visitor Information Centre

➕ 199 F5 ✉ West End, Kaikoura
☎ (03) 319 5641; info@kaikoura.co.nz; www.kaikoura.co.nz 🕐 Daily 8–6, Nov–Mar; 9–5, Apr–Sep

Whale Watch Kaikoura

✉ Old Railway Station, Kaikoura
☎ (03) 319 6767, 0800 655 121 toll-free; res@whalewatch.co.nz; www.whale-watch.co.nz 🕐 Daily 7:15, 10, 12:45; also 3:30, Sep–Apr 💲 Expensive

Fyffe House

✉ 62 Avoca Street, Kaikoura ☎ (03) 319 5835; fyffe.bill@xtra.co.nz; www.nzmuseums.co.nz/museums/fyffe_house.html 🕐 Daily 10–6, Nov–May; Mon–Fri, 10–4 Jun–Oct 💲 Inexpensive

🔢 Hanmer Springs

At the thermal reserve in this small alpine resort, natural hot springs feed a sequence of pools and you can choose how hot you want your soak. The mineral pools have been used for more than a century and are particularly popular in winter, when you can have a hot bath while it snows all around you. If the health spa and aqua therapy centre (with saunas and steam rooms) prove too relaxing, walking, mountain biking and horse-riding are also popular.

➕ 199 E5 ✉ Amuri Road, Hanmer
☎ (03) 315 7511; info@hotfun. co.nz; www.hotfun.co.nz 🕐 Daily, 10–9 💲 Day pass: moderate

Where to... Stay

Prices
Expect to pay for two people sharing a double room
£ under NZ$150 ££ NZ$150–$300 £££ more than NZ$300

CHRISTCHURCH

Bangor Country Estate £££
Half an hour from Christchurch, on the way to the West Coast, Bangor was once part of a vast pioneer farming estate. The six suites are individually themed, with views over park-like grounds. Five-course dinners feature local produce, matched with wines from the cellar. Breakfasts are bountiful.

➕ **199 E4** ◻ **Bangor Road, Darfield, Canterbury** ☎ **(03) 318 7588; fax: (03) 318 8485; www.bangor.co.nz**

Dorothy's Boutique Hotel £
Sam Beveridge and Tony Downes offer warm hospitality and good value at this hotel, popular with both gay and straight clientele. A lovingly restored 1916 villa with immaculate gardens, it has six *en suite* rooms, including one with twin queen beds. The décor is an unusual mix of Wizard of Oz memorabilia, period furniture and the owners' fine collection of Japanese art. There are two guest lounges, a 45-seater restaurant and a Rainbow Bar.

➕ **199 E4** ◻ **2 Latimer Square, Christchurch** ☎ **(03) 365 6034; fax: (03) 365 6035; www.dorothys.co.nz**

The Château on the Park ££
This 190-room hotel is unashamedly romantic, with architecture reminiscent of a French château. Guest rooms looking out on 2ha of manicured gardens. The swimming pool is surrounded by lavender bushes, there's a suit of armour in the lobby, and you cross a moat to get to the bar. Located in a residential suburb beside Hagley Park, it's a short drive from the city centre. Rooms range from standard to de luxe king. The Camelot restaurant is recommended.

➕ **199 E4** ◻ **189 Deans Avenue, Riccarton, Christchurch** ☎ **(03) 348 8999; fax: (03) 348 8990; www.chateau-park.co.nz**

The George £££
A small luxury hotel on the banks of the Avon, The George has 57 de luxe rooms and suites with views over Hagley Park. Some have balconies, spas and butler service, and the Residence wing is set in an English garden. The emphasis is on understated elegance and good service. The fine-dining Pescatore, which specialises in seafood, has been named one of New Zealand's top ten restaurants, and 50 on Park brasserie, also an award-winner, is known particularly for its breakfasts.

➕ **199 E4** ◻ **50 Park Terrace, Christchurch** ☎ **(03) 379 4560; fax: (03) 366 6747; www.thegeorge.com**

AORAKI/MOUNT COOK

The Hermitage £–££
Spectacularly situated at the foot of the Alps, The Hermitage is one of New Zealand's most famous hotels. Its isolation is part of the mystique: the original hotel was destroyed in a flood in 1913; the second burned down in 1957. The present hotel is a stone alpine lodge at the centre of a complex that includes chalets and motels. For a spectacular view of Aoraki/Mount Cook, book one of the 18 queen rooms or, during the summer, a table at the fine-dining Panorama Room. There's a choice of restaurants and bars, a gift shop, spa, sauna and tennis courts.

➕ **198 C4** ◻ **SH80, Aoraki Mount Cook National Park** ☎ **(03) 435 1809; fax: (03) 435 1879**

Where to...
Eat and Drink

Prices
Expect to pay for a three-course meal, excluding drinks
£ up to NZ$45 ££ NZ$45–$60 £££ more than NZ$60

CHRISTCHURCH

Annie's Wine Bar and Restaurant ££
Annie's makes the most of its picturesque setting in the Arts Centre. You can eat outside in the cloistered quadrangle, or inside, where there's a fire in winter, exposed brick walls, and furniture made from recycled wood. The food is a creative New Zealand mix of East and West, from rabbit ravioli to Szechuan-infused scallops. The ostrich pâté is a favourite. Annie's is noted for its wine list, with more than 70 Canterbury and other New Zealand wines available. It's a popular spot so bookings are advisable.

✚ 199 E4 ⊠ Arts Centre, Christchurch ☎ (03) 365 0566 ⏰ Mon–Fri 11–9; Sat–Sun 9 am–10 pm; closed 25, 26, 31 Dec, 1–2 Jan

Saggio di Vino £££
Lisa Scholz is the ebullient host and Yommi Pawelke the cellar master at this Mediterranean-style wine bar. As the name suggests there is an extensive list of international and New Zealand vintages, in various glass sizes. The small menu focuses on quality ingredients. Expect eye fillet ordered by weight, lobster, mini abalone, scallops and seasonal specials like truffles, whitebait and oysters. Bookings are necessary.

✚ 199 E4 ⊠ 185 Victoria Street, Christchurch ☎ (03) 379 4006 ⏰ Daily 5–11; closed 1 Jan

Tiffany's £££
In a Tudor-style villa, with lawns sweeping down to the river, Tiffany's is like a bit of old England. The restaurant has discreet service and the menu focuses on regional wine and food, like roasted Cervena venison, Akaroa salmon with Asian greens, and Canterbury rack of lamb. Bookings are necessary.

✚ 199 E4 ⊠ Corner Durham and Lichfield streets, Christchurch ☎ (03) 379 1350 ⏰ Daily 6–10:30 pm; closed 26 Dec

BANKS PENINSULA

French Farm Winery and Restaurant £
Make a detour just to visit this striking French provincial-style building in its beautiful rural setting. Wines from the little vineyards in the valley are made on site and feature on the wine list. The *à la carte* menu features West Coast lamb and beef, Akaroa salmon, local cheeses and home-grown herbs. In summer, an alfresco restaurant serves pizzas.

✚ 199 F4 ⊠ French Farm Valley Road, Duvauchelle, Banks Peninsula ☎ (03) 304 5784 ⏰ Daily 10–5; La Pizza noon–8 in summer

WEST COAST

Café de Paris £–££
French chef Pierre Esquilat and his Kiwi wife Joy run this little bit of *rive gauche* on the West Coast. An airy café during the day, serving coffee and pastries and blackboard lunches, it offers an *à la carte* menu in the evening. Look for classics like French onion soup and *canard à l'orange*, West Coast deer and wild pig.

✚ 199 D5 ⊠ 19 Tancred Street, Hokitika ☎ (03) 755 8933 ⏰ Daily 7:30–late

Where to…
Shop

CHRISTCHURCH

City Centre

Christchurch's main shopping area is a pleasant network of pedestrian malls intersecting Colombo Street and fringing Cathedral Square. Between the Bus Exchange and the Avon River, **City Mall** is a landscaped pedestrian precinct that takes in parts of High and Cashel streets and arcades like **Shades Atrium** and the **Guthrey Centre**. Here you will find speciality shops, international fashion and lifestyle chains, food courts, cafés, bookshops and department stores. **Ballantynes** (corner City Mall and Colombo Street, tel: (03) 379 7400) is a Christchurch institution, an old-fashioned, family-run department store where you can buy anything from perfume to fashions, crockery to carpets.

Browse High Street for bargains in books and music, antiques, art and funky fashion. The precinct is also home to top designers **Victoria Black** (201–203 High Street, tel: (03) 379 1197) and **Panache** (232 Tuam Street, tel: (03) 366 5979).

Pick up picnic ingredients at **Good Things** (163 High Street, tel: (03) 366 3894), which specialises in Canterbury food and wine.

Sheepskins and knitwear, leather goods, All Blacks paraphernalia, paua and greenstone jewellery can be found in the souvenir shops clustered around Cathedral Square. There's also a craft market here on Fridays. Nearby New Regent Street boasts boutiques and cafés, built in Spanish Mission style. The centre of New Zealand's high-tech sports and leisurewear industry, Christchurch is the home of labels such as Fairydown, Macpac, and Canterbury of New Zealand. Major outlets are **Mainland Great Outdoors Centre** (54 Lichfield Street, tel: (03) 365 2178), **Bivouac Outdoor** (76 Cashel Street, tel: (03) 366 3197), **Kathmandu** (36–46 Lichfield Street, tel: (03) 366 7148) and **Canterbury of New Zealand** (corner Colombo and Armagh streets, tel: (03) 379 9687). The **Swanndri Retail Shop** (123 Gloucester Street, tel: (03) 379 8674) has traditional bush shirts.

The Arts Centre (Worcester Boulevard, tel: (03) 366 0989), picturesquely situated in the Gothic-Revival buildings of the old Canterbury University, has galleries, shops, theatres, cinemas, cafés and bars. Take a guided Retail Therapy Tour, or browse around the 40 art and craft outlets. You can also meet the artists, watch them at work and buy direct. The weekend **Arts Centre Market** has 70 stalls, with entertainment and food vendors.

Suburbs

Merivale, north of the city, is a chic shopping centre, with 40 boutiques in **Merivale Mall** (189 Papanui Road, tel: (03) 355 9692), top designer fashion store **Quinns** (195 Papanui Road, tel: (03) 355 7349), and antique shops, cafés and bars. **Traiteur** (corner Aikmans and Papanui roads, tel: (03) 355 7750), is a European-style butchers.

The **Riccarton Rotary Market**, held on Sunday mornings at Riccarton Park Racecourse (Racecourse Road, tel: (03) 339 0011), has more than 300 stalls selling craft, food, clothing, jewellery, bric-a-brac and produce. **Dressmart Factory Outlet Centre** (409 Main South Road, Hornby, tel: (03) 349 4980) has more than 30 stores, each, with 30–70 per cent of normal retail prices on popular brands of fashion, sportswear, accessories and music.

Near the airport, **Untouched World** (155 Roydvale Avenue, tel: (03) 357 9399) is a striking complex of retail shops, restaurant, native garden and wine bar. It carries its own-brand merino/possum blend knitwear and lifestyle clothing, skincare products, craft and food.

Where to...
Be Entertained

CHRISTCHURCH

Look for listings in the Arts section of *The Press* on Wednesdays and its *Entertainment Guide* on Fridays. For a lively night out, try The Strip – one look at the midnight queues gives the lie to any idea that Christchurch is a stolid city.

Arts

The Court Theatre (Arts Centre, Worcester Boulevard, tel: (03) 963 0870) usually has at least one production in season on its two stages. The heritage **Theatre Royal** (145 Gloucester Street, tel: (03) 371 9452) is used by visiting theatre and dance companies, and **Canterbury Opera** (tel: (03) 366 9932).

The **Town Hall** (Kilmore Street, tel: (03) 377 8899) is the venue for concerts by **Christchurch Symphony** (tel: (03) 379 3886), the **Christchurch City Choir** (tel: (03) 366 6927) and visiting performers. Lunchtime concerts are held at the **Arts Centre Great Hall** (tel: (03) 363 2836), and the **Music Centre of Christchurch** (140 Barbadoes Street, tel: (03) 377 5000). For jazz, try informal venues like **Sammy's Jazz Review** (Bedford Row, tel: (03) 377 8618) and the **Blue Note** (20 New Regent Street, tel: (03) 379 9674). Rock bands play at the **Dux de Lux** (Arts Centre, tel: (03) 366 6919).

The **Robert McDougall Art Gallery** (➤ 133) and **CoCA** (66 Gloucester Street, tel: (03) 366 7261) often have exhibitions of New Zealand work. Follow the **Artisans' Trail** of Banks Peninsula craftspeople. For a brochure, contact the Akaroa Information Centre (80 Rue Lavaud, tel: (03) 304 8600).

Sports

Major rugby fixtures and test cricket are played at **Jade Stadium** (Wilsons Road, tel: (03) 379 1765), and the **Canterbury Crusaders** (Super 12 rugby union) have a passionate local following. Book tickets through **Ticketek** (tel: (03) 377 8899). For horse-racing, go to **Riccarton Park Racecourse** (Racecourse Road, tel: (03) 342 8928), or catch the harness racing at **Addington Raceway** (Jack Hinton Drive, tel: (03) 338 9094).

The Estuary at Ferrymead is popular for windsurfing and parasailing, while Sumner has surf and swimming beaches. Canterbury rivers offer salmon-fishing, jet boating and rafting. In the city, there's punting and boating on the Avon. Head to the Port Hills for walkways, mountain biking and paragliding. Christchurch is 90-minutes' drive from the ski fields. **Mount Hutt** (tel: (03) 302 8811) is the largest commercial field, or for a real Kiwi experience, try the club fields in the **Craigieburn ranges** (Canterbury Ski Association, tel: (03) 377 1749), where the facilities are more basic and you can stay overnight.

Golfers should try the picturesque city links in **Hagley Park** (tel: (03) 379 8279) or the 36-hole twin course at **Harewood** (371 Mcleans Island Road, tel: (03) 359 8843).

Wine and Beer Trails

Canterbury and Waipara (an hour's drive north of Christchurch) are distinctive wine-growing regions. Most wineries welcome visitors. Contact the visitor centre for a wine trail map. **Canterbury Brewery** offers tours of its Heritage Centre (36 St Asaph Street, tel: (03) 379 4940).

Festivals

Romance, jazz, comedy, buskers, flowers, wine and food, winter, summertime – Christchurch has festivals for all of them, and more.

Wild South

Getting Your Bearings

The southern regions of the South Island are often bypassed by visitors – yet they feature some of the wildest and most scenic places on earth. Many of the more remote areas may have remained unexplored to this day, had it not been for a stampede of fortune-seekers, attracted by the lure of gold.

Like moths heading for the flame, miners swarmed to the southern parts of New Zealand in the mid-19th century, abandoning the exhausted gold fields of California and New South Wales. Their picks and shovels shaped the landscape from Queenstown to Dunedin and their adventurous spirit is still alive in Queenstown, where you can challenge your body and mind amid stunning scenery – and then relax and enjoy the deserved rewards of fine food and wine.

This Fiordland track explores the Hollyford Valley

Lake McKerrow
Darran Mts
Yates Point
Milford Sound
Milford Sound
1692m
Mitre Peak
George Sound
Charles Sound
Te Wahipounamu
Secretary Island
Doubtful Sound
Fiordland **2**
WESTLAND
94
Lake Te Anau
Eglinton Valley
Te Anau
Manapouri
Lake Manapouri
Resolution Island
Takitimu Mts
SOUTHLAND
West Cape
Lake Monowai
Chalky Inlet
Lake Poteriteri
Lake Hauroko
Puysegur Point

Queenstown is also a gateway to Fiordland, New Zealand's largest national park and a World Heritage area of majestic mountains and seascapes. Towering peaks, icy lakes and sheer-sided fiords, carved by glaciers and separated by narrow, densely forested valleys, combine to create a landscape of unmatched grandeur.

Fiordland harbours some of New Zealand's last untouched landscapes

The central part of the southern South Island is where the gold-miners' heritage is best preserved by a dry and sunny climate. Here, modern pioneers have successfully established the southernmost vineyards and orchards. On the southern east coast, Dunedin is a delightful city that combines Scottish charm with scenic appeal and easy access to rare wildlife.

★ Don't Miss

Page 151: Wilderness pure at Milford Sound, with its towering peaks and brooding skies

At Your Leisure

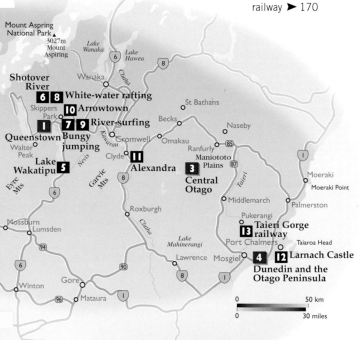

The Wild South is the place to challenge your body and mind

Experience the stunning scenery of New Zealand's wild south, from the grandeur of the Southern Alps and the remote rainforests of Fiordland to the romantic haven of wildlife that surrounds Dunedin.

In Five Days

Day 1

Morning

Explore the buzzing downtown of
1 Queenstown (pictured below; ➤ 156–157).
Walk along the shores of beautiful **5 Lake Wakatipu** (➤ 168) and join a cruise on the vintage steamship **TSS *Earnslaw*** (➤ 156). Have lunch on board or at a café in town.

Afternoon

Drive to **6 Shotover River** (➤ 168) to see the magnificent canyon or to test your nerves with a bungy jump. Then explore the region's gold-digging history at Winky's Museum. Try **8 white-water rafting**, jet boating (right), **9 river-surfing** or other adventure sports (➤ 168–169) on the Shotover or Kawarau rivers, or visit the old gold-mining town of **10 Arrowtown** (➤ 169).

Catch the **Skyline gondola** (➤ 156) for evening views of the lake and city. Have dinner at one of restaurants downtown or visit the nearby Gibbston Valley Winery (➤ 172).

Day 2

If you want to experience the scenic road to **Milford** (➤ 186–188), fly to Te Anau and drive from there. Otherwise fly directly to Milford and spend the day exploring **2 Fiordland** and the majestic **Milford Sound** (➤ 158–160). Join a cruise to see the

Fiordland crested penguins and resident dolphins and to get close to Mitre Peak (right) and the 146m **Stirling Falls** (➤ 159). Other activities you can try at Milford Sound include kayaking excursions and a ride in a submarine to see Fiordland's awe-inspiring underwater world. Return to Te Anau in the evening.

Day 3

Drive through ruggedly scenic **3 Central Otago** (➤ 161–163) and visit orchards or vineyards to taste the produce of New Zealand's fruit bowl. Stop in small rural places such as **Cromwell**, **Clyde** and **11 Alexandra** (➤ 170) for meal breaks and to explore the area's gold rush history. Continue driving to the wildlife capital, **4 Dunedin** (➤ 164–167).

Day 4

Explore the southern city's Victorian architecture and Scottish heritage. Spend the morning investigating the Octagon, St Paul's Cathedral, the Dunedin Public Art Gallery and the University of Otago campus. Take the train journey along the **13 Taieri Gorge** (left; ➤ 170) in the afternoon.

Day 5

Explore the untamed beauty of the **4 Otago Peninsula** (➤ 166–167), with its seaside towns and easily accessible wildlife. Visit **12 Larnach Castle** (➤ 170) and the royal albatross colony at **Taiaroa Head** (➤ 166). On the way back, join a tour to see yellow-eyed penguins, or walk down to Sandfly Bay to watch the birds return from the ocean and waddle uphill to their nests. Take a break at the enchanting coastal town of **Portobello**.

❶ Queenstown

For a few crazy years after the discovery of gold there in 1862, Queenstown's fortunes were extracted from the Shotover River. But, with its rugged beauty and wild waters, the river has become Queenstown's modern gold-mine, and the gold rush has given way to the adrenaline rush.

Queenstown is a magnet for thrill-seekers. Every year it welcomes a million international visitors, most coming to part with their money so that they can swoop down a river in a raft, whizz off in a jetboat, take a gut-wrenching freefall or a hair-raising helicopter ride – and that's just for starters. With ubiquitous tour operators promising adventure activities ranging from bungy jumping to snowboarding, the alpine resort buzzes all year round (see At Your Leisure, ➤ 168–170 for individual recommendations). Queenstown is only the size of a sprawling village, but it has a cosmopolitan atmosphere and rivals the capital Wellington in the number of downtown cafés and restaurants it boasts.

There's a proud gold-mining heritage too. Of all the Wakatipu diggings, the most reliable was **Skippers Canyon**, a beautiful gorge cut by the Shotover into soft schist about 27km from Queenstown. The area around Skippers was still being dredged for gold in 1992, but now only the school building and cemetery remain. The last gold-digger, Joe Scheib, established **Skippers Park**, a starting point for jet boat rides and bungy jumps (➤ 168–169), and his family continues to gather gold rush relics at **Winky's Museum**.

The TSS *Earnslaw* in full steam on Lake Wakatipu

Queenstown's enviable position on the shores of Lake Wakatipu, framed by the majestic Southern Alps, means that some of New Zealand's most picturesque scenery is within reach. So, if you are looking for something less energetic, take a cruise on the vintage steamship **TSS Earnslaw**. The ship has been ploughing Lake Wakatipu since 1912, transporting goods for run-holders (farmers) and conveying passengers. You can explore the engine room and fireboxes, browse through historic photographs or just watch the stunning scenery go by. The *Earnslaw* makes daily excursions to a high country farm at Walter Peak, where you can help feed the deer and Highland cattle, try your hand at spinning wool or watch sheepdogs in action. A gondola ride up **Bob's Peak** is a perfect finale to an action- and scenery-filled

day. Evening light colours the panoramic view across the city, Lake Wakatipu and Coronet Peak, and the Remarkables to Cecil and Walter peaks on the other side of the lake.

TAKING A BREAK

Try some wholesome foods, check your email and hang out with the cool crowd at funky **Vudu Café** (23 Beach Street, tel: (03) 442 5357; www.vudu.co.nz).

Never mind the adventure sports – just admiring the views can take your breath away

Queenstown Visitor Information Centre

198 B3 ✉ Clocktower building, corner of Shotover and Camp streets, Queenstown ☎ (03) 442 4100; qvc@xtra.co.nz; www.queenstown-vacation.com ⏰ Daily 7–7, Oct–Mar; 7–6, Apr–Sep

TSS *Earnslaw*

✉ Steamer Wharf, end of Shotover Street ☎ (03) 442 7500 ⏰ Daily 10, noon, 2, 4, 6, 8, Oct–mid-Apr; noon, 2, 4, mid-Apr–Sep 💲 Expensive

Steamer Wharf village on the edge of Lake Wakatipu

WILD SOUTH: INSIDE INFO

Top tips It would be difficult to visit Queenstown without sampling some of the adventure sports on offer. If you want to try **white-water rafting** but aren't so sure about the risks, opt for the **Kawarau River** rather than the Shotover. The Kawarau is a high-volume river with no exposed rocks in the rapids and is therefore safer.

Hidden gem Queenstown's gardens rarely feature on tourist brochures but they are worth a visit. Extensive lawns and rose gardens mix with sports grounds on a small peninsula on the eastern side of the Queenstown Bay, off Park Street.

In more depth Taste some of the **award-winning wines** from this southernmost wine-growing region. Pick up a wine trail map from the visitor centre.

② Fiordland

Fiordland is pure wilderness. The best way to discover the raw beauty of New Zealand's largest national park is to explore Milford Sound. Brooding and serene, it's the most northern of Fiordland's 14 glacier-carved fiords and the only one accessible by road. Although Milford Sound and its landmark Mitre Peak are often photographed, the mountains, rainforests and waterfalls still leave visitors in awe.

The South Island's southwestern tip is New Zealand's least explored part, and is one of the greatest wildernesses of the southern hemisphere. Together with the Westland/Tai Poutini (➤ 141), Mount Aspiring and Aoraki/Mount Cook (➤ 137–138) national parks, Fiordland makes up the World Heritage Area called **Te Wahipounamu** – "the place of greenstone". The scenery is the result of over 500 million years of sculpting, with hundreds of waterfalls dancing to a changing tune as the landscape is relentlessly ground, split, pressurised and washed down by the elements.

Te Wahipounamu covers 10 per cent of New Zealand's total area and most of its 2.6 million hectares of wilderness is difficult, sometimes almost impossible, to reach. **Milford Sound's** dramatic splendour provides a window to this natural wonderland. You can reach Milford by air, road or on foot. The sound is the end point of a four-day walk established by 19th-century pioneers who discovered New Zealand's highest waterfall, the

Mitre Peak towers above the splendour of Milford Sound

Cledday Valley is a hint of landscapes to come on your way to Milford

Sutherland Falls, and were the first to cross overland to Milford. Because the track is so popular, numbers are strictly limited and accommodation is only in huts along the route (no camping is permitted). You will have to organise the walk well ahead, particularly if you are interested in taking a guided tour during the summer months.

The road to Milford (➤ 186–188) is one of the most spectacular alpine drives, with many points of interest and short nature walks along the 120km from Te Anau. The road is open to campervans and trailers, but presents challenging driving: it is sometimes closed to traffic because of avalanche danger or high winds, so check with the **visitor information centre in Te Anau** first.

After the remoteness and relative tranquillity of the journey, the crowds and bustle of Milford's main bus terminal and car park may come as a bit of a shock. Milford's small wharf is the departure point for all cruises, which vary from one-hour boat trips to overnight voyages in vessels modelled on traditional trading scows and equipped with kayaks for evening excursions. The exact route depends on weather conditions, but generally each trip will take you to Milford Sound's mouth and a short distance out on to the Tasman Sea. On the way, the boats pass below towering **Mitre Peak** (1,692m) and cruise close to lush and dripping rainforests that cling to the sound's sheer rock walls. Chances are that a group of bottlenose

Pause for a moment's reflection: Mirror Lakes on Milford Road

dolphins will join the boat within a short distance of the wharf; sightings of seals and Fiordland crested penguins, clambering around secluded rocky beaches, are also common. Weather permitting, the ship will be steered under the magnificent **Stirling Falls**, which drop a sheer 146m into the sea. Thanks to this layer of fresh water, courtesy of the phenomenal six metres of annual rainfall, Milford Sound is a special ecosystem below the surface, as well as above. The turbid top layer allows rare marine organisms, such as black coral, to grow at shallower depths than elsewhere and you can get a glimpse of them at an underwater observatory in **Harrison Cove**, accessible by cruise. Another spectacular, albeit expensive, option is to dive through this tea-coloured top layer in a submarine for a panoramic view of the marine life at a depth that would be otherwise inaccessible. If that isn't enough splendid scenery, you can fly back to Queenstown and see the entire national park stretched out below.

Adventure and beauty at Doubtful Sound

TAKING A BREAK

Walk to Bowen Falls, about ten minutes from the wharf, to have a **picnic at Cemetery Point**. The area was named after its mounds of debris brought from the falls, which resemble graves. However, there are actually three real graves there, containing fatalities from the old whaling and sealing days.

Queenstown Visitor Information Centre

198 B3 ✉ Lakefront Drive, Te Anau ☎ (03) 249 8900; vin@fiordlandtravel.co.nz
Daily 8:30 am–6 pm SH94 to Te Anau branches off the main Invercargill to Queenstown Road (SH6). Intercity offers regular bus services to Te Anau

Fiordland Travel

198 B3 ✉ Lakefront Drive, Te Anau ☎ (03) 249 7416, 0800 656 501 toll-free;
info@fiordlandtravel.co.nz; www.fiordlandtravel.co.nz Daily 7:30 am–9 pm Moderate
 Bus tours and cruises of Milford and Doubtful sounds and Lake Manapouri; bookings essential

Red Boat Cruises

198 B3 Milford Wharf, Milford Sound ☎ (03) 441 1137, 0800 657 444 toll-free;
rbinfo@redboats.co.nz; www.new-zealand.com/RedBoats/index.html Daily 9, 10:30, 11, 12:25,
1, 1:30, 3, Oct–Apr; 11, 12:25, 1:30, May–Sep
 Inexpensive

Mitre Peak Cruises

198 B3 ✉ Milford Wharf, Milford Sound ☎ (03) 249 8110; in@mitrepeak.com;
www.milfordsound.org Daily 10, 1:15, 3:30, 5:15 Inexpensive

FIORDLAND: INSIDE INFO

Top tips Milford Sound changes its mood as quickly as the weather, so **bring rain gear and sun protection**. Don't forget an **insect repellent**, as sandflies can be a nuisance throughout Fiordland.
• Consider a coach-cruise-fly combination to get the best out of a short visit. There are a number of operators who offer trips from Te Anau or Queenstown.

Hidden gem Doubtful Sound, further south, will appeal to those looking for an experience with fewer companions. Doubtful is not as easily accessible and can only be reached by crossing Lake Manapouri by boat and taking a bus over Wilmot Pass, but its unspoiled and remote wilderness makes up for the effort.

In more depth Overnight cruises will give you an idea of Milford Sound after daytime visitors have gone – and you might hear an unforgettable dawn chorus.

❸ Central Otago

Central Otago stretches out across a rugged plateau sheltered by the Southern Alps. The wide, open landscape is fringed only by rolling foothills and luminous skies. There is something romantic about "Central", with its Tuscan-style golden hills and tiny villages, old stone buildings and gold rush relics.

Remnants of the goldrush days still haunt romantic Central Otago

Summer temperatures can climb well over 30°C and parch the landscape, while in winter they regularly drop below freezing and the foothills get a dusting of snow. The arid climate has helped preserve many gold-mining remnants, and also provides ideal conditions for fruit-growing and viticulture.

Plan at least a day to cover the 285km between Queenstown (▶ 156–157) and Dunedin (▶ 164–167), allowing time for frequent stops. Several old gold-mining sites along the way are worth exploring and you may want to visit some of the wineries and orchards. The banks of the Clutha River, which drains the southern lakes around Queenstown and Wanaka, provide ideal picnic spots and there are opportunities for short walks.

On your way out of Queenstown, stop at the visitor information centre for a guide to **Central Otago's wineries** and a map of the **Otago Goldfields Heritage Trail**, which links more than 20 sites with gold-mining history.

From Queenstown, follow State Highway 6 along the Kawarau River. If you want to explore one of the best-preserved Chinese gold-mining settlements, make a short detour to the charming **Arrowtown** (▶ 169); otherwise, drive along the **Kawarau Gorge** to see the river's **Roaring Meg** rapids and stunning 1,200m canyon. About 18km from Queenstown you will pass another gold rush legacy – a stone-piered suspension bridge, which was built in 1880 and today doubles as a platform for bungy jumpers (▶ 168–169).

The steep slopes of the gorge are in stark contrast to the flat valley area of **Gibbston**, planted with row after row of grapevines, and the expansive **Cromwell Flats**. Cromwell, about 30 minutes from Queenstown, was originally known as

**Right:
Mitchell's
Cottage, near
Alexandra, is a
fine historic
stone building**

The Junction, at the confluence of the Clutha and Kawarau rivers. When gold was discovered there in 1862, several thousand miners arrived within days and transformed the settlement. More recently, Cromwell experienced another major – and controversial – transformation when the Clyde Dam was built as part of the Clutha River hydropower scheme. Parts of Cromwell disappeared under Lake Dunstan, which was created by the dam, and many historic huts had to be painstakingly removed and re-erected in what is now called **Old Cromwell**, a popular attraction. The giant fruit sculpture at the town entrance indicates Cromwell's modern economic focus.

From Cromwell, State Highway 8 will take you to **Clyde**, a small town whose streets are lined with stone buildings dating back to the 1860s, and **Alexandra**, a pleasant town on the banks of the Clutha and the district's commercial hub (▶ 170).

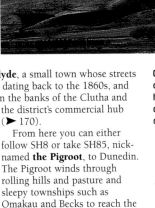

**Central
colours: ochre
hills, white
dust of snow,
open blue skies**

Golden Opportunity

Central Otago's gold rush isn't over yet, and the Macraes mining company still extracts about 100,000 ounces of gold each year.

From here you can either follow SH8 or take SH85, nick-named **the Pigroot**, to Dunedin. The Pigroot winds through rolling hills and pasture and sleepy townships such as Omakau and Becks to reach the vast, moody and dramatic **Maniototo plains**. The faster

way to Dunedin is along SH8 and the mighty **Clutha**, New Zealand's largest river. The Clutha is 16km shorter than the Waikato River in the North Island but it carries almost twice as much water to the ocean. Between Alexandra and Roxburgh, the Clutha flows through a narrow gorge that can only be seen from a boat or a foot track, but even a short walk provides some stunning views. During the gold rush era, Roxburgh had 20 dredgers working the Clutha and one of them can still be seen from the north end of town when the river is low.

TAKING A BREAK

The roadside **Fruitlands Gallery** (tel: (03) 449 2192), between Alexandra and Roxburgh, was once a pub serving weary travellers and gold-miners. The stone building, dating from the 1870s, has been restored and now offers food and crafts.

Visitor Information Centre
✚ 198 C3 ✉ 22 Centennial Avenue, Alexandra ☎ (03) 448 9515; info@tco.org.nz; www.tco.org.nz ◉ Mon–Fri 9–5, Sat–Sun 10–3

CENTRAL OTAGO: INSIDE INFO

Top tips The most beautiful time to see Central Otago is **autumn**, when the poplars and willows turn amber and gold. Another good time to visit is when the Otago Goldfields Heritage Trust holds its **annual cavalcade**, usually in November or March, and hundreds of people re-enact history by travelling along the old gold-mining routes on horseback and in wagons.

Hidden gem If you are taking the Pigroot, visit St Bathans and have a snack at the reputedly haunted **Vulcan Hotel**. The Blue Lake, near by, was formed after gold-diggers sluiced away an entire hill.

4 Dunedin and the Otago Peninsula

Set between rolling hills and the rugged coastline, Dunedin is the capital of the southern province of Otago, which is best known for its pioneering gold-mining history, rugged scenery, and fertile orchards and vineyards.

The city clings to the walls of a natural amphitheatre, enclosing a harbour whose narrow channel extends to the tip of the Otago Peninsula and beyond Port Chalmers. Dunedin's wealth in the latter half of the 19th century produced a grand Victorian city in the middle of the South Pacific and, despite modern intrusions, much of the original architecture remains intact. Historic buildings have been given a new lease of life, serving as public venues and municipal buildings. Many grand old homesteads are restored to their former glory and wooden villas are scattered through the hilly suburbs.

Dunedin's Scottish heritage is also evident throughout the city. This is the only place in New Zealand – possibly anywhere along the Pacific Rim – with a kilt shop. Dunedin also boasts its own

The Octagon is a favourite lunchtime spot in the middle of Dunedin

The Other Side of the World

Dunedin is the old Gaelic name for Edinburgh, but, apart from street names and the original architecture, it has little in common with the Scottish capital. Locals claim that Dunedin is hillier, smaller and closer to the sea – and that it has a better climate than Edinburgh.

whisky, and still has haggis ceremonies and a population that speaks with a distinctly rolling accent. Much of Dunedin's architecture is modelled on Scottish and other British examples: New Zealand's first university, the University of Otago, resembles the University of Glasgow buildings; the college buildings of Otago Boys' High School have the air of a British public school, and even the police station was modelled on architect Norman Shaw's design for Scotland Yard in London.

Start your exploration in the heart of the city, the eight-sided **Octagon**, through the middle of which runs Dunedin's main street, changing from Princes Street on the south to George Street in the north. Rather fittingly, a sculpture of poet Robert Burns overlooks the Octagon's small central park – "with his back to the kirk and his face to the pub". The Oban Hotel, which Burns once faced, is no more, but behind him

Academic pursuits in a historic setting: University of Otago

towers **St Paul's Anglican Cathedral**. Walk up the marble steps to see its soaring limestone-vaulted nave. Apart from Italian marble floor tiles, most of the stone and timber used to build the cathedral came from New Zealand, most notably the near-white Oamaru limestone, which you will find in public

buildings and sculptures throughout the country. Next to the cathedral, the ground floor of the **Municipal Chambers** house Dunedin's **visitor information centre**. On the other side of the cathedral is the **Dunedin Public Art Gallery**, which has the largest collection of paintings by the popular painter Frances Hodgkins.

It is a short walk along George Street to the **University of Otago** campus. Dunedin is very much a university town – during

Dunedin is close to some wild, southern beaches

term time its population of just under 120,000 swells by about 17,000 and students are one of the driving forces behind the city's vibrant café and cultural scene. The campus itself is constantly bursting at the seams, with new buildings going up

on the fringes, but a walk through the inner group of historic slate-roofed bluestone buildings, huddled beside the Leith stream, will give a sense of its Victorian origins.

If you're going to take the vintage train journey to the Taieri Gorge (➤ 170), allow time to inspect Dunedin's **railway station**, a monument to Edwardian architecture and testimony to the settlers' faith in railways. Inside, the Royal Doulton mosaic tile floors and intricate stained-glass windows depict railway motifs and the monogram of New Zealand Railways.

A tour of the Otago Peninsula is a must, even if you only have time to drive to **Taiaroa Head**. You should get a chance to observe albatrosses, penguins, seals and sea lions in the wild, just a few minutes from the city. Taiaroa Head is the only mainland breeding colony of royal albatrosses in the world. Albatross chicks are raised here every year but can only be seen as part of a guided tour to the glass-covered observatory. It takes about 45 minutes to drive to Taiaroa Head along the coastal route, which winds past many bays on the harbour side of the peninsula, each with spectacular views of the city. If you take the inland route, the views are even better, as you're overlooking the entire peninsula, with its rocky shores within the harbour and its steep cliffs and secluded sandy beaches on the seaward side. You can also inspect Larnach Castle (➤ 170) before you reach the peninsula's main settlement, **Portobello**, where the road continues to Taiaroa Head. A few minutes before you reach the albatross colony, a sign points to **Penguin Place**, an ecotourism venture where visitors can observe yellow-eyed penguins from deep trenches dug into the dunelands.

TAKING A BREAK

Visit **Glenfalloch Woodland Gardens**, about 9km from Dunedin along the coastal route to Portobello. The Gaelic name means "hidden glen". Narrow walking tracks wind through 30ha of shrubs, trees and herbaceous borders. The gardens have a café and restaurant (tel: (03) 476 1006).

Dunedin's student population is a catalyst for its lively pub scene

If you want to see penguins, seals and albatrosses, take a boat cruise around Otago Peninsula

Dunedin Visitor Information Centre
➕ 199 D3 ✉ 48 The Octagon, ground floor of the Municipal Chambers, Dunedin ☎ (03) 474 3300; visitor.centre@dcc.govt.nz; www.cityofdunedin.com ⏰ Mon–Fri 8:30–6, Sat–Sun 8:45–6, Jan–Mar; Mon–Fri 8:30–5, Sat–Sun 8:45–5, Apr–Dec

Royal Albatross Colony
➕ 199 D3 ✉ Taiaroa Head, Otago Peninsula ☎ (03) 478 0499; reservations@albatrosses.com; www.albatrosses.com ⏰ Wed–Mon tours every half hour 9:30–7, Tue tours every half hour 12:30–7, Nov–Feb; tours daily 10–4, Mar–Oct; closed 25 Dec; bookings essential 🚌 Peninsula bus, tour buses 💰 Expensive

Yellow Eyed Penguin Conservation Area
➕ 199 D3 ✉ Penguin Place, Harington Point Road, Otago Peninsula, about 5km from Taiaroa Head ☎ (03) 478 0286; www.penguin-place.co.nz ⏰ Several 90-min tours daily, bookings essential 🚌 Peninsula bus, tour buses 💰 Expensive

Early Settlers Museum
➕ 199 D3 ✉ Queens Gardens, Dunedin ☎ (03) 477 5052 ⏰ Daily 10–5; closed 25 Dec and Good Fri 💰 Inexpensive

Otago Museum
➕ 199 D3 ✉ 419 Great King Street, Dunedin ☎ (03) 474 7474; www.otagomuseum.govt.nz ⏰ Daily 10–5; closed 25 Dec and Good Fri 💰 Free

DUNEDIN AND OTAGO PENINSULA: INSIDE INFO

Top tip Many of Dunedin's **historic homesteads** have been restored to offer bed and breakfast accommodation, and staying the night in a place full of character will add to your visit.

In more depth Visit the **Early Settlers Museum** to find out more about some of the Scottish families who influenced Dunedin's development. If you're interested in natural history or Maori cultural heritage, the **Otago Museum** has good displays.

Hidden gem **Sandfly Bay** is an enchanting beach on the seaward coast of the Otago Peninsula, where people can watch yellow-eyed penguins return to their nests in the evening.

At Your Leisure

Relics of the difficult gold-mining days have been restored at Winky's Museum

5 Lake Wakatipu

In summer, Lake Wakatipu's shoreline is pleasant for picnics; in winter, it adds drama to the already majestic alpine landscape. The town hugs a corner of the Z-shaped lake, which fills an 84km long, narrow and deep glacial valley. Lake Wakatipu and the rivers that feed it are popular with anglers and watersports fans. The old steamer TSS *Earnslaw* (➤ 156) sails to a farm at Walter Peak, where you can join a lakeside horse trek.

➕ 198 B3

6 Shotover River

The Shotover River gorges are the mini Grand Canyons of the south but some of their landscaping was done by hand, pick and shovel during the gold-mining days. The most stunning gold rush relics are at Skippers Park, about 27km from Queenstown. At Winky's Museum in the park you'll find rusty horseshoes, century-old bath taps, pots and bottles, handcuffs and – bizarrely – a miner's boot with the poor fellow's foot bones still in it. Try your luck with a gold pan for a few minutes and you will almost certainly take a home a flake or two. The road to Skippers Park is as spectacular as it was when there was only a bridle path. Sometimes it can be equally dangerous, and hire cars are generally not insured.

Skippers Canyon/Winky's Museum
➕ 198 B3 ✉ Skippers Canyon, Shotover River ☎ (03) 442 9434; winkys@skipperscanyon.co.nz; www.skipperscanyon.co.nz 🕐 Tours depart daily 8 am, 2 pm 💲 Expensive

7 Bungy jumping

Thrill seekers inspired by the exploits of A J Hackett (➤ 26) will be satisfied near Queenstown. The original bungy site is a bridge across the Kawarau River, 43m high and the only site where jumpers can splash headfirst into the water. The next highest jump is from a bridge across Skippers Canyon, 71m above the river. A few metres further down the spectacular canyon is the Pipeline Bridge, built during the gold-mining boom to transport water across the gorge and converted into a 102m bungy adventure – surpassed only by a 134m highwire jump from a gondola, where the Nevis River, meets the Kawarau River. Packages combining other adventure activities are available from many operators.

Few things will raise your adrenaline levels as quickly as a bungy jump

A J Hackett Bungy

198 B3 ✉ Bungy Centre, cnr of Camp and Shotover streets, Queenstown ☎ (03) 442 4007, (03) 442 7100; bungyjump@ajhackett.co.nz; www.AJHackett.com ⏰ Daily; courtesy transport to bungy jump location 💲 Expensive; video of jump included

Pipeline Bungy

198 B3 ✉ Skippers Canyon, Shotover River ☎ (03) 442 9434; bunjy@pipeline.co.nz; www.skipperscanyon.co.nz ⏰ Daily from Pipeline Bridge, transport part of tour to Skippers Canyon 💲 Expensive

🎱 White-water rafting

Expect to get wet during this swirling ride through rapids with names such as Shark Fins, Jaws and Cascade. Rafting companies operate year-round on the Kawarau and Shotover rivers, except when the water levels are too high. Up to eight people – confident swimmers only – fit into each boat. There's a brief introduction on how to paddle, how to float safely downriver, and how to help scoop others out. Generally, the Kawarau River is the safer option, not having exposed rocks. Book at the visitor information centre (► 157).

198 B3

🎱 River-surfing

River-surfing, or sledging, gives you a degree of control over how you navigate the rapids, equipped with a wetsuit, helmet, fins and a body board. Each trip starts in calm water with an introduction to the equipment and techniques. From there you can either stay in the quieter sections, slowly floating down the Kawarau River, or tackle four rapids of varying difficulty. Basic swimming skills are required.

Serious Fun River Surfing

198 B3 ✉ 43 Camp Street ☎ (03) 442 5262, 0800 737 468 toll-free; sfun@voyager.co.nz ⏰ Daily, bookings required, courtesy transport to river 💲 Moderate

River-surfing: hold on tight and go with the flow

🔟 Arrowtown

Arrowtown is a faithfully restored early gold-mining settlement, set against the backdrop of a majestic mountain range and the golden, tussock-covered high country. The town's main street, lined with historic houses, shops and saloons, could be mistaken for a Western film set. A few minutes from the centre, on the banks of Bush Creek, are the remains of a Chinese gold-mining camp, indicating the harsh life of Chinese diggers, who often came to work the tailings for any gold undetected by earlier miners.

198 B3

It may be small but Arrowtown has more than 50 listed buildings

⑪ Alexandra

Like most Central Otago towns, Alexandra sprang up almost overnight after the discovery of gold. While many of the historic buildings remain, Alexandra has developed into a tranquil but modern town and the commercial hub of Central Otago. It's now an oasis of orchards among rocky hills, owing its current prosperity to fruit production and the growing reputation of local wines.

✚ 198 C3

⑫ Larnach Castle

Built by the 19th-century banker and merchant baron William Larnach, this is New Zealand's only castle, and was one of the most expensive buildings in the country when construction began in 1871. Larnach employed more than 200 workmen for five years and spent a reputed £150,000. The castle's best-known features are its elaborate ceilings, carved by English and Italian craftsmen. After Larnach's suicide in 1898, the castle was used as a cabaret venue, a tourist resort and a psychiatric hospital. The Barker family bought it in 1967, restoring it and the extensive gardens to their former glory.

✚ 199 D2 ✉ Camp Road, Otago Peninsula ☎ (03) 476 1616; larnach@larnachcastle.co.nz, www.larnachcastle.co.nz ◷ Daily, castle 9–5, gardens 9–7, Oct–Easter; castle and gardens 9–5, Easter–Sep; closed 25 Dec 🎟 Castle: moderate, gardens: inexpensive

Taieri Gorge: where nostalgia combines with scenic appeal

⑬ Taieri Gorge railway

A vintage train with refurbished traditional carriages takes passengers for a sightseeing journey through the spectacular Taieri Gorge, inland from Dunedin's railway station. As the railway winds for 58km to Pukerangi, the landscapes change from rolling pastures to increasingly steeper cliffs of layered schist rock. In the narrowest part of the gorge, the train passes between sheer cliffs on one side and a sudden drop on the other. From Pukerangi, the land flattens into the Taieri river plains that continue to Middlemarch, a small rural settlement. The train has an open viewing carriage and makes frequent stops at sightseeing spots. Most people take the four-hour return trip to Pukerangi or Middlemarch but you can continue to Queenstown by bus.

✚ 199 D2 ✉ Dunedin railway station, Anzac Avenue ☎ (03) 477 4449; reserve@taieri.co.nz; www.taieri.co.nz ◷ To Pukerangi: 2:30 pm, Oct–Mar; 12:30 pm, Apr–Sep. To Middlemarch: Sun 2:30 pm, Oct–Mar. Check for extra departures

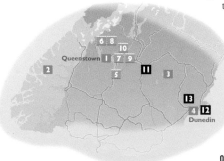

Where to... Stay

Prices

Expect to pay for two people sharing a double room

£ under NZ$150 ££ NZ$150–$300 £££ more than NZ$300

Millbrook Resort ££–£££

Set in 200ha of landscaped grounds near Arrowtown, Millbrook is a luxury resort with a golf course and fitness centre. Accommodation is in self-contained cottages, villas, suites and rooms. Most have super-king beds, living and dining areas, kitchen and laundry. There are four restaurants and bars on site.

🚹 198 B3 ⊠ Malaghans Road, Queenstown ☎ (03) 441 7000; fax: (03) 441 7007; www.millbrook.co.nz

The Heritage Queenstown £–££

Built in the style of a European alpine lodge, this 178-room hotel complex is a short walk from the town centre, with views over Lake Wakatipu and the Remarkables mountain range. Suites with kitchen and laundry facilities are a speciality. In winter, there's a roaring fire in the restaurant and bar; in summer, dining on the balcony. Guests can use the swimming pool and health club.

🚹 198 B3 ⊠ 91 Fernhill Road, Queenstown ☎ (03) 442 4988; fax: (03) 442 4989; www.heritagehotels.co.nz

Olivers of Clyde £–££

This atmospheric collection of old stone buildings was once Clyde's general store, built in the 1860s gold rush. It's reminiscent of an English country inn, with creeper-covered walls and nooks crammed with country produce. The old shop is a restaurant, with a bar in the grain store, and accommodation is in the converted outhouses. The smoke-house is now a suite with an open fire, half-tester bed and sunken bath. In the barn, the Stairs Suite has an antique bed and stairs leading to a balcony. Smaller stable rooms retain the original doors and stone floors.

🚹 198 C3 ⊠ 34 Sunderland Street, Clyde ☎ (03) 449 2860; fax: (03) 449 2862; www.olivers.co.nz

Castlewood Bed and Breakfast £

A ten-minute walk from the city centre, this grand early 20th-century homestead, restored in Tudor style, is home to Peter and Donna Mitchell. Peter is a painter, and the house is decorated with both his own art and that of other New Zealand artists. Upstairs, the largest of the three guest rooms has a queen bed, en suite bathroom and the best views. The downstairs rooms share a bathroom. There's a large guest lounge and also a travellers' library. The house is insulated from noise, with a walled garden for privacy.

🚹 199 D2 ⊠ 240 York Place, Dunedin ☎ (03) 477 0526; fax: (03) 477 0526; www.castlewood.co.nz

Larnach Lodge £–££

This re-created colonial wooden farm building in the grounds of Larnach Castle (▲ 170) has a stunning view of the harbour and the Otago Peninsula. The 12 rooms are *en suite* and decorated in period style. Six more rooms with shared bathrooms are in the converted coach house. Guests can have dinner in the castle (arrange it by 5 pm), and a free tour during opening hours. Breakfast is available by arrangement.

🚹 199 D2 ⊠ Larnach Castle, Camp Road, Dunedin ☎ (03) 476 1616; fax: (03) 476 1574; www.larnachcastle.co.nz

Where to...
Eat and Drink

Prices
Expect to pay for a three-course meal, excluding drinks
£ up to NZ$45 **££** NZ$45–$60 **£££** more than NZ$60

Gibbston Valley Winery £

One of Central Otago's pioneering vineyards, Gibbston Valley makes the most of its site in the scenic Kawarau Gorge. There's a stylish restaurant, a tasting facility and a shop. Local ingredients feature, from a Mediterranean platter to pasta, chargrilled lamb and salmon. Each dish has a suggested wine match. There's also a guided tour of the underground cellars.

✚ 198 B3 ⊠ Queenstown–Cromwell Highway ☎ (03) 442 6910 ◉ Daily 10–5 (lunch noon–3)

McNeills Cottage Brewery £

Situated in a historic stone cottage in central Queenstown, McNeills is an atmospheric pub and café. It's popular at lunchtime, especially under the parasols in the garden. You can choose from hearty pub fare like beer-battered fish and chips, kumara (New Zealand sweet potato) fries and venison sausages, or lighter salads and open sandwiches. McNeills also specialises in New Zealand wines.

✚ 198 B3 ⊠ 14 Church Street, Queenstown ☎ (03) 442 9688 ◉ Daily 11:30 am–midnight; closed 25 Dec

The Coronation Bathhouse ££

Built to commemorate the coronation of King George V in 1911, the bathhouse is now a nostalgic café on the beach. Steamer chairs sit invitingly on the boardwalk, and the glass frontage gives views over the lake and mountains. Drop in for coffee or afternoon tea, or linger over an evening meal. The menu features beef, lamb and seafood in a blend of European and Asian flavours, from eye fillet in puff pastry to salmon on udon noodles. Desserts include a selection of daily baking. Bookings are necessary.

✚ 198 B3 ⊠ Marine Parade, Queenstown ☎ (03) 442 5625 ◉ Tue–Sun 10 am–late (dinner from 6); closed 13 May–28 Jun, 25 Dec

Bell Pepper Blues and Chile Club ££

The names of Michael Coughlin's restaurant and bar are tributes to his passion for chillis and the flavours of Mexico and the southern United States. He doesn't go for killer heat, but uses subtle seasonings, and his innovative cuisine has made him one of New Zealand's best-known chefs. Bookings are necessary.

✚ 199 D2 ⊠ 474 Princes Street, Dunedin ☎ (03) 474 0973 ◉ Mon–Sat from 6:30; Wed–Fri lunch from noon; bar and snack menu Mon–Fri from 5; closed 25 Dec–2 Jan

High Tide ££

The setting is not romantic, but the view from this waterfront restaurant is. Once inside, you can forget the surroundings and look through the picture windows across the lawn to the harbour's edge. The focus is on seafood and local specialities such as queen scallops from the harbour, muttonbird from the Titi Islands, and pickled walnuts from Central Otago. There's a small wine list or you can bring your own.

✚ 199 D2 ⊠ 29 Kitchener Street, Dunedin ☎ (03) 477 9784 ◉ Tue–Sat from 6 pm

Where to... Shop

QUEENSTOWN

Queenstown is geared for tourists, with most shops in the Queenstown Mall area. These are usually open till late every day, and many offer packing and posting services. Prices may be on the high side.

Whether you mountain bike, climb, ski, snowboard, kayak, walk, fish, play golf or play tennis, you should be able to find the equipment you need in Queenstown. Try **Outside Sports** (Top of the Mall, tel: (03) 442 8883) or **Queenstown Sportsworld** (17 Rees Street, tel: (03) 442 8452). **O'Connell's Shopping Centre** (corner Camp and Beach streets, tel: (03) 442 7760) has 25 stores under one roof, offering everything from food to fashion.

Stroll down the leafy pedestrian Queenstown Mall for rugby paraphernalia at **Champions of the World** (11 The Mall, tel: (03) 441 1122), a branch of **Louis Vuitton** (12 The Mall, tel: (03) 441 8002), souvenirs, books and cafés.

At the **Jade Factory** (22 Beach Street, tel: (03) 442 8688) you can watch carvers produce jewellery and sculptures in traditional and contemporary designs. The gift centre also sells woodcarvings.

Pick up the ingredients for a picnic from **Wine Deli** (40 Shotover Street, tel: (03) 442 4482), which specialises in Otago and other New Zealand wines, cheese and preserves.

ARROWTOWN

The main street of Arrowtown is lined with boutiques, galleries and souvenir shops housed in pretty cottages. Strolling along Buckingham Street you can relive Arrowtown's gold-mining past at **The Gold Shop** (29 Buckingham Street, Arrowtown,

tel: (03) 442 1319), which has gold nugget jewellery. You can watch the craftsmen at work at the **Jade and Opal factory**. For knitwear, there's **High Country**, and the **Wool Press** has leather and sheepskin garments, and knitwear. Follow the **Wakatipu Arts Trail** to buy direct from artists and craftspeople in their studios. Ask at the Lakes District Museum (49 Buckingham Street, tel: (03) 442 1824).

DUNEDIN

The main shopping area in Dunedin is George Street. There's a mix of chain stores and highly individual local stores. Dunedin celebrates its Scottish roots at **The Scottish Shop** (187 George Street, tel: (03) 477 9965). From tartans to shortbread, if it's Scottish, they'll have it. **Meridian Shopping Mall** (267–287 George Street, tel: (03) 474 7500) houses Arthur Barnett's department store, K-Mart, fashion chains and food outlets. For designer clothing, head for

Plume (310 George Street, tel: (03) 477 9358). Browse for designer objects at **Things** (326 George Street, tel: (03) 477 4427) and **Acquisitions** (286 George Street, tel: (03) 477 0623). For collectables, try **Pendlebury Antiques** (165 George Street, tel: (03) 479 2670).

Near the Octagon, **Fluxus Contemporary Jewellery** (99 Stuart Street, tel: (03) 477 9631) has handmade jewellery made of gold, silver, bone, shell, wood and kauri gum. For work by New Zealand artists, try **Milford Galleries** (18 Dowling Street, tel: (03) 477 7727), **Moray Gallery** (55 Princes Street, tel: (03) 477 8060) or **Marshall Seifert Gallery** (1 Dowling Street, tel: (03) 477 5260).

Up near the University, **Everyday Gourmet** (446 George Street, tel: (03) 477 2045) is a good place to find deli food. The **University Book Shop** (378 Great King Street, tel: (03) 477 6976) has two floors of books for all ages and interests and a continuous clearance sale.

Where to...
Be Entertained

QUEENSTOWN

For listings of what's on, see *Mountain Scene*, published every Thursday, or call in at the Queenstown visitor centre (corner Shotover and Camp streets; tel: (03) 442 4100).

of them in spectacular sites. Get a wine trail map from the visitor centre or enquire about guided tours.

Skiing

Queenstown is one of New Zealand's major ski resorts, with two fields on its doorstep: **Coronet Peak** and **The Remarkables** (tel: (03) 442 4620). Several more are about an hour away near Wanaka. You can hire gear in Queenstown or on the field.

Wine Trails

Central Otago, the world's southern-most wine-making region, has more than 30 vineyards in the area, some

Golf

There are four golf courses around Queenstown: **Millbrook Resort** (tel: (03) 441 7000), **Queenstown Golf Club** (tel: (03) 442 9169), **Frankton Golf Club** (tel: (03) 442 3584) and **Arrowtown Golf Club** (tel: (03) 442 1719).

Nightspots

The Wharf Casino (Steamer Wharf, tel: (03) 441 1495) is open till 3 am and **Sky Alpine Casino** (Beach Street, tel: (03) 441 0400) till 4 am. No passport is required but you may be asked for ID. **The Edge Niteclub** has three floors of entertainment, open from 10 pm. **Fraser's** (Steamer

Wharf, tel: (03) 442 5111) offers music, theatre and comedy.

Festivals

The **Central Otago Wine and Food Festival** is held in February, while July brings the annual **Queenstown Winter Festival**.

DUNEDIN

For listings of what's on, see *Pulse* in Thursday's edition of the *Otago Daily Times*. Ask for further information at the visitor centre (48 The Octagon, tel: (03) 474 3300).

Arts and Entertainment

Dunedin's professional theatre company, **Fortune** (231 Stuart Street, tel: (03) 477 8323, has regular seasons of plays. Concerts of classical music are given by the **Dunedin Sinfonia** (110 Moray Place, tel: (03) 477 5623). **Dunedin Casino** operates in the restored 1880s Southern Cross Hotel (118 High Street, tel: (03) 474 4545). There's a dress code.

Sports

Otago boasts more than 100 rivers, streams, lakes and dams where you can go fishing for brown and rainbow trout. Professional guides supply transport, gear, tackle, and the necessary fishing licence. Golf is available at several courses; contact the visitor centre. **Carisbrook Sporting Complex** (Burns Street, tel: (03) 455 1191) is the venue for national and international rugby and cricket matches.

Festivals

The city holds a **Scottish Festival** in March, when the whole city becomes involved in ceilidhs and concerts, curling, conferences, poetry-readings, tossing the caber and country dancing shows. There's also a chance to banquet on haggis patties, shortbread, oatcakes and black bun. March is also the month of the **Dunedin Wine and Food Festival**. October brings the **Rhododendron Festival** and the biennial **Dunedin Arts Festival**.

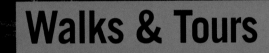

Walks & Tours

1 WELLINGTON CITY TO SEA WALKWAY

Walk

DISTANCE 4km **TIME** 1.5–2 hours
START POINT Bolton Street Memorial Park ✚ 197 B4
END POINT Aro Street ✚ Off 197 A1
GETTING BACK From Aro Street, catch the No 8 bus

This walk, with its stunning views of the city and harbour, covers the first third of a 12km route that leads from the heart of central Wellington to the capital's southern coastline and the picturesque suburb of Island Bay. You can pick up a detailed description and map of the entire walkway at the Wellington Visitor Information Centre (▶ 110).

Modern developments loom over the chapel on Bolton Street

1–2

Turn from The Terrace, one of Wellington's central arteries near Parliament (▶ 108–110), into Bolton Street. The **Bolton Street Memorial Park** is just a few metres uphill on your right. From 1840 to 1892 this was the only cemetery for non-Catholics in Wellington, unusually allowing all faiths in one burial ground.

Walk up the steps to the small **chapel**, a replica of the original, 1866 Anglican mortuary. Inside are displays about the main killers of the 19th century – disease, fire,

Page 175: New Zealand's highest mountains, Mounts Aoraki/Cook and Tasman, are reflected on Lake Matheson

poverty, earthquakes, tides and battle – and burial records of prominent citizens, including some of the founders of Wellington, who are interred in the cemetery (chapel open daily 10–4).

When a motorway was built through the cemetery in the 1960s, the original chapel was removed and the remains of almost 4,000 early settlers were shifted to a mass grave below the current chapel. On the left side of the

The Botanic Garden offers respite from the pace of city life

0 | 300 metres
0 | 300 yards

Kelburn Park

Mount Street Cemetery

SALAMANCA RD

Victoria University

MOUNT STREET

TERRACE

THE

WAITEATA ROAD

KELBURN PARADE

RAWHITI TERR

Boyd Wilson sports field

Te Aro School

ABEL SMITH STREET

STREET

ARO ST

4

FRONT

To the sea

chapel, the Anglican part of the old cemetery is still mostly intact and you'll find some beautiful tombstones. On the right, there is a memorial plaque for the people in the mass grave below.

Follow the walkway on the right of the chapel to the **Denis McGrath Bridge**, which crosses the motorway. Turn right after the bridge to follow Robertson Way through a heritage rose garden and uphill past the Jewish cemetery to a lookout point over Thorndon (▶ 117). A few metres further uphill, at an iron gate, is the **Seddon Memorial**, a tall obelisk in honour of Richard John Seddon, who arrived in New Zealand as a gold-miner and eventually became the country's premier in 1893.

2–3

From the Seddon Memorial veer to your right after the gate towards Anderson Park. As you pass the sports grounds on your right you can already see the Lady Norwood Rose Garden and the Botanic Garden's **Begonia House** (open daily 10–5). Here the traffic noise finally subsides, particularly around the small Japanese-style Peace Flame watergarden to the left of the rose garden.

Leave the Begonia House and café on your right, and follow the Serpentine Way uphill (a sign points to the Cable Car) as it winds through remnants of native forest. After about five minutes, it meets a narrow track; turn left into the Junction Path towards the **Sculpture Park**. Path names are not always on raised signposts so look for flat plaques on the lawn. Pass several sculptures, then continue along Manuka Way for a few metres before turning right into Scrub Path. The path skirts around the hilltop, where you'll see the large **meteorological station**. Follow the markers along Scrub Path, then turn right onto Hill Path and climb up the steps (made of railway sleepers) and, at the top, turn right into Australian Path. This takes you to the top of the hill and the **Sundial of Human Involvement** (where you can tell the time using your own shadow), the **Carter**

Observatory (▶ 118), several smaller historic observation domes and the top terminal of the **Cable Car** with its museum (▶ 118).

3–4

The magnificent views from the Cable Car take in Wellington's central city, the waterfront, Matiu/Somes Island (▶ 119) and the distant Rimutaka Ranges.

Walk out on to the road and past a planted traffic island to turn left onto a footpath signposted to Rawhiti Terrace. Cross Rawhiti Terrace and continue down another footpath to Kelburn Parade and the Victoria University buildings. Veer left to Salamanca Road and

The distinctive Cable Car links central Wellington with its hilly suburbs

cross the road to enter Kelburn Park. Walk around the left side of the sports field and turn left and downhill at the large fountain. Follow the track through bush, past squash courts, through another part of Wellington's green belt and up a few steps to Salamanca Road. Then turn left and cross the road, and walk back up on the other side to Mount Street.

At the top of Mount Street, at the Student Union Building, turn left and stroll through the **Roman Catholic Cemetery**, where about 800 early settlers were buried. When you reach Waiteata Road, at the bottom of the cemetery hill, turn right and follow the markers past university buildings, around the back of a student apartment block, its car park and a gym to the Boyd Wilson sports field. Walk along the field and turn left down a path past Te Aro School to the southern and more residential end of The Terrace. From there, turn right to follow The Terrace for a few metres until it intersects with Abel Smith Street. Cross the street and walk past several small houses to Aro Street Park and the Aro Valley. **Aro Street**, with its colonial villas, its shops and its cafés, is one of Wellington's favourite historic streets. This walk ends here, so stop for a coffee unless you want to take the long official route all the way to the sea.

2 LAKE MATHESON
Walk

DISTANCE 2.5km for lake circuit **TIME** 1.5 hours for lake circuit **START/END POINTS** Car park at Lake Matheson ✚ 198 C4 **GETTING THERE** At Fox Glacier turn into Cook Flat Road and after about 5km turn right to Lake Matheson car park.

Lake Matheson is renowned for providing the best opportunity to see New Zealand's highest mountains without having to brave the harsh alpine environment. On a calm day, the reflections on the lake are magical, but even if the surface is ruffled, the views to the Southern Alps are magnificent. Gillespies Beach, meanwhile, represents the wild essence of the West Coast, with pounding surf and enchanted landscapes of bleached driftwood.

1–2

The best time to see the reflections of Aoraki/Mount Cook and Mount Tasman on Lake Matheson is early in the morning or late in the evening, when the winds are silent, the light is soft and the tour buses are elsewhere. The lake circuit starts from a car park about 6km from Fox Glacier village. The comfortable and partly

Koromoko, rimu, lancewood and kahikatea trees are among those forming Lake Matheson's primeval forests

first time. Lake Matheson was carved out by the retreating Fox glacier, which left a hole at the head of a small side valley about 18,000 years ago. It used to be an important food-gathering place for Maori people, who put out eel traps in the lake and hunted the forest for wood pigeons and the weka (wood hen). When the Europeans arrived, they cleared the grassy river flats for farmland, but the lake's forest fringe remains and is now part of Westland/Tai Poutini National Park.

As you continue from the jetty, the lake disappears from view briefly. After about ten minutes, a raised boardwalk brings you to the water's edge, as it skirts around the lakefront and crosses the swampy outlet at the back of the lake. From there a few steps lead up to the **View of Views** platform, which overlooks the entire lake, across to the Fox valley and mountain ranges. You'll get good views of the mountains from any of the viewpoints, but this is the best spot to get the postcard image of the reflected mountains.

Sheltered by dense forests, the lake's surface is calm on most days. Reflections are particularly clear on this lake because tannin leached from fallen vegetation and the humus-rich soil has stained the water a dark brown tea colour.

At the start, the track crosses a swing bridge over Clearwater River and cuts through dense, low forest along the outlet stream, sometimes giving way to patches of towering flax bushes, until it reaches the lake and the jetty after about 20 minutes.

At the **jetty lookout**, the entire lake comes into view for the

The lagoons at Gillespies Beach are backed by rimu forests, a habitat rich in native birdlife

boarded path skirts around the entire lake, undulating between the swampy shoreline and forest, to three main viewing platforms.

The wetlands around the lake are home to introduced waterfowl, as well as native songbirds such as the melodious bellbird, which you are likely to hear during this section of the walk.

2–3

From the View of Views it is five minutes to the next lookout, **Reflection Island** – not really an island but a small platform jutting out onto the water. The rest of the loop track keeps to the forest and eventually brings you back out to the farmland, punctuated by the tall kahikatea swamp tree. On frosty, misty mornings, these isolated, gnarled trees are another scenic setting for photographs of the mountain ranges.

Wild Gillespies Beach was once a thriving goldminers' settlement

Walking at Gillespies Beach

From Lake Matheson, drive along Cook Flat Road for 9km, turn right and follow Gillespies Beach Road (unsealed) for 11km; then turn right to the car park. Walk through the dunes to the beach and head north. The beach has a wild beauty, with roaring surf and skeletal trees scattered along the high-tide mark. It's named after James Edwin Gillespie, who detected gold here in 1865. Rusting gold dredgers are still visible, but they are gradually sinking into the mire. After about an hour you'll reach the estuary fed by the Waikowhai Stream. Cross the trestle bridge and either explore the lagoon's dark tidal swamps or follow the path further north to the tunnel and lookout point. From there you can drop back down to the beach and walk for 30 minutes to the fur seal colony at Galway Beach. This is mainly a winter haul-out for immature males, so while there may be hundreds there in winter, it can be difficult to find any during the summer.

3 Around East Cape

Drive

DISTANCE 334km **TIME** 1–2 days for a leisurely tour
START POINT Opotiki, eastern Bay of Plenty ⊞ 201 E4
END POINT Gisborne, Poverty Bay ⊞ 201 E3

The Maori name for White Island is Whakaari

The East Cape, the first to greet the rising sun, remains isolated and sparsely populated. A tour along the Pacific Coast Highway, (SH35), takes you along a string of azure bays and deserted beaches, interspersed with small Maori townships. The area is steeped in Maori history and you will find numerous meeting houses and churches. The jagged Raukumara Ranges provide a formidable backdrop to the coastal scenery.

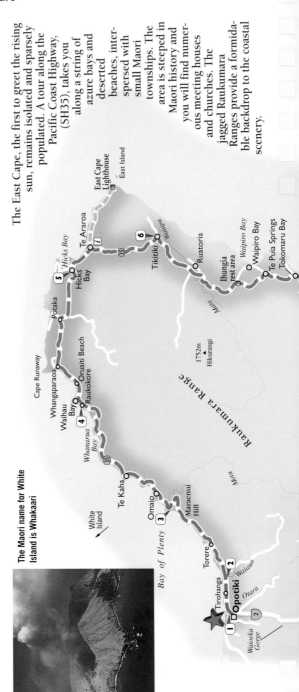

East Cape Lighthouse
East Island
Te Araroa
Hicks Bay
Hicks Bay
Potaka
Cape Runaway
Whangaparaoa
Waihau Bay
Oruaiti Beach
Raukokore
Whanarua Bay
Te Kaha
Omaio
Maraenui Hill
Torere
Tirohanga
Opotiki
Waioeka Gorge
Otara
Waiaua
White Island
Bay of Plenty

Raukumara Range
1752m Hikurangi
Moto
Moto
Waiapu
Tikitiki
Ruatoria
Ihungia rest area
Waipiro Bay
Te Puia Springs
Tokomaru Bay
Waipiro Bay

1-2

Start your journey at **Opotiki**, a small farming township at the confluence of the Waioeka and Otara rivers. The extensive coastline at this eastern end of the Bay of Plenty is lined with safe, sandy beaches, and punctuated by rocky volcanic outcrops. Opotiki marks the intersection between SH2, which continues to Gisborne through the Waioeka Gorge, and the more scenic SH35, which winds its way around the spectacular East Cape to the same destination.

As you leave Opotiki, you'll get good views out to **White Island** (➤ 95), 48km offshore. About 6km from Opotiki, at the sandy beaches of **Tirohanga**, there are remnants of terraces of an ancient and extensive *pa*, a Maori fortified village, clearly visible on Tirohanga Bluff. The

narrow, unsealed Motu Road, now a popular mountainbike track along the Waiaua River, turns off from SH35 about 11km from Opotiki, climbing through rugged, bush-covered country to Matawai, on SH2, which is about two hours' drive away.

2-3

After passing several stretches of sandy beaches and rocky inlets, you reach **Torere**, about 23km from Opotiki. Holy Trinity Church, beside the meeting house, is worth a short stop in order to compare its relative simplicity with the ornate wooden St Mary's Church at Tikitiki, further along the route.

For the next 20km the road follows the coast, opening up to sweeping views across the Bay of Plenty at Maraenui Hill, until you reach the mouth of the Motu River, renowned for white-water rafting and jet boating.

St Mary's in Tikitika is highly ornate in comparision with the simple churches passed on earlier on the route

from Opotiki, offering viewpoints, bushwalks and deep-sea fishing excursions. The grey shell of the derelict freezing works (an abattoir) near the old wooden wharf recalls days of intensive coastal shipping at the cape before the road was developed.

Snorkel, hike or just pause to admire the tranquility of idyllic Whanarua Bay

meeting house features an intricate lintel. Pretty **Whanarua Bay**, about 18km further along the Pacific Coast Highway, has many secluded beaches if you fancy stretching your legs or sunbathing.

About 10km from Whanarua Bay, at **Raukokore**, the Anglican Church stands imposingly on a lone promontory near the sea. Built in about 1894, it shows a strong European influence in its architecture.

4–5

For the next 15km the road snuggles into the curves of the coastline, looking out to the rocky inlets and glistening beaches of **Waihau Bay** and **Oruaiti Beach**, until it turns away from the coast at Whangaparaoa, near **Cape Runaway**, the eastern extremity of the Bay of Plenty. It was named by Captain Cook in October 1769 when five Maori warrior canoes paddled out towards his ship. Cook ordered grapeshot to be fired over the warriors' heads, scaring them into a quick retreat.

Whangaparaoa is a place of mythical significance to Maori as the landing place of two of the seven ancient canoes that brought the first people to populate Aotearoa (New Zealand). From Whangaparaoa, SH35 briefly leaves the coast as it skirts across to **Hicks Bay**, 148km

Te Kaha is well known for its fine beaches and its fishing, diving and watersports opportunities

3–4

Te Kaha, 70km from Opotiki, is a small town set in a delightful cove that was once the scene of inter-tribal battles. As recently as 1930, open-boat whaling still operated here and whales were landed on the beach. It's now a holiday resort. Te Kaha's richly carved Tukaki

5–6

From Hicks Bay continue for another 12km to **Te Araroa**, which has a visitor information centre, postal facilities, shops, a petrol station and, in its school grounds, reputedly the oldest pohutukawa tree in the country, thought to be 600 years old. It has a girth of over 19m and is named Te Waha o Rerekohu after an old tribal chief.

At Te Araroa, you'll find the turn-off to the

Mount Hikurangi is sacred to the Ngati Porou tribe and is the focus of several Maori legends

East Cape lighthouse, at mainland New Zealand's most eastern point. The detour, a 44km return trip on an unsealed road, takes about 50 minutes, and you'll have to walk up 700 steps from the car park to the lighthouse, but the effort is more than rewarded with stunning views towards **East Island**. Originally, the lighthouse was on East Island but the rocky outcrop has no beaches, and when four men drowned trying to land supplies, the lighthouse was shifted to its present site.

Tikitiki, 25km from Te Araroa, is a small settlement on the banks of the Waiapu River, best known for St Mary's Church, one of the most ornate Maori churches in New Zealand. It was built in 1924 as a memorial to World War I soldiers from the local Maori tribe, Ngati Porou, still the main tribe on the East Coast; the carved panels and rafter patterns tell their story.

6–7

The centre for the Ngati Porou is the small town of **Ruatoria**, 20km further on at the foot of

the tribe's sacred mountain **Mount Hikurangi**. At 1,752m, Mount Hikurangi is the North Island's highest non-volcanic peak and the first point in New Zealand to see the sun each morning. You can get good views from the Ihungia rest area, about 20km further along the highway; because of the peak's sacred status you need permission to climb it.

Further along, **Waipiro Bay village**, reached via an unsealed loop road off the highway, was once the busiest town on the coast; today, it's a slow-paced settlement where most activity revolves around the *marae*. **Te Puia**, 231km from Opotiki, has a pretty lake and hot pools near by, and **Tokomaru Bay**, 242km from Opotiki, is a crumbling but picturesque town with a beach and sandstone cliffs at the end of the bay. For the next 40km you'll pass several exquisite beaches before reaching **Tolaga Bay** and the **Cooks Cove** walkway, south of the township. The easy 5km return trip crosses private land to visit a pretty bay where Cook dropped anchor to repair the *Endeavour* and take on water supplies (allow 2.5 hours; walk is closed during lambing season, August to September). For the rest of the 54km journey to Gisborne, the road passes several tranquil beaches popular with surfers.

4 Scenic Drive on Milford Road

Drive

Driving on State Highway 94, the road to Milford Sound, is a journey of superlatives. It leads through the Te Wahipounamu World Heritage area, one of the greatest wilderness areas left in the southern hemisphere, with the highest mountains, largest glaciers, tallest forests, wildest rivers, most rugged landscape and deepest lakes.

DISTANCE 120km

TIME 2.5 hours driving time; allow about 6 hours to take in sights and short walks along the way

START POINT/END POINT Te Anau ✚ 198 B3

with fenced paddocks, grazing livestock and pockets of native forests dominated by the small-leaved southern beech.

After about 50km, you reach the first

The unmistakable profile of Mitre Peak towers above Milford Sound

1–2

For the first 30km to Te Anau Downs, the road follows the shoreline of **Lake Te Anau**, a long, narrow lake with three side arms stretching out towards the soaring peaks of the Southern Alps.
From the small wharf, the road leaves the lake to wind gently through pastures

lookout point out to the **Eglinton Valley**, a wide, frequently mist-shrouded river valley. The ranges and forests close in as you reach **Mirror Lakes**, about 58km from Te Anau. Stretch your legs on a five-minute boardwalk beside several small glacial lakes surrounded by wetlands. The lakes provide outstanding reflective views of the Earl Mountains. Look out for the Mirror Lakes sign, which is upside down so that you can read the reflection. This is a favourite

habitat for waterfowl and wetland plants. Beech trees are the main feature of Fiordland forests.

From the Mirror Lakes, it's only 5km to **Knobs Flat**, which has campsites, toilets and the last card phone before Milford.

2-3

Take a break at Knobs Flat to see the displays on local nature and on the history of the road to Milford, particularly the construction of Homer Tunnel, which you'll enter later (see panel below).

As you leave Knobs Flat, the landscape starts changing from hilly pastures to an increasingly dense native rainforest and soaring, partly snow-covered peaks. About 78km from Te Anau, just before the road meets Lake Gunn, a 45-minute **nature walk** provides an opportunity to see typical vegetation before the tree line.

A few minutes into the nature walk, a 500-year-old beech log has a mark on one of its year rings to indicate its size when Captain Cook made his first visit to New Zealand.

Several longer walks fork off Milford Road, including the popular **Routeburn and Greenstone tracks**, before you reach the junction with the unsealed no-exit Lower

A Difficult Job

Homer Tunnel was started in the 1930s Depression, and the men endured unimaginable hardship, working in an area prone to landslides, earthquakes and avalanches. It took almost 20 years to hew the tunnel through the sheer rock, and several men died when the air blast from an avalanche destroyed most of their camp.

Knobs Flat · Mirror Lakes · Earl · Eglinton Valley · National · Park · Te Anau Downs · Lake Te Anau · Te Anau · Manapouri · Waitiounamu

0 — 15 km
0 — 10 miles

Hollyford Road. This leads to the **Humboldt Falls** and the head of the **Hollyford Track**.

3–4

The last few kilometres before Milford are undoubtedly the most scenic of the journey (though the risk of avalanche means you can't stop until you get to the Chasm). Turn your lights on as you approach **Homer Tunnel**, about 19km from Milford. Here, the mountains form a solid rock wall in front of you, free of vegetation but awash with hundreds of waterfalls fed by snowfields and glaciers clinging to the peaks. The water runs through the rock and drips down inside the tunnel, as the hand-hewn passage was left unlined. Sections of the 1,270m tunnel now have large sheets of metal to divert the water down the sides, where it forms two small creeks running alongside the traffic. As you come out of the tunnel the view opens out to a narrow U-shaped valley and the road continues a steep downhill run to Milford, through a precipitous zigzag past imposing mountains streaming with water. The road frequently narrows to one-way bridges to cross creeks that can swell to roaring rivers after rain. One of the best short walks along Milford Road is **the Chasm**, about 9km from Milford, a 20-minute walk along the Cleddau River to two

footbridges with spectacular views of a series of waterfalls that have sculpted the rock into beautiful round shapes and basins.

From the Chasm, the road passes a stretch of steaming beech forest and a river viewpoint at the Tutoko Bridge, before finally reaching **Milford Sound** (➤ 158), with Mitre Peak dominating the view.

Before You Set Out…

● Milford Road can be busy in high season, so an early start is a good idea.

● The road may be closed due to winds or avalanches (mostly June to November); check roadside information signs in Te Anau.

● Fill your tank and buy food and drink in Te Anau. There are no petrol stations or shops on the road.

● For more information, read The *Milford Road World Heritage Highway Guide* (available from Fiordland National Park Visitor Centre, Te Anau)

● For up-to-date road advice and weather reports: AA/Transit Highway Information Line: 0900 33 222 www.milfordroad.co.nz; www.fiordland.org.nz; www.transit.govt.nz/news/content_files/ Newsletter46_pdfFile.pdf

The Mirror Lakes are typical of the beauty of Fiordland National Park. Opposite: Hands-on natural history at Te Papa's Mountain to Sea exhibition

Practicalities

GETTING ADVANCE INFORMATION
Websites
- Pure New Zealand (Tourism New Zealand) www.purenz.com
- Tourism Auckland www.aucklandnz.com
- Tourism Rotorua www.rotoruanz.co.nz
- Christchurch and Canterbury Marketing www.christchurchnz.net
- Totally Wellington Tourism www.wellingtonnz.com
- Destination Queenstown www.queenstown-nz.co.nz

BEFORE YOU GO

WHAT YOU NEED

- ● Required
- ○ Suggested
- ▲ Not required
- △ Not applicable

	UK	Germany	USA	Canada	Australia	Ireland	Netherlands	Spain
Passport/National Identity Card	●	●	●	●	●	●	●	●
Visa	▲	▲	▲	▲	▲	▲	▲	▲
Onward or Return Ticket	●	●	●	●	●	●	●	●
Health Inoculations (tetanus and polio)	▲	▲	▲	▲	▲	▲	▲	▲
Health Documentation	▲	▲	▲	▲	▲	▲	▲	▲
Travel Insurance	○	○	○	○	○	○	○	○
Driving Licence (national, International for Spanish nationals)	●	●	●	●	●	●	●	●
Car Insurance Certificate (included if car is hired)	▲	▲	▲	▲	▲	▲	▲	▲
Car Registration Document	▲	▲	▲	▲	▲	▲	▲	

WHEN TO GO

Auckland

High season   Low season

JAN	FEB	MAR	APR	MAY	JUN	JUL	AUG	SEP	OCT	NOV	DEC
23°C	23°C	22°C	20°C	18°C	15°C	13°C	14°C	16°C	18°C	19°C	22°C

☀ Sun   🌦 Sunshine and showers   🌧 Wet   ☁ Cloudy

Temperatures are the **average daily maximum** for each month.
New Zealand's main travel season is during the warmer months, generally from November to March, but ski resorts like Queenstown are also busy throughout the year. The warmest months are December, January and February, and the coldest are June, July and August. The north of New Zealand is often described as "Mediterranean", with short winters and long summers. The south is temperate, with occasional winter frosts. The best time to travel is after January, as the weather in late summer and autumn tends to be more stable than during spring. Winter and spring have more rain, which can cause floods in some areas.

For information on New Zealand, a copy of the New Zealand vacation brochure, or the contact details of the nearest travel agent with New Zealand expertise:

In the UK
☎ 0 9069 101010

In the USA/Canada
☎ 1 866/639-9325 toll-free

In Australia
☎ (02) 9728 5801

GETTING THERE

By Air Auckland, Wellington and Christchurch are the main international airports.
From the UK Air New Zealand has direct flights to Auckland, and Qantas, Cathay Pacific and Singapore Airlines have good connections.
From the rest of Europe Flights from many European cities to Los Angeles, Singapore and Hong Kong give good connections to New Zealand.
From the US and Canada United Airlines, Air New Zealand and Qantas offer direct flights to Auckland, with other airlines providing code-share services.
From Australia Air New Zealand and Qantas fly trans-Tasman between all main centres, and Freedom Air serves smaller locations.

Travel times New Zealand is a 3.5-hour flight from eastern Australia. From the west coast of the United States, a direct flight to New Zealand takes 12 hours. Flights from Europe take either the route via the US, or destinations on the Pacific Rim, such as Singapore and Hong Kong, from where flights take around 10 hours.

Ticket prices Prices are highest in December and January, but you can get cheaper tickets between Christmas and New Year. Prices drop during the cooler months from May to August.

TIME

New Zealand Standard Time is 12 hours ahead of Greenwich Mean Time (GMT), and 2 hours ahead of Australian Eastern Standard Time.
Daylight Saving Time Clocks are put forward by one hour on the last Sunday of October and wound back on the first Sunday of the following March.

CURRENCY AND FOREIGN EXCHANGE

Currency The unit of New Zealand currency is the dollar; $1=100 cents. Notes are printed in English and issued in 5, 10, 20, 50 and 100 dollar denominations. Coins are issued in denominations of 5, 10, 20 and 50 cents (all silver), 1 and 2 dollars (gold). The New Zealand dollar (also referred to as the kiwi dollar) has declined markedly against major overseas currencies in recent years, making the country a low-cost holiday destination. There is no restriction on the amount of foreign currency that can be brought in or taken out of New Zealand but every person who carries more than $10,000 in cash in or out is required to complete a Border Cash Report. **Foreign currency** can be exchanged at banks, some hotels and Bureau de Change kiosks, which are found at international airports and most city centres. The best **exchange rates** are given by the trading banks: BNZ, National Bank, ANZ, WestpacTrust. You can withdraw money from **ATM machines** with international credit cards and ATM cards as long as they have a four-digit PIN encoded. All major **credit cards** can be used. **Travellers' cheques** are accepted at hotels, banks and some stores. All goods and services are subject to 12.5 per cent **Goods and Services Tax** (GST), included in the displayed price. You can't claim this tax back, but when a supplier ships a major purchase to your home address the GST will not be charged.

GMT	New Zealand	USA (East)	USA (West)	Germany	Australia
12 noon	12 midnight	7 am	4 am	1 pm	(Sydney) 10 pm

WHEN YOU ARE THERE

CLOTHING SIZES

UK	New Zealand	USA	
36	36	36	Suits
38	38	38	
40	40	40	
42	42	42	
44	44	44	
46	46	46	
7	7	8	Shoes
7.5	7.5	8.5	
8.5	8.5	9.5	
9.5	9.5	10.5	
10.5	10.5	11.5	
11	11	12	
14.5	14.5	14.5	Shirts
15	15	15	
15.5	15.5	15.5	
16	16	16	
16.5	16.5	16.5	
17	17	17	
8	8	6	Dresses
10	10	8	
12	12	10	
14	14	12	
16	16	14	
18	18	16	
4.5	4.5	6	Shoes
5	5	6.5	
5.5	5.5	7	
6	6	7.5	
6.5	6.5	8	
7	7	8.5	

NATIONAL HOLIDAYS

1 Jan	New Year's Day
2 Jan	New Year's Holiday
6 Feb	Waitangi Day
Mar/Apr	Good Friday
Mar/Apr	Easter Sunday
25 Apr	Anzac Day
1st Mon Jun	Queen's Birthday
Last Mon Oct	Labour Day
25 Dec	Christmas Day
26 Dec	Boxing Day

Each region also observes an Anniversary Holiday.

OPENING HOURS

○ Shops   ● Post Offices
● Offices   ● Museums/Monuments
● Banks   ● Pharmacies

8 am 9 am 10 am noon 1 pm 2 pm 4 pm 5 pm 7 pm

Day   ▨ Midday   ▨ Evening

Shops Most have a late night, usually Fri, until 9 pm; Sat 9 am–4 pm; Sun 10 am–4 pm. In cities, supermarkets often open daily from 8 am–9 pm. Convenience stores (dairies) open 8 am–9 pm.
Banks Open weekdays 9 am–4:30 pm; city branches increasingly open during weekends.
Post offices At weekends and at night, services may be available from dairies, video shops and other stores.
Museums Tend to follow shop hours, and most are open on weekends and public holidays. See individual opening hours in this guide.
Pharmacies Some open 24 hours in major centres.

PERSONAL SAFETY

- New Zealand is generally safe, but don't take safety for granted. Thieves are attracted to areas where tourists congregate so take care with valuables.
- In the outdoors, the weather can change quickly from one extreme to the other.
- Prepare carefully for outdoor excursions: take appropriate clothing for any kind of weather, protect yourself from the sun and bring a first-aid kit. For automatic weather forecasts call 0900 99909.
- Leave an itinerary with friends and family.

Police assistance:
☎ 111 from any phone

ELECTRICITY

New Zealand operates on a 230V AC, 50 hertz mains supply, three-pin plug system.

 Most hotels provide 110V AC sockets for shavers only, and hardware or electronics shops stock adaptors.

TELEPHONES

Local calls are free from most private phones but are charged at 50c per call from public telephone booths. Almost all pay phones are card-operated and accept $5, $10, $20 and $50 cards, and are available from visitor information centres, some supermarkets, post shops and most accommodation. Many pre-paid telephone cards offer discounted rates for international calls. Some cards can be recharged with a credit card. In New Zealand, the national directory number is 018; the international directory is 0172. The area code for Auckland is 09, for Wellington 04, and for all South Island destinations 03. The phone numbers in this guide that begin with 0800 are free to call within New Zealand. Most accommodation will provide access to email and the internet. There are also many internet cafés and copy shops in most towns and cities, which charge about $2 for 15 minutes.

POST

Auckland's main post office is at 24 Wellesley Street, tel: (09) 379 6714. In Wellington, the main office is at 7–27 Waterloo Quay, tel: (04) 496 4065; in Christchurch, at 53–59 Hereford Street, tel: (03) 353 1899, and in Dunedin at 233 Moray Place, tel: (03) 474 0932.

TIPS/GRATUITIES

New Zealanders do not expect tips for normal service. However, tipping for special service is discretionary.

EMBASSIES and HIGH COMMISSIONS

UK
☎ (04) 472 6049
(Wellington)

USA
☎ (04) 472 2068
(Wellington)

There is no Irish embassy in New Zealand

Australia
☎ (04) 473 6411
(Wellington)

Canada
☎ (04) 473 9577
(Wellington)

HEALTH

Insurance A doctor's visit costs about $40. Make sure your travel insurance covers hospital care at least. Accidents (but not illnesses) are covered by the Accident Compensation Corporation (ACC), which ensures that residents and tourists alike are not charged for any medical treatment required as a consequence of an accident suffered in New Zealand. This covers both physical and psychological damage. In cases of minor injuries, for example a sprained ankle, you may have to contribute to the cost of the initial doctor's visit and physiotherapy. The ACC scheme means you can't sue anybody for damages.

Dental Services Dentists are expensive, so make sure your travel insurance covers dental treatments.

Weather The sun can be harsh in New Zealand, even through cloud. Make sure you apply sunscreen and wear a hat.

Drugs Painkillers can be bought over the counter at pharmacies, but antibiotics have to be prescribed.

Safe Water While tap water is safe to drink, some streams are infected with giardia and E-coli, which can cause serious intestinal illness. If you're unsure, treat the water before drinking.

WILDLIFE SOUVENIRS

Importing wildlife souvenirs sourced from rare or endangered species may be illegal or require a special permit. Check your country's customs rules.

CONCESSIONS

Students/Children Most museums offer discounted prices for children between five and 14 as well as university students (with valid ID). There are also family concessions, which cover two adults and up to four children, and under-fives can usually get in free.
Senior Citizens Discounted prices are available for some attractions, public transport and accommodation.

TRAVELLING WITH A DISABILITY

Wheelchair access and toilet facilities for people with disabilities are a legal requirement for new accommodation establishments. Many government facilities and attractions are similarly equipped. Quarantine laws prevent overseas visitors from bringing guide dogs. Cities have a Total Mobility (wheelchair transporter) taxi service operated by the main taxi companies. Some tour companies can adapt adventure activities for people with disabilities. For further information, contact the Disability Information Service, at 314 Worcester Street, Christchurch, tel: (03) 366 6189.

CHILDREN

Most attractions, particularly museums, have hands-on activities designed for children. Hotels and restaurants are generally child-friendly, but some bed and breakfasts are designed for couples, rather than families.

TOILETS

All attractions have public toilets, which can also be found in many public areas, such as city squares, parks and playgrounds. Most public toilets have access for wheelchairs and many have baby-changing facilities.

Atlas

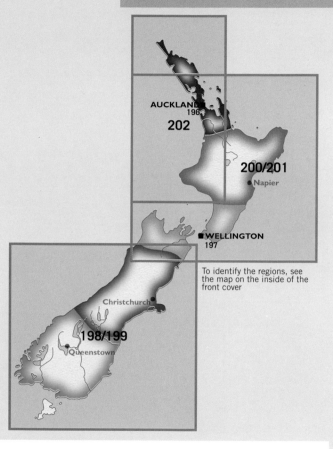

AUCKLAND
196
202

200/201

● Napier

■ WELLINGTON
197

To identify the regions, see
the map on the inside of the
front cover

Christchurch

198/199

Queenstown

Regional Maps

0	20	40	60	80	100 km
0		20		40	60 miles

━━━ Major route

━━━ Motorway

──── Main road

──── Other road

□   City

▫   Major town

○   Large town

○   Town, village

■   Featured place of interest

▪   Place of interest

✈   Airport

    Glacier

City Plans

▨   Pedestrian street

▨   Steps

■   Important building

■   Featured place of interest

ⓘ   Information

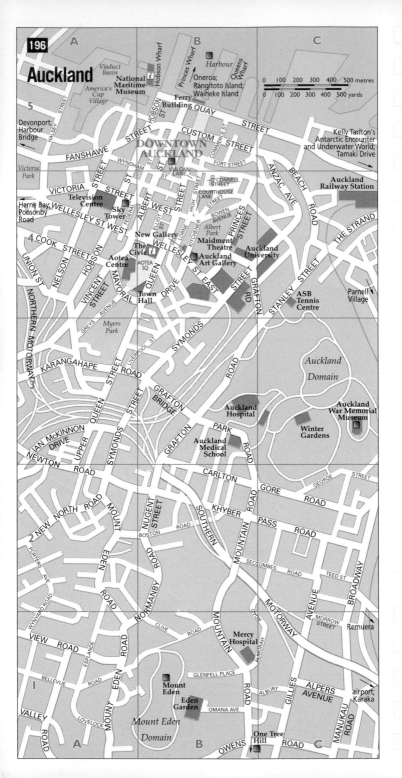

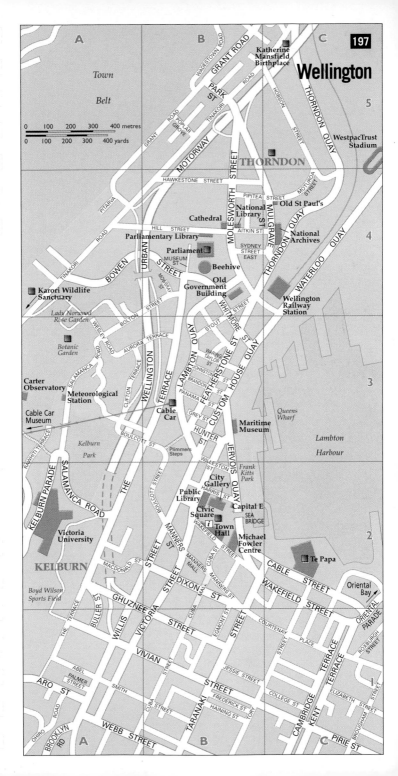

Wellington

A **B** **C**

5

Town

Belt

GRANT ROAD

WADESTOWN ROAD

Katherine Mansfield Birthplace

PARK ST

TINAKORI ROAD

POPLAR GROVE

MOTORWAY

GRANT ROAD

PITARUA

HOBSON STREET

THORNDON QUAY

WestpacTrust Stadium

THORNDON

STREET

HAWKESTONE STREET

PIPITEA STREET

MOTUROA STREET

4

Cathedral

National Library

Old St Paul's

MOLESWORTH

MULGRAVE ST

HILL STREET

AITKIN ST

National Archives

Parliamentary Library

SYDNEY STREET EAST

Parliament

MUSEUM ST

Beehive

THORNDON QUAY

WATERLOO QUAY

Karori Wildlife Sanctuary

BOWEN STREET

URBAN

MOWBRAY ST

Old Government Building

WHITMORE ST

Wellington Railway Station

Lady Norwood Rose Garden

BOLTON STREET

WESLEY ROAD

STOUT STREET

Botanic Garden

AURORA TERRACE

LAMBTON QUAY

WARING TAYLOR ST

FEATHERSTONE ST

CUSTOM HOUSE QUAY

JOHNSTONE ST

3

Carter Observatory

SALAMANCA

CLIFTON TERRACE

WELLINGTON TERRACE

BRANDON ST

PANAMA

Queens Wharf

Meteorological Station

Cable Car

GREY ST

Lambton Harbour

Cable Car Museum

BOULCOTT ST

HUNTER ST

JERVOIS QUAY

Maritime Museum

RAWHITI TERRACE

Kelburn Park

Plimmers Steps

WILLESTON STREET

Frank Kitts Park

KELBURN PARADE

SALAMANCA ROAD

THE TERRACE

BOULCOTT STREET

City Gallery

HARRIS ST

Capital E

2

Public Library

Civic Square

SEA BRIDGE

Victoria University

MANNERS ST

Town Hall

CUBA ST

WAKEFIELD ST

Michael Fowler Centre

KELBURN

MACDONALD ST

DIXON ST

MANNERS MALL

CABLE STREET

Te Papa

Boyd Wilson Sports Field

THE TERRACE

BULLER ST

GHUZNEE STREET

VICTORIA STREET

MANNERS ST

WAKEFIELD STREET

Oriental Bay

ORIENTAL PARADE

WILLIS

VIVIAN STREET

EGMONT STREET

CUBA STREET

COURTENAY PLACE

CAMBRIDGE TERRACE

KENT TERRACE

ROXBURGH STREET

1

ARO ST

ABEL PALMER STREET

SMITH

STREET

JESSIE STREET

FREDERICK ST

COLLEGE ST

ELIZABETH STREET

BROUGHAM STREET

OHIRO ROAD

BROOKLYN RD

WEBB STREET

CUBA STREET

TARANAKI STREET

HAINING ST

PIRIE ST

A **B** **C**

0 100 200 300 400 metres

0 100 200 300 400 yards

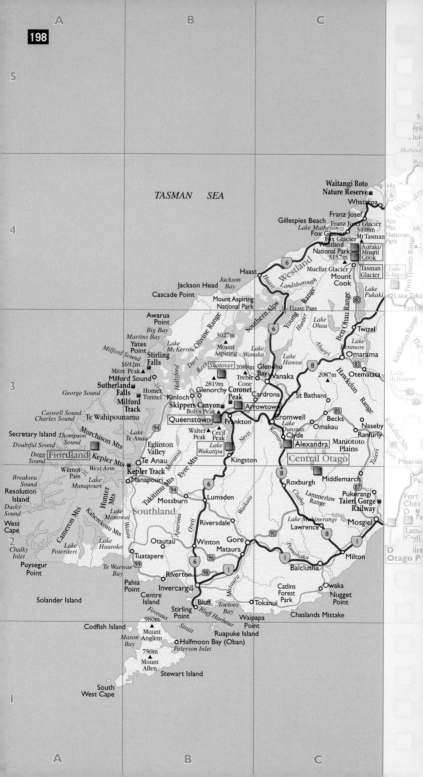

TASMAN SEA

Waitangi Roto
Nature Reserve
Whataroa
Ha
6
Franz Josef
Gillespies Beach
Franz Josef Glacier
Lake Matheson
3498m
Fox Glacier
Mt Tasman
Fox Glacier
Westland
National Park
Aoraki/
3157m
Mount
Cook
Muellar Glacier
Tasman
Mount
Glacier
Cook
Haast
Jackson
Bay
Jackson Head
Cascade Point
Landsborough
Mount Aspiring
National Park
Haast Pass

Westland
Southern Alps
Young
Range
Ben Ohau Range
80
Lake
Pukaki
Lake Tek
Lake
Ohau
Twizel
Lake
Benmore
Omarama
83

Awarua
Point
Big Bay
Olivine Range
3027m
Yates
Lake
Point
McKerrow
Mount
Martins Bay
Aspiring
Lake
Stirling
Dart
Wanaka
Falls
Milford
Hunter
Mitre Peak
Sound
1692m
Rees
Shotover
2088m
Glenorchy
Hawkdun
Sutherland
Treble
Wanaka
2087m
Hollyford
Cone
Bay
Otematata
Falls
Homer
Glenorchy
Coronet
Cardrona
Range
Milford
Tunnel
Peak
St Bathans
Track
Kinloch
Skippers Canyon
Arrowtown
82
Caswell Sound
Te Wahipounamu
Bob's Peak
Cromwell
Charles Sound
Queenstown
Frankton
Becks
83
Murchison Mts
94
Clyde
Omakau
Naseby
Secretary Island
Walter
Cecil
Lake
Peak
Peak
Dunstan
Ranfurly
Thompson
Lake
Lake
Doubtful Sound
Sound
Te Anau
Wakatipu
Alexandra
85
Dagg
Kepler Mts
Nevis
Maniototo
Sound
Fiordland
Eglinton
Kingston
Central Otago
Plains
Valley
Te Anau
Breaksea
Kepler Track
Taieri
Sound
Wilmot
West Arm
Manapouri
Moerak
Resolution
Pass
Lake
Takitimu Mts
Middlemarch
Island
Manapouri
Mossburn
87
Dusky
Hunter
Roxburgh
Sound
Mts
6
Pukerangi
West
Kaherekoau Mts
Lumsden
Lammerlaw
Taieri Gorge
Cape
Lake
Range
Railway
Monowai
Riversdale
Chalky
Cameron Mts
94
Lake
Lake
Mahinerangi
Mosgiel
Inlet
Lake
Hauroko
Gore
Lawrence
D
Poteriteri
Otautau
Winton
90
Otago P
Puysegur
Tuatapere
Mataura
8
Milton
Point
99
Te Waewae
6
96
Balclutha
Lake
Bay
I
Solander Island
Pahia
Riverton
98
Point
Invercargill
Centre
Owaka
Island
Bluff
Catlins
Nugget
Codfish Island
Stirling
Toetoes
Forest
Point
980m
Point
Bay
Tokanui
Park
Mount
Bluff Harbour
Mason
Anglem
Waipapa
Chaslands Mistake
Bay
Halfmoon Bay (Oban)
Point
750m
Paterson Inlet
Ruapuke Island
Mount
Allen
Stewart Island
South
West Cape

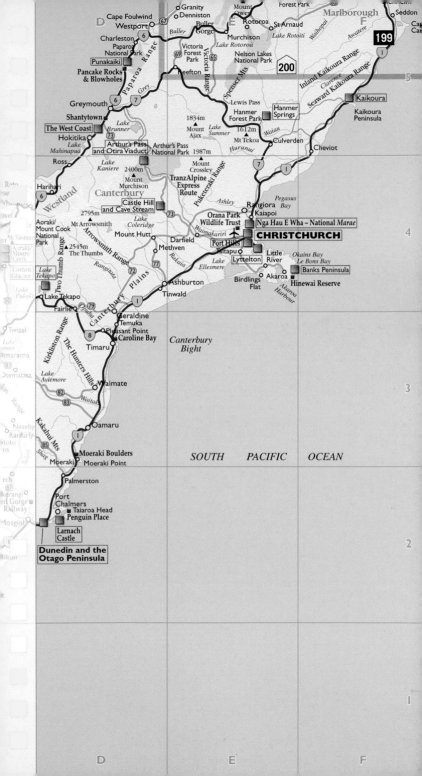

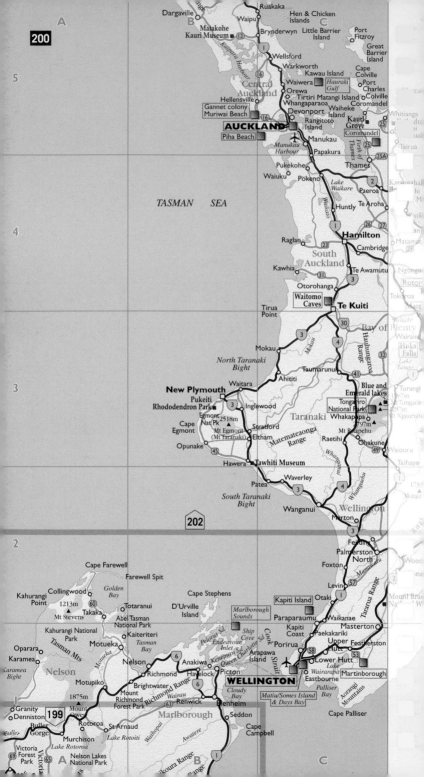

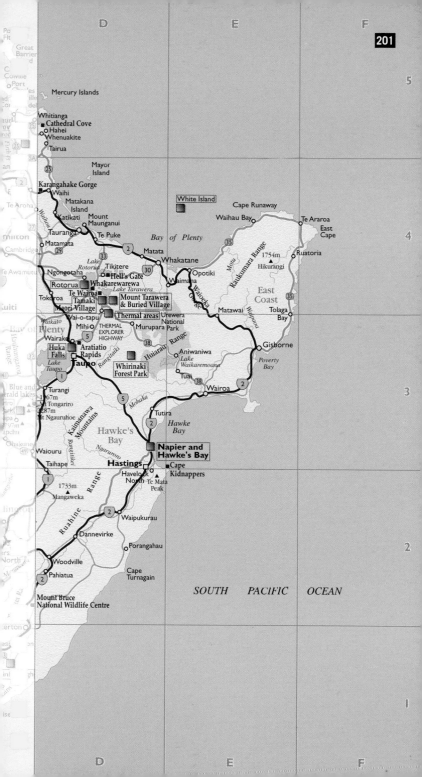

D   E   F

5

Mercury Islands

Whitianga
Cathedral Cove
Hahei
Whenuakite
Tairua

Mayor
Island

White Island

Cape Runaway

Te Araroa
East
Cape

Waihau Bay

Karangahake Gorge
Waihi
Matakana
Island
Katikati
Mount
Maunganui
Tauranga
Te Puke
Matamata
Bay of Plenty
Matata
Whakatane
Opotiki
Waimana

Ruatoria

Ngongotaha
Lake Rotorua
Tikitere
Hell's Gate
Rotorua
Whakarewarewa
Te Wairoa
Lake Tarawera
Tamaki
Village
Maori Village
Mount Tarawera
& Buried Village
Thermal areas
Wai-o-tapu
Mihi
THERMAL
EXPLORER
HIGHWAY
Murupara
*Urewera
National
Park*

Hikurangi 1754m

*East
Coast*

35

4

Tokoroa
Wairakei
Huka
Falls
Aratiatio
Rapids
Taupo
Whirinaki
Forest Park
*Lake
Taupo*
38
Rangitaiki
Ihuaru Range
Aniwaniwa
*Lake
Waikaremoana*
Tuai

Matawai

Tolaga
Bay

Gisborne
*Poverty
Bay*

Te Awamutu
Matamata
Cambridge

3

Turangi
Mt Tongariro
1967m
2287m
Mt Ngauruhoe
*Kaimanawa
Mountains*
38
Mohaka
Wairoa
2

Tutira
*Hawke's
Bay*

Waiouru
Taihape
*Hawke's
Bay*
Napier and
Hawke's Bay
Hastings
Havelock
North
Te Mata
Peak
Cape
Kidnappers

Mangaweka 1733m
Ruahine Range
Waipukurau

Dannevirke
Porangahau

Woodville
Pahiatua
Cape
Turnagain

Mount Bruce
National Wildlife Centre

SOUTH   PACIFIC   OCEAN

2

1

D   E   F

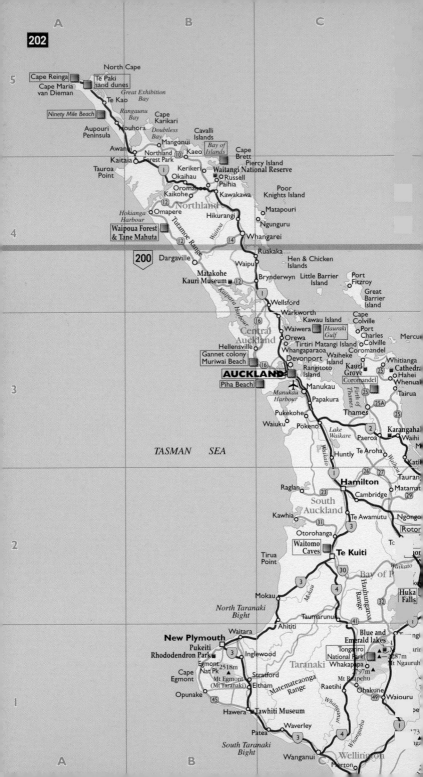

Picture credits

Abbreviations for terms appearing below: (t) top; (b) bottom; (l) left; (r) right; (c) centre.

The Automobile Association wishes to thank the following photographers and libraries for their assistance in the preparation of this book:

Front and back cover (t) AA Photo Library/Andy Belcher; (ct) AA Photo Library/Andy Belcher; (cb) AA Photo Library/Andy Belcher; (b) AA Photo Library/Andy Reisinger and Veronika Meduna; Spine AA Photo Library/Paul Kenward

ANDY BELCHER 81b, 82, 83c, 86t, 86cr, 87ct, 91, 128, 131t, 138, 141b, 145c, 162–163; THE ANTHONY BLAKE PICTURE LIBRARY 13, 15cr; AUCKLAND WAR MEMORIAL MUSEUM 57t; 57b; 58l, 58r, 59l, 59r; BLACK WATER RAFTING 95; BRUCE COLEMAN COLLECTION 16–17, 17t, 17b; EMPICS 24–25, 26b, 27; MARY EVANS PICTURE LIBRARY 10; FOCUS NEW ZEALAND PHOTO LIBRARY 182, 183, 184tl, 184r, 185; GREENPEACE IMAGES 19t; HULTON ARCHIVE 21; IMAGESTATE LTD 3iv, 175; CAROLINE JONES 50; REX FEATURES 23b; THE RONALD GRANT ARCHIVE 23t; TE PAPA TONGAREWA MUSEUM OF NEW ZEALAND 3v, 107t, 111t, 112t, 112c, 119c, 120, 189; TOPHAM PICTUREPOINT 11t, 11b; TRAVEL INK 176, 177; POPPERFOTO 6–7, 8, 10–11 (background), 25t; WORLD PICTURES 179; BOB McCREE/WORLDWIDE PICTURE LIBRARY 65c, 66, 68t; JAMES TIMS/ WORLDWIDE PICTURE LIBRARY 168b.
The remaining pictures are held in the Association's own library (AA PHOTO LIBRARY) and were taken by ANDY BELCHER, except 2ii, 3iii, 6, 9, 22, 28t, 28b, 29t, 29b, 33, 51t, 51b, 56c, 65b, 67, 68c, 69c, 70, 78b, 83b, 84c, 86cl, 92, 93, 94, 97m, 97 inset, 113, 130t, 132l, 132r, 137, 146, 151, 152t, 156, 157t, 157b, 159t, 159b, 160, 164, 180, 186, 188, which were taken by PAUL KENWARD; 26c, 153, 154t, 168t, 169t, which were taken by ANDY REISINGER AND VERONIKA MEDUNA; and 159, 144t, 144b, 154b, which were taken by NICK HANNA.

Acknowledgements

The authors would like to thank the regional tourist boards of New Zealand for their help in researching this book.

SPIRAL GUIDES

Questionnaire

Dear Traveler

Your comments, opinions and recommendations are very important to us. So please help us to improve our travel guides by taking a few minutes to complete this simple questionnaire.

Send to: Spiral Guides, MailStop 66, 1000 AAA Drive, Heathrow, FL 32746–5063

Your recommendations...

We always encourage readers' recommendations for restaurants, nightlife or shopping – if your recommendation is added to the next edition of the guide, we will send you a FREE AAA Spiral Guide of your choice. Please state below the establishment name, location and your reasons for recommending it.

_____

_____

_____

_____

_____

Please send me AAA Spiral_____
(see list of titles inside the back cover)

About this guide...

Which title did you buy?

_____ **AAA Spiral**

Where did you buy it? _____

When? mm/ y y

Why did you choose a AAA Spiral Guide? _____

_____

_____

_____

Did this guide meet your expectations?

Exceeded ☐   Met all ☐   Met most ☐   Fell below ☐

Please give your reasons _____

_____

_____

_____

continued on next page...

Were there any aspects of this guide that you particularly liked?

Is there anything we could have done better?

About you...

Name (Mr/Mrs/Ms)

Address

Zip

Daytime tel nos.

Which age group are you in?

Under 25 ☐ 25–34 ☐ 35–44 ☐ 45–54 ☐ 55–64 ☐ 65+ ☐

How many trips do you make a year?

Less than one ☐ One ☐ Two ☐ Three or more ☐

Are you a AAA member? Yes ☐ No ☐

Name of AAA club

About your trip...

When did you book? m m/ y y When did you travel? m m/ y y

How long did you stay?

Was it for business or leisure?

Did you buy any other travel guides for your trip? ☐ Yes ☐ No

If yes, which ones?

Thank you for taking the time to complete this questionnaire.

All information is for AAA internal use only and will NOT be distributed outside the organization to any third parties.